D0046265

Asking for a Friend

Asking
for a Friend

Three Centuries *of* Advice *on* Life, Love, Money, *and* Other Burning Questions *from* a Nation Obsessed

Jessica Weisberg

NATION
BOOKS
New York

Nation Books
116 East 16th Street, 8th Floor
New York, NY 10003
www.nationbooks.org
@NationBooks

Printed in the United States of America
First Edition: April 2018
Published by Nation Books, an imprint of Perseus Books, LLC, a subsidiary of Hachette Book Group, Inc.

Nation Books is a co-publishing venture of the Nation Institute and the Perseus Books.

The Hachette Speakers Bureau provides a wide range of authors for speaking events. To find out more, go to www.hachettespeakersbureau.com or call (866) 376-6591.

The publisher is not responsible for websites (or their content) that are not owned by the publisher.

PRINT BOOK INTERIOR DESIGN BY LINDA MARK.

The Library of Congress has cataloged the hardcover edition as follows:
Names: Weisberg, Jessica, author.
Title: Asking for a friend : three centuries of advice on life, love, money, and other burning questions from a nation obsessed / Jessica Weisberg.
Description: First edition. | New York : Nation Books, 2018. | Includes bibliographical references and index.
Identifiers: LCCN 2017044117 (print) | LCCN 2017056186 (ebook) | ISBN 9781568585352 (ebook) | ISBN 9781568585345 (hardcover)
Subjects: LCSH: Advice columnists—United States—Biography.
Classification: LCC BJ1589 (ebook) | LCC BJ1589 .W43 2018 (print) | DDC 070.4/44092273—dc23
LC record available at https://lccn.loc.gov/2017044117

ISBNs: 978-1-56858-534-5 (hardcover); 978-1-56858-535-2 (e-book)

LSC-C

10 9 8 7 6 5 4 3 2 1

For Ben

And yet, inside a year, five years, a decade, five decades, people will be asking, "How *could* they have believed that?"

—Doris Lessing, *Prisons We Chose to Live Inside*

Contents

Contents

Preface

I'LL BEGIN BY GETTING SOMETHING OUT OF THE WAY: I have no clear and easy tricks for a happier, healthier you. I have no instant remedies for sluggishness, or shyness, or social discomfort. I possess no secrets to success. My morning routine, which I am not suggesting you imitate, can be summarized as (1) Wake up. (2) Hurry.

But this book tells the stories of sixteen people who made their names, and sometimes their fortunes, by telling people what to do. They are all professional advice-givers, and their job is to answer Americans' thorniest, most intimate questions.

You've probably heard of many of the individuals profiled in the pages ahead, like Benjamin Franklin, "Dear Abby," Dale Carnegie, and Elisabeth Kübler-Ross. Others may be new to you, like John Dunton, William Alcott, Dorothy Dix, Sylvia Porter, and Joan Quigley. All of them wrote, in one form or another—books, columns, letters, almanacs—and their words and ideas were so popular that they rumbled across all spheres of American popular culture, their maxims stitched on pillows, printed on mugs, recited at dinner; their faces fixtures on magazine covers and cable channels; and their books docked permanently on the bestseller list. They dislodged long-established norms about how Americans ought to date, mourn, work, and raise their children, and defined, and redefined, what was "right" and what was not.

Most so-called serious writers diagnose but never prescribe. A memoirist might probe her own experience with mourning for her readers' benefit, but she's unlikely to offer explicit instructions. Listening to Lena Dunham talk about her struggles as a woman in Hollywood may inspire you, but even she, with her porous definition of personal boundaries, stops short of providing a step-by-step guide. Advice-givers don't have these hang-ups—as a group, they tend not to have many hang-ups.

And yet few writers come close to possessing the power and influence advice-givers wield. They literally tell people what to do! And people listen! Even though they often aren't licensed to be giving advice; frequently their only qualifications are their imperviousness to embarrassment and their penchant for popularity. Most of them entertain as they counsel; they are skillful at coining catchy one-liners and composing sentences that play in your mind like a pop song. Often, their advice columns are designed to be playful. There is no telling if correspondents like End of the Line or Losing It are the melancholic people they claim to be or if they are pranksters, or editors making backhanded assignments. Still, columnists have become the arbitrary authors of social rules, helping readers decide what is required of them. After Pauline Phillips, or "Dear Abby," wrote about the importance of writing a will, hundreds of thousands of people signed one for the first time. With one column, she normalized the idea that preparing for death, while one is still young and healthy, is not morbid but prudent. This book is filled with stories like this, of not particularly credible people issuing mandates that millions of Americans followed.

America is unique in its hankering for advice. The British have their "agony aunts"—their equivalent of advice columnists—but rarely do they reach the same level of prominence as their American colleagues. The American self-help empire has been sprawling aggressively for decades, overtaking bookstores and the internet. It's estimated that Americans spend eleven billion dollars a year on self-help books. ("Here's Sound Advice: Write a Book, Become Rich," went one headline in *Forbes*.)

This multibillion-dollar industry employs many, many advice-givers. There are experts on finance and car maintenance and dog obedience. But the advice-givers profiled in this book are of a more ambitious ilk: they attempt to provide concrete solutions to the murkiest problems; they are brave—or foolish—enough to seek answers that have escaped philosophers, poets, and religious scholars for centuries, and to bill themselves as experts on topics as broad and impossible as love, health, and life itself.

The typical story about an advice-giver, the one you've likely heard before, is about a phony or hypocrite. A person incapable of following his own sage wisdom, who espoused knowledge on subjects like dating or friendship even as he remained perennially single and friendless, or who encouraged moral or fiscal restraint while he was millions in debt with a family on every continent.

Miss Lonelyhearts, the 1933 novel by Nathanael West, is the classic example. It tells the story of an anonymous advice columnist for a New York paper. The novel begins with letters from the people seeking advice from Miss Lonelyhearts: there's one from a woman being pressured by her husband to have an eighth child against her and her doctor's wishes, another from a teenage girl born without a nose and bullied by the other teenagers at her school, and one pained letter from a boy who suspects that his deaf-mute little sister was molested and isn't sure what to do. Each letter is its own distinct melodrama, but their authors are all people who don't need just advice but an empathetic friend—someone who can say "It's going to be okay" with conviction. Then we're introduced to the individual behind

Miss Lonelyhearts, who is tasked with performing these significant feats of emotional labor. *He* is a depressed middle-aged man who dulls his loneliness with alcohol and chain-smoking and despises his colleagues and his readers. He churns out columns dense with mawkish one-liners such as, "When old paths are choked with the debris of failure, look for newer and fresher paths." Miss Lonelyhearts's advice is clear and straightforward, presumably helpful to those seeking direction, but also a symptom of the columnist's own emotional limitations. He's an expert at dismissing dangerous feelings. "Her sureness was based on the power to limit experience arbitrarily," West writes of Miss Lonelyhearts.

Straight Talk, the 1992 film starring Dolly Parton, depicts a different kind of ruse: a hick with a heart of gold falls into a job as a radio psychologist in Chicago and claims to hold a PhD though she never went to college. One of the more notable advice-givers from the last few decades is Donald Trump, a person and brand that has become almost synonymous with deceit. (This isn't a political statement: every reality television star traffics in flash.) Trump's 1987 bestseller *The Art of the Deal* painted him as a cautious and expert deal maker, but within five years of its publication, four of Trump's companies had filed for bankruptcy.

The advice columnists in this book aren't just hypocrites and narcissists, even if they do display those tendencies once in a while. They're all well-intentioned people who tend to get in the way of their own noble instincts. Many of them are social reformers who upended the status quo, expanded rights for women and minorities, and proselytized greater acceptance for different ways of living. Dorothy Dix, for instance, was an advice columnist at the turn of the twentieth century who strove to legitimize domestic work, urging wives to strike until their husbands offered them a living wage. All of the individuals in the pages ahead are idealists, eager to change the world, or at least get people to change their behavior. They share a curiosity for giant moral and emotional questions and an instinct for controversy.

I should get something else out of the way: I don't necessarily recommend that you follow all of the advice in this book. Some of it is extreme, outdated, or downright insane. William Alcott, an early dieting expert, urged his followers to avoid tomatoes under all circumstances. Dorothy Dix advised against divorce, no matter how miserable the relationship had become.

While their wisdom may not always seem relevant today, the advice-givers in this book were all, at some point, responding to Americans' emotional needs. This book is a history of Americans seeking the answers to their generation's hardest questions, their parents being just as out of touch as ours are. Their questions are a window into the particular and universal torments of being alive in the 1810s or 1910s or 2010s. I am as interested in the advice-givers as I am in the millions of Americans who *needed* them.

FIVE OR SO years ago, in my midtwenties, I became disquietingly addicted to an advice column. It was called "Dear Sugar," and it was published on *The Rumpus*, a website geared to emerging writers. I was, as they say, "between things"—that joyless euphemism for having more time on one's hands than one wants. I didn't know then that "Sugar" was Cheryl Strayed, the novelist and memoirist who would soon publish *Wild*, a memoir about the months she spent hiking the Pacific Crest Trail. "Dear Sugar" had no clear publishing schedule, so I checked the site every day. I never missed a column. I never sent Sugar a letter, but I felt connected to those who did. They were lonely, too.

If you were looking for straightforward advice, Sugar was not the person to turn to. She would call you a "warrior" or even a "sweet arrogant beautiful crazy talented tortured rising star glow-bug," which may or may not have made you feel better. She would offer you anecdotes—some harrowing, some charming—from her own life, but she was unlikely to tell you what to do. And that was precisely what made her columns so appealing. Sugar was the internet's greatest relief from itself. The internet is like a garrulous friend—entertaining and inattentive, carrying on regardless of who's around. Sugar, in turn, liked to listen. Thousands of people wrote to Sugar seeking not her advice but her attention. She received a letter early on in her tenure that went, "WTF, WTF, WTF? I'm asking this question as it applies to everything every day. Best, WTF." And then other letters like it—vague, existential pleas for Sugar's companionship—started flowing in. "I don't have a definite question for you. I'm a sad, angry man whose son died. I want him back. That's all I ask for and it's not a question," one reader wrote, in a letter that went on for pages. She had both male and female readers, but their questions recalled what Betty Friedan, in *The Feminine Mystique*, called "the problem that has no name." Friedan wrote about the "strange stirring, a sense of dissatisfaction" among American housewives in the fifties who spent too much of their days alone. Sugar's readers, similarly, had trouble naming what plagued them. They were self-centered enough to think that their problems merited attention but too shy or unpracticed to ask the right questions. They seem atomized, listless, and chronically lonely. If confronted with this kind of existential angst, Miss Lonelyhearts would have given actionable, straightforward advice. ("Try to have lunch with a friend!") Sugar, on the other hand, was an aficionado of dangerous, complicated feelings, a glutton for experience. She said "I'm sorry" a lot and offered her condolences in lyrical prose. "How painful. I'm sorry this happened to you," she told Mourning and Raging, whose husband had cheated on her. "Though we live in a time and place and culture that tries to tell us otherwise, suffering is what happens when truly horrible things happen to us," she wrote to another advice-seeker.

I wrote above that I was "disquietingly" obsessed with "Dear Sugar." As far as addictions go, reading is a fairly anodyne one. But advice or self-help, despite its ubiquity, still carries a whiff of shame.

It's an embarrassment, for many, to be caught in the self-help aisle; they would rather be caught reading a worn paperback with a woman in a red bustier on the cover. (Those posing the questions have always been granted anonymity, but even reading these exchanges seems to demand a degree of privacy.) Advice books are considered undignified reading material and, at the same time, too edifying to be excused as a guilty pleasure.

But seeking advice should never be shameful. Needing advice means you have yet to learn something that others seem to know— what to wear to an interview, what to give someone as a wedding present. And not knowing something is a sign that you're entering a world different from the one in which you were raised, or a world that recently discriminated against people who look like you. We need professional advice because we don't know any other women in our industry, or because we're the first person in our family to attend college. Americans' interest in advice reflects our cultural tendency toward optimism: we tend to believe that with a bit of direction and a small boost, the future can be bright. Seeking advice is for strivers, for people who want to better themselves, land a new job, get in shape.

The fact that Americans want advice is proof that the American dream still exists, at least in people's imaginations. Who doesn't want to believe that with hard work, determination, and a bit of advice, that anything is possible? It's an idea that advice-givers have been peddling for centuries. Benjamin Franklin wrote *Poor Richard's Almanack,* his annual compendium of life lessons, with the hopes that anyone, from any background, would be inspired by it.

Over the centuries, the advice changes, as do the people supplying it, but the questions largely remain the same. Should I stay with my husband after learning he's cheated? How do I get out of debt? How do I seem more confident than I really am? There's never been a time when life hasn't been mind-bogglingly hard, or a time when we didn't hope for someone or something to come along to make sense of it all. The past was never as simple as it now seems. Many of the most confusing questions—How do I mourn my loved one? What's the secret to a happy marriage?—have been confusing us for hundreds of years.

There is a community of historians concerned with what's called "emotional history" who study how people throughout time have communicated their feelings. I am not a historian, but I consider this book a work of emotional history, one that examines the flawed and fascinating people who have offered Americans comfort and wisdom over the past three hundred years as well as the people who turned to them when they wanted to be told that everything was going to be fine, when they sought someone—like Sugar—who could say "I'm sorry" and sound like they meant it. History is, typically, a chronology of great accomplishments and the figures who helmed them, but advice columns offer a different kind of history: one that looks at the anxieties quietly suffered by innumerable Americans and that they revealed, exclusively in some cases, to a pseudonymous stranger. In the early twentieth century, many women started advice columns because they offered a rare shot at a byline. The history of advice centers around these influential women who amassed power through their assiduous emotional labor—work that was quintessential to formation of American identity but is rarely, if ever, mentioned in textbooks.

～ ⚬ ～

ADVICE-GIVERS HAVE directed their audience to be obedient or rebellious, disciplined or free-spirited, fiercely self-reliant or unfailingly generous, depending on the decade. If you pick up an etiquette book from the 1790s, you will not learn how to be less anxious at a party but how to make those around you enjoy themselves. Particularly during times of war or upheaval, advice-givers stressed the importance of honoring social binds, whereas today the emphasis is more on self-actualization, or "self-help." Selfishness has gone from a categorical sin to something more complicated, something that can even be worth fighting for.

In the colonial era, advice-giving was the job of the genteel. Today, we want advice-givers to be accessible; we want to be spoken to in the first person. There's been a cultural shift favoring vulnerability over expertise. This book maps the transformation of the advice-giver from the buttoned-up pundit to the tell-all peer, from Benjamin Franklin to Top Writers on Quora. The barriers to achieving authority—an elusive but necessary quality for those who give advice for a living—have loosened over the past few centuries. There's always been advice geared toward women or toward specific immigrant groups or ethnic communities—Jewish advice columnists, black advice columnists—but until the twentieth century, advice marketed to a general, all-genders audience was almost exclusively written by white men. In recent years, the internet and podcasting have lowered the barriers for aspiring advice-givers. But aside from Oprah, who politely declined to be interviewed for this book, mass-market life advice is still largely dispensed by white people.

I've grouped the advice-givers in this book into four loosely chronological categories. The first group are men who dispensed nonreligious advice from the late 1600s to the mid-1800s, when most social guides were written by preachers or religious scholars. These men referenced the Bible but based their ideas on a range of other texts, conversations with friends, and their own experiences. Even though they were all white, male, and pedigreed, they still grappled with their claims to authority. The second group, mostly women, all worked in the twentieth century and distinguished themselves by striking the tone of a friend, of someone who resembled the reader and related to their pains and fantasies. They sought recognition not for their merits or achievements but for their capacity for empathy. The third group, who also worked in the twentieth century, were experts in their field, possessed PhDs or other impressive credentials, and believed that they were uniquely qualified to give advice in their subject area, whether that be child rearing, mourning, or astrology. The fourth group are contemporary advice-givers, all of whom walk a fine line between friendliness and authority; they want to be relatable, but they also want your respect. Compared to their predecessors, they are far more willing to share stories from their own lives, citing their mistakes to prove their credibility. But they are also quick to formalize their services, bestowing themselves with made-up titles like "life coach" so that they're not mistaken for laity.

But the most well-received advice-givers throughout history have tended to be those who argue that following your heart too steadfastly is a lonely enterprise, but abiding too closely to external demands will harden you. The goal of most advice, ultimately, is to find a compromise between an individual's needs and those of the society she lives in. It's a compromise that fuels America's most idealized vision of itself: a country where everyone can express their differences but still get along.

part one

Old, Wise Men

There is nothing so beautiful and legitimate as to play the
man well and properly, no knowledge so hard to acquire
as the knowledge of how to live life well and naturally.

—Michel de Montaigne, *Of Experience*

THE IDEA THAT THERE IS SOMETHING SUSPECT ABOUT
professional advice-givers has a history, and that history begins with
John Dunton. In the 1690s, Dunton invented the advice column as
we now know it and counseled Londoners on all varieties of spiritual
and moral questions. Dunton had never been known as an especially sage or accomplished person. He was a middling publisher,
and the resounding consensus among his peers was that he was an
acquired taste of a human being. Most of his readers, presumably,
had grandfathers, parents, teachers, and pastors they could turn to
for guidance; if they were readers, they had the works of Plato and
Shakespeare, the Bible. Why, then, seek advice from someone they
didn't know?

Before Dunton, there was no such thing as advice literature. Its closest approximation was philosophy written as a dialogue. Plato originated the form with a series of wide-ranging conversations about love, government, and relationships, most of which feature his mentor, Socrates, replying to his students' questions. The question-and-answer format is grounding: it turns the philosopher from a high-minded scholar, immersed in a universe of abstractions, into an accessible teacher responding to real-life concerns. (Like nutrition. In one conversation, Socrates recommends a diet heavy in barley, wheat, olives, cheese, and figs.) The conversational format was parroted by many religious scholars and philosophers, such as Cicero and St. Augustine; the Milindapañha, one of the earliest Buddhist texts, was written as a dialogue between a king and a priest. These are not conversations among equals: they are interviews; one person asks the questions, the smarter person responds to them. But there is a sense of trust, of kinship, of being honored to simply be in the room.

Dunton, and the many advice-givers who succeeded him, was never in the same room as the people who sought his advice. The exchanges occurred anonymously and by mail. Dunton was a skillful pitchman who had the instinct to sell his readers on a completely new kind of intimacy—intimacy among strangers. He recognized that though it is ennobling to be in the room among scholars, to be cradled by one's mentors and guides, there is something uniquely freeing about a correspondence among strangers, whose judgments can be kinder or blunter than those of a close friend and whose opinions bear a detachment that can feel like omniscience. He realized, many centuries before the invention of the internet, that it can be easier to trust someone who has no reason to care. There are no humiliations, no dumb questions, in this nameless, epistolary space.

In the late 1680s, just before Dunton began his advice column, King James II was ousted in a coup and replaced by his son-in-law. The other three men in this section, Lord Chesterfield, Benjamin Franklin, and William Alcott, rose to prominence during similarly turbulent moments in history. War, in any decade, has a theatrical quality, requiring citizens to perform temporary roles in the name of patriotism: teenage boys become soldiers, women join the work-force. Lord Chesterfield was an accomplished British statesman, but in his role as a politician, he had no influence on America—he never even visited the colonies. But his book arrived in America in 1775, a time of profound open-mindedness and upheaval, when readers were hungry for new ideas, when any book could be The Book. Benjamin Franklin, too, found a ready audience in prerevolutionary America. Amid the chaos of Philadelphia, which was the second-largest city in the colonies and had no newspaper, fire department, or hospital, Franklin created a new role for himself—the secular moralist, the policeman of everyday ethics—and found a ready audience. Some decades later, William Alcott, a doctor and an early evangelist for vegetarianism, wrote nutritional advice during the lead-up to the Civil War and connected his theories on healthy eating to the abolitionist movement.

These men provided advice at a moment when power was newly splintered and available for the taking. They were each deliberate in their plans to acquire some for themselves. They were experimenting with new ideas, nothing blasphemous, but different from what your father or pastor would tell you. They were not fire-breathing activists—the status quo had treated them well. But they initiated conversations that weren't happening elsewhere.

None of them were terribly concerned about their lack of qualifications. They were all preternaturally confident. They did not have elaborate arguments or any great evidence for why everyone should take their word on how to behave. *Trust me*, they said, essentially. And people did.

ONE

In Praise of the Maggot

John Dunton

THERE WAS ONCE A GROUP OF MEN WHO HAD THE answer to every question. They were based in London and called themselves the Athenian Society. Membership was kept secret, but they claimed to be thirty-odd strong and to include experts in religion, astronomy, math, and philosophy. From 1691 to 1697, with the occasional hiatus, the Athenian Society published the *Athenian Mercury*, a twice-weekly magazine in which members responded to readers' questions. Their readers wanted to know why alcohol killed erections and made people slur, why horse excrement was square, if people born with missing body parts were also missing pieces of their soul, and if the sun was made of fire. They also asked ethical, "was it okay" questions. Like, was it okay for a man and woman to live together before they were married, or to have adulterous thoughts if you never acted on them, or to masturbate, or to throw a witch in a pond, or for a Jew to marry a Christian? The Athenians delivered harsh and clear determinations of what was acceptable and what was not. They showed the moral clarity of a priest and the worldliness of a diplomat. They condemned adultery, masturbation, mixed marriages, and impure thoughts.

The Athenians' founder, John Dunton, was a publisher with a small bookstore in the Poultry, an industrial London neighborhood named for its unwelcoming smell. He was known to be impatient and arrogant. He had few friends. A colleague once described Dunton's mind as being like a "table, where the victuals were ill-sorted and worse dressed." In portraits, he appears gangly, with a pointy nose and a bulbous chin and a face so narrow that it's unclear, if he were to smile, where a smile might fit.

In his memoir, Dunton writes that he learned to lie before he learned to speak. In elementary school, in a small town near London, he paid no attention to the teacher and instead perfected the art of avoiding things he did not want to do. "The advances I made in school went on very slowly," he writes. "For I had a thousand little things to say, that would excuse my absence or at least abate the rigor of punishment." He was a serial daydreamer who spent days lost in his own detailed fantasies and armchair adventures. He had an instinct for "rambling." "I have been a Rambler ever since I was 14 years Old," Dunton wrote. "I was always moving from one Stage to another, rummaging every corner and neuke [nook] of the World." Dunton didn't actually travel all that much, but he was fidgety and restless and had an especially vivid strain of wanderlust.

Dunton's mother died when he was a baby and he was raised by his father, an Anglican minister from a long line of Anglican ministers. His father likely assumed that John would join the clergy, but by his teenage years, it must have been obvious that he lacked the discipline for religious life. When he was thirteen, Dunton had such a raving crush on a girl in the neighborhood that he couldn't bring himself to study or pay attention to his classes. Finally, when he was fifteen, his father allowed him to drop out of school and found him an apprenticeship with a religious bookseller in London.

Three days into the apprenticeship, Dunton returned home—he didn't like having a boss any more than he liked having a teacher. His father wrote a letter to the publisher, Thomas Pankhurst, asking that he give his son a second chance. Dunton returned to London, and this time, he stuck around. "I began to love books to the same excess that I hated them before," he wrote. Dunton worked for Pankhurst from 1676 to 1684 and then opened his own publishing house and bookstore. He sold books and pamphlets by popular preachers; "The Sufferings of Christ" by Reverend Mr. Doolittle was one of his top sellers.

Books were Dunton's life. He not only published and sold them but wrote them too. One of his biographers, J. Paul Hunter, wrote that Dunton was a "conscious reader of public tastes and trends." He had endless complaints about the book business, but only because he loved it—with the exception of working his store: "Were I to begin the Trade of Bookselling once again, I would never give myself the trouble to keep open shop. Unless a man can haggle half an hour for a farthing, be dishonest, and tell lies, he may starve behind his shopboard for want of subsistence."

The Athenian Society was, in many ways, Dunton's chance to be the reverend his father thought he'd never be: he became someone people turned to with their moral quandaries, even though the entire Athenian project was founded on a lie.

THE IDEA CAME to him on a winter day in 1691. He was on a stroll with two friends through St. George's Fields, a marsh in central London. Dunton wasn't talking much—rare for him. He broke his silence to tell his friends that he'd just had a brilliant idea, but because Dunton took pleasure in annoying people, he refused to tell his friends what the idea was, only that it was so good he would "not exchange [it] for Fifty Guineas." This was the exact sort of thing that earned Dunton the nickname "the maggot"—he had an instinct for getting under people's skin.

Dunton's big idea was to start a magazine composed of readers' questions. Or, as he put it, "concealing the Querist and answering his question."

Dunton had a habit of starting magazines, though none of them lasted. *The True Protestant Mercury* lasted two months and the *Coffee House Mercury* three weeks. He'd sold both of them at coffee shops for a penny. Despite these failures, Dunton was certain that magazines were good business, much better than books. Readers, he'd found, were "unwilling to lay out a shilling or a crown on a Journal of Travels bound together, but will not grutch to part with a Penny at a time for a single sheet."

Like any publisher, Dunton tried to understand why certain books sold and others did not, and, as Hunter wrote, he seemed to have a potent instinct for the zeitgeist. The question-and-answer format made his job far easier: it allowed him to respond directly to whatever readers wanted to know.

The 1690s were a turbulent but liberating time in Great Britain. In 1688, the Whig Party staged a coup in which King James II, a converted Catholic, was replaced by his Protestant daughter Mary and her Dutch husband, William of Orange. When William assumed the crown, he implemented measures to expand religious freedom and the rights of the press; he allowed for Presbyterians and other non-Anglican Christians to gather and pray in groups and reduced the licensing requirements for publishers.

It was a moment of possibility, and Dunton wanted his publication to be a place for the curious and disoriented to ask whatever was on their minds. He would need to censor any question that even mildly insulted or critiqued King William or Queen Mary—the new freedoms King William afforded the press did not include the right to critique the crown. But Dunton was eager to tackle just about anything else. His magazine was intended, he wrote, for "lovers of Novelty."

There was one problem: Who would answer the questions? Dunton realized that the person supplying the answers had to appear wiser than their readers' favorite teacher, pastor, or grandfather. He had to offer rare and exclusive knowledge—or, at least, *seem* like the kind of person with access to rare and exclusive knowledge. He needed someone mysterious and enticing, but trustworthy, too.

Dunton didn't know anyone who met all these requirements, so he decided that the answers would come from an intellectual society: the Athenian Society. The first person Dunton approached about joining was Richard Sault, who was married to Dunton's sister. Sault was a moody math teacher with particular passion for algebra. He was not the most impressive man, but he was around. Dunton and Sault put out the first issue of what was then called the *Athenian Gazette* in March of 1691, though their names are nowhere to be found in it. The issue included a lengthy introductory letter: "The Design is briefly, to satisfy all ingenious and curious Enquirers into Speculations Divine, More, and Natural, &c and to remove those Difficulties and Dissatisfactions that shame or fear of appearing ridiculous by asking Questions." No question was too scandalous, no subject off the table, anonymity was ensured.

The first issue included seven questions, four of them about the human soul. ("Whether all souls are alike?" one reader asked.) The other questions concerned the existence of angels, the ethics of wife beating, and the origin of the spots on the moon. There were too many questions for Dunton and Sault to handle on their own, and since many of them begged for a religion expert, Dunton wrangled the only one he knew—Samuel Wesley, who was married to his wife's sister. Wesley was an ordained priest of the Church of England but had not been assigned a parish. By May, Dunton had courted the society's fourth and final member: Dr. John Norris. There's little record of Norris; even Dunton was never completely sure what kind of "doctor" he was. Unlike Sault or Wesley, Norris refused to accept any compensation; he just liked being in the club.

The Athenian Society took no more members; it stayed confined to Dunton, his two in-laws, and a man who may or may not have been a doctor. About a year after the release of the first issue, the writer Charles Gildon published *The History of the Athenian Society,* a paean to this elusive intellectual community. The book, which Dunton likely commissioned, includes an illustration that shows twenty-six stately men in curly wigs and long robes arguing around a rectangular table. *These* were supposed to be the men answering the questions.

It's unknown whether Dunton and his team ever felt guilty for misleading their readers or if they were having too much fun poring through all manner of intimate questions. The four of them became the sounding board for the nameless masses of London. Readers wrote them about their anxieties and fantasies too humiliating to say aloud but too urgent to ignore. The *Athenian* became a place for people to air their grievances and horrors, a place where they could be vulnerable and weird. When it came to people's personal lives in the 1690s, the Athenian Society had an incomparable view.

THERE WERE QUESTIONS about nature, about God, marriage, sex, archeology, astronomy, the Bible, and dreams. There was one reader who'd had a dream about a comet and then saw a real one in the sky a month later and wondered if that made him a prophet. The Athenians told him that it had been a cosmic coincidence. There was a letter from a woman in love with a clueless man who never seemed to catch her hints. The Athenians recommended that she be more obvious. "Pull 'em by the Nose, write to 'em, or if neither of those will do . . . show 'em this Question and Answer," they wrote. Someone wanted to know if it was normal for a woman to cry after sleeping with her husband for the first time. The Athenians wrote that consummating a marriage was stressful and that there was no reason to feel ashamed. Did the Bible forbid suicide? Yes, the Athenians said. Did angels have bodies? The Athenians weren't sure. One man had proposed to his girlfriend, but only so she'd sleep with him. Did he really have to keep his word? "Whether I had not best immediately marry her to put her out of her Fear, and endeavor also to make her sensible of the Crime we have together been guilty of: Pray give a speedy answer?" The Athenians said to marry her, immediately. There was a man who saw no point or pleasure in kissing. The Athenians told him he was doing it wrong.

There's no record of how many questions they received—over their six years, they published nearly six thousand—but the magazine appears to have been something of a cultural phenomenon given the number of imitations and parodies it inspired. Dunton and his colleagues became so overwhelmed by submissions that they had to set a cap on questions, asking readers to send no more than two at a time. They also set some ground rules about the types of questions they published. "Send no more Obscene Questions, for we shan't answer 'em," they wrote. "Some *Questions* . . . we think not proper to take any notice of, our Design being to answer only what is a *fitting entertainment for the Ingenious,* or what does consist with *Faith and good manners.*"

But the dirty questions kept coming, and the Athenians kept printing them. Their readers needed clarity on all sorts of sexual, emotional, and bodily matters that they couldn't take to a priest. One man was in love with a woman promised to another, much older man. Another man had two wives, sisters, and wanted to know if he was allowed to take a third. Another wanted to know why women preferred soldiers to intellectuals. ("His legs be well proportioned," the Athenians reasoned.) Dunton had opened the floodgates; he couldn't shut them now.

The questions could be probing, even scandalous, but the answers were stale and reflexive. One reader, ahead of his or her time, asked why there was no male synonym for "whore": "Why the word to express the Sin of Lewdness in our English Tongue, is of a feminine Signification being call'd Whoring, from the Word Whore? Why mayn't it be better call'd Roguing, and so made masculine, since Men are, at least commonly, the Tempters and of consequence have the greater Share in the Sin?"

The Athenians replied: "If words were by Institution, 'tis proba-
ble that Men made most of 'em, though now they are made, Women
have a pretty large Share in the use of 'em. The Greek and Latin
words *Titpuet* and *forincatio* seem to have a larger sense than the
English. However Roguing here won't do because it has too large a
Signification." Or, to put it a little differently: that's what the men
who invented words decided. The Athenians had no qualms with
arbitrary power.

Athenians believed adultery was wrong, masturbation was wrong,
and the king was right. They generally instructed their readers to
abide by whatever the Bible said—it was advice, perhaps, that Dunton imagined his father might give in the same situation. The tone
of the replies was stoic and self-serious, with gratuitous and frequently inaccurate sprinkles of Latin. The *London Mercury*, one of
the parody rags, reprinted all the questions that had appeared in the
previous issue of the *Athenian* with their own snappier replies. They
theorized that the only explanation for the Athenian Society's dry
prose was that all of its members were undertakers. (They also took
unbridled delight correcting the *Athenian's* Latin.) Occasionally, the
Athenians broke character: when someone wrote in with the question, "When shall I be marry'd?" the Athenians replied, "When you
can find any that's Fool enough to have ye."

The Athenians were mocked by their competitors for publishing
so many questions from women. In response, Dunton started the
Ladies Mercury. In the first issue, published in February 1693, the
editors explained that the *Ladies Mercury* would only accept questions about love and relationships, which left "the examination of
learning, nature, arts, sciences, and indeed the whole world" to the
Athenian. One question in the first issue came from a woman who
wanted to know if she should tell her fiancé she was a virgin even if
it wasn't true. (She had once been seduced by a "lewd and infamous
Rifler.") The Athenians strongly recommended, in this particular
instance, that she ignore the Bible and lie.

Dunton shut down the *Ladies Mercury* after four issues. Maybe their staff of four couldn't handle two publications; maybe they didn't have enough readers. The *Athenian* continued to publish letters from women, many of them about love. One woman rejected one of her suitors and then he died unexpectedly. Was she to blame? Was a married woman allowed to keep love letters from former flings? Dunton also introduced a new poetry column, written by Elizabeth Singer Rowe, a seventeen-year-old from Somerset. Her poems were far more virtuous than most contributions to the *Athenian*. ("Who could, and yet out-live the Amazing sight? / Oh, who could stand the stress of so much Light!") Dunton was a devoted fan. Volume fifteen of the *Mercury*, published in 1694, was wholly dedicated to her verses, and Dunton later published her first collection.

Dunton and his fellow Athenians were surprisingly forward-thinking not only in their inclusion of women's letters but in their responses to them. Dunton believed that women should be educated just as men were—a progressive position at the time. He also took on the question of whether men and women can be friends, and he had a distinctly post–*When Harry Met Sally* take. "Such a friendship is not only innocent but commendable, and as advantageous as delightful," the Athenians wrote. "Souls have no sexes, nor while those only are concerned can anything that's criminal intrude."

THE ATHENIANS KEPT up the ruse until 1695. From that point forward, every issue was signed "John Dunton, proprietor of the *Athenian Mercury*." It's not clear how the Athenians lost their anonymity, when the other three members were found out, and if their outing was Dunton's intention, or mistake, or the work of one of their muckraking competitors. The disclosure marked the beginning of the end of the *Athenian Mercury*. The issues started coming out less frequently, and at the end of that year, they took a seventeen-month hiatus so that Dunton could care for his dying wife, Elizabeth.

The final issue was published on June 14, 1697, some weeks after Elizabeth's death. There was the usual range of questions: What gives gunpowder its strength? Why are some wines stronger than others? Why do some people have curly hair? "According to Aristotle, this may proceed from the double Motion of the Matter of Hairs," the Athenians wrote. "Partaking both of an Earthy and Fiery quality, the Earthy tending downwards; and the Fiery upwards: It must necessarily follow, that by this double and contrary motion the Hair be Curled."

By that point, the other three Athenians were no longer speaking to Dunton. Elizabeth had bankrolled the project, and after her death, Dunton could no longer afford to pay his contributors. Wesley and Sault were furious, but what made matters worse was that Dunton remarried four months after Elizabeth's death, while the rest of the family was still mourning. Dunton's second wife, Sarah, looked and behaved so much like Elizabeth that Dunton blithely described her as his "first wife in a new edition . . . in a new frame." He appears to have meant it as a compliment.

Dunton published more than sixty books in his lifetime—"a most Voluminous writer," as one of his colleagues recollected. One of his last books, a memoir called *The Life and Errors of John Dunton, Citizen of London*, is written as an advice book to himself. He writes about every period of his life—his childhood, his apprenticeship, his marriage—and what he wishes he'd done differently. Every chapter is broken into two parts: in the first section, he tells the reader what happened, and in the second, he writes about what he wishes had happened instead. The second, self-chastising sections he calls "An idea of a new life." He wishes that he'd listened to his elders, been more cautious, obedient. He's humiliated by his wayward ways, his eccentricities. "My first great care under the relation of Apprenticeship should be diligence; for no sooner does an Apprentice drop his diligence, but he is on the high road to every irregularity, he is exposed to every vice, lies open to temptation," he writes. Again and again, he admonishes himself for not playing by the rules.

Dunton says he couldn't help himself, that he was born with squishy morals. "Long before I had any articulate use of my tongue, I gave the world sufficient evidence of a child of Adam; and the certain tokens of corrupt nature and intemperate passion were more and more apparent, as I made advances both in strength and age: all the signs of disobedience and revenge, of impatience and immoderate desire, were seen in me," he writes. In the *Athenian*, he'd given advice that he was too indolent to follow: respect authority, respect the king.

Dunton didn't have the patience for a traditional education; he couldn't force himself to follow in his father's clerical footsteps. Yet he took an opportunity in which he could have challenged social norms—anonymously!—and reinforced them instead. He could have instigated a sexual revolution: Masturbate! he could have said. Marry whoever and however many people you please! But he didn't. Instead, he evangelized rules he did not follow.

Dunton was thirty-eight when the *Athenian* shuttered. He continued to write and sell books out of his shop in London, mostly religious texts. He started an oral history project with the prostitutes of downtown London, but he never completed it. He set out to create an epistolary service for men and women to exchange ideas on politics and books—a kind of matchmaking project for people seeking a pen pal of the opposite sex. It didn't take off. Nothing did, after the *Athenian*.

Dunton was seventy-four when he died. He had no children. The *Athenian* was his only legacy, and it's largely remembered as an elaborate trick. "There is nothing here without which English literature has suffered any serious deprivation," the critic Cecil A. Moore wrote in 1902 of the *Athenian Mercury*. "They are of some importance, however, for the additional light they shed upon the egregious dishonesty of the author and, incidentally, also upon the taste of a large English public to which he catered, with evident success, during the closing years of the seventeenth century. It is a safe generalization that the further we penetrate through the elaborate deceptions Dunton built up round his character and work the more plainly it will appear that he deserves no attention whatever as a creative writer." Dunton was, in this view, a talentless hypocrite who deserved to be expunged from history.

But the point of the *Athenian* was never Dunton's answers, it was the questions. A little bit outside of things is where people go to fend off despair. And, for nearly a decade, the *Athenian Mercury* served as such a haven. The Athenian Society were humorless sticklers, but the magazine they created was morally capacious, the one place where people could question what was normal. Dunton recognized the rare comfort created in an anonymous chat room. The *Athenian Mercury* was the precursor to "Dear Abby," Reddit, and Quora, and the many advice columns that proliferated across America. For a penny, readers could pick up a copy and know there were other people out there with the same strange questions. And, for a minute, they might feel a little less alone.

TWO

Politeness vs. Honesty, Part 1

Lord Chesterfield

> True Republicanism requires that every man shall have an equal chance—that every man shall be free to become as unequal as he can.
>
> —Samuel Wells, *How to Behave*

LORD CHESTERFIELD NEVER LIKED HIS DAUGHTER-IN-law. Her name was Eugenia Peters and she was the illegitimate daughter of some Irishman. She was two years older than Philip, Chesterfield's only son. She was well-read, a quality that Chesterfield could appreciate, but she was also "plain almost to ugliness," as one cruel observer noted. Chesterfield felt he had raised his son to do better. He had always coached Philip to keep two French girlfriends, one for "gallantry" and the other for "attachment."

Little has been written about Philip, except that he was mild-mannered and often ill. I imagine him as handsome and helpless, easily stomped on. His father, on the other hand, was boisterous and commanding. He was known as one of the more engrossing public speakers in the House of Lords; in 1728, he was appointed ambassador to the Netherlands, and in 1745 he was named Lord Lieutenant—the second in command—of Ireland. Chesterfield retired from government young, and by the time Philip met Eugenia in 1750 while they were both traveling through Rome, he was spending his days minding his horses and writing his son letters. He had written Philip a letter almost every day since before his son could read. Philip was born out of wedlock, and to quell the gossip mill, Chesterfield kept his distance. The letters were Chesterfield's way of compensating, of staying connected while remaining discreet. He largely parented his son by mail.

Eugenia and Philip knew that Chesterfield would never approve of their relationship. Philip said nothing to his father when Eugenia gave birth to his son in 1760 and said nothing three years later when she gave birth to his brother. In 1767, Eugenia and Philip eloped and kept their marriage a secret from Philip's family. They knew that Philip's father would find out eventually, but they hoped by then he'd have no choice but to accept them—however begrudgingly. Chesterfield sensed that Philip was hiding something from him; his son's letters had become distant and vague. He pleaded for the details of his son's life. "Admit me to your fireside, in your little room; and as you would converse with me there," Chesterfield wrote. But Philip's letters didn't change: he wrote about work, the weather, their shared acquaintances.

In 1768, at the age of thirty-six, Philip died unexpectedly, and only then did Chesterfield find out about his son's family. Biographers say that Chesterfield was a doting grandfather. But he wanted little to do with Eugenia. When he died a few years later, at the age of seventy-nine, he left her nothing.

Eugenia was broke, with no way to earn a living. Some months after Chesterfield's death, she decided to sell his letters for cash. Philip had saved virtually every one. She took them to James Dodsley, a top English publisher, who offered her fifteen hundred guineas. *Finally*, she must have thought. Chesterfield had finally done something useful for his son.

Lord Chesterfield's Letters to His Son was published in Britain in 1774 and sold out three printings within the year. When the book reached America the following year, it was met with the same rabid interest. It is said to be America's first best-selling advice book, even though its advice was never intended for a mass audience. It was a brutish father's attempt to help his son compete in a ruthless world, his tips conniving and offensive. The book was met with a combination of delight and disgust. And it made Chesterfield, unwittingly, America's first expert on how to behave.

IN 1726, WHEN he was thirty-two years old, Lord Chesterfield inherited his family's seat in the House of Lords. He was a short, boxy man with an oversized head, an icy voice, and teeth so black that he was ashamed to smile. A friend once told him that he "looked like a stunted giant." He compensated with charm. "Lord Chesterfield was allowed by everybody," as one colleague said, "to have more conversible entertaining table-wit of any man of his time." He practiced his public-speaking skills and became known as a tactful statesman, witty and poised, with a way of putting others at ease. He learned to string sentences together in such a stylistic way that no one even paid attention to the content of what he said. "I discovered that of the five hundred and sixty [members of the House of Commons] not above thirty could understand reason and that all the rest were *peuple* that those thirty only required plain common sense dressed up in good language and that all the rest only required flowing and harmonious periods whether they conveyed any meaning or not; having ears to hear but not sense to judge." He had a talent for lightening a heavy mood, for coining the line that would bring men on the verge of taking a swing to crack a smile instead. He was a workaholic who hardly drank, though he was known to get carried away at the card table, always up for another round.

Chesterfield had skill but no integrity. Sir John Chester, a character in Charles Dickens's novel *Barnaby Rudge*, is a thinly veiled portrayal of Chesterfield. The character is a vapid aristocrat, "more proud, indeed, than wealthy," whose success is entirely attributed to brownnosing. "He caught the fancy of the king, knelt down a grub, and rose a butterfly," Dickens writes. Chester is eerily placid, heartless, and smooth, "no mark of age or passion, envy, hate or discontent." He has no enemies, but no friends either. He's killed in a duel at the end of the book, and no one is especially sad about it.

It's a harsh depiction but probably a fair one. Chesterfield's biographer, William Henry Craig, determined that his subject's only redeemable trait was his prudency. "Lord Chesterfield rarely or never acted on impulse, and was incapable of strong emotion. This type of man is very common and very useful too. It is by such calm, self-governed natures that the world's business is best conducted; by men who act from principle and not from feeling. Such men are often admired and trusted, but they are rarely loved," Craig writes in his 1907 book *Life of Lord Chesterfield*. "To be loved, one must be lovable, which his lordship neither was or affected to be."

In 1728, Chesterfield was able to talk his way into a plum assignment as ambassador to the Netherlands. There, he met a French woman named Madelina Elizabeth du Bouchet. In 1732, Bouchet gave birth to Philip, Chesterfield's first and only child, and Chesterfield returned to London, where he married another woman, Petronilla Melusina von der Schulenburg. She was King George I's daughter with one of his long-term and favorite mistresses; Petronilla had all the connections of a bona fide princess, even if she lacked the title. It was a *smart* marriage, a shrewd move for Chesterfield's diplomatic career, and it was clear to all involved that it was nothing more than a political arrangement. For years after their wedding,

Chesterfield and Petronilla lived in neighboring houses. They never had children. Bouchet, meanwhile, raised Philip in Holland, alone.

Chesterfield considered himself an intellectual and sophisticate. He billed himself as a patron of the arts, though he despised music and had little interest in architecture or painting. He was a man who liked titles, and "patron" had a certain ring to it. He liked being *seen* with artists. He offered his patronage to the writer Samuel Johnson as he completed his *Dictionary of the English Language* and seemed surprised that Johnson expected something from him, that "patron" wasn't an honorific bestowed by a writer or artist. "I have been pushing on my work through difficulties of which it is useless to complain, and have brought it at last to the verge of publication without one act of assistance, one word of encouragement, or one smile of favour. Such treatment I did not expect, for I never had a patron before," Samuel Johnson wrote in a letter to Chesterfield when the dictionary was nearly complete—no thanks to him. Chesterfield displayed Johnson's angry letter on his mantel for all to see. He believed any conflict, no matter how tense, could be spun into an entertaining anecdote. There was no purpose, in Chesterfield's view, in dwelling on emotions, or really in expressing emotions at all.

Chesterfield was desperate to see Philip succeed and believed he would if only he tried. "From the time you have had life, it has been the principle and favorite object of mine, to make you as perfect as the imperfections of human nature will allow," he once wrote Philip in a letter. He feared that Philip would have to be tenacious to overcome the social handicap of having been born out of wedlock and also recognized that his son was among the least tenacious people he knew.

In 1746, when Philip was seventeen, Chesterfield decided that his son had reached the age for his first grand tour of Europe. Chesterfield would not chaperone. Chesterfield's illegitimate son was an open secret in London, but traipsing through Europe together was not how things were done. Philip traveled with a tutor but stopped to meet Chesterfield's colleagues and acquaintances along the way. These weren't friendly stopovers; they were exams. Chesterfield would write to his friends asking for reviews of Philip—of his manners and conversational skills. "I am told you speak very quick and not distinctly," Chesterfield wrote in April of 1748, while Philip was in Leipzig. "This is a most ungraceful and disagreeable trick, which you know I have told you of a thousand times; pray attend carefully to the correction of it." Over time, Philip received more positive reviews. "I have lately had extraordinary good accounts of you, from an unexpected but judicious person, who promises me that, with little more of the world, your manners and address will equal your knowledge," Chesterfield wrote him on September 5, 1749.

The journey was Philip's coming-out party, his introduction to the continent's aristocracy. Chesterfield's letters were full of tips on how to make people forget the circumstances of Philip's birth: flatter, avoid arguments, never show the slightest hint of emotion. He prescribed a daily grooming regimen, instructing his son to clean his ears, nose, and fingernails each morning. He urged Philip to be punctual and appropriately dressed. "Dress yourself fine where others are fine; and plain where others are plain," he told his son.

Chesterfield wished for his son to be the kind of person who could easily transmute his personality, who could become whomever he needed to be. Chesterfield's school of etiquette had a distinctly anthropological bent: he encouraged Philip to notice social rules and then follow them closely. When in doubt, he told Philip, imitate. For Chesterfield, the highest possible compliment was "easy." He urged Philip to be flexible, to be the kind of person who's easy to be around, easy to talk to, easy to bring anywhere. "Lord Chesterfield had two admirable qualities at least; he always recognized the fact of his own ignorance when it was forced upon him and he was not above learning his business from those who were capable of teaching it," wrote William Henry Craig in what is among the most spiteful biographies ever written. These were qualities Chesterfield hoped that Philip would inherit: a capacity to identify what he didn't know and the confidence to learn on the fly.

"Nothing is more engaging than a cheerful and easy conformity to other people's manners, habits, and even weaknesses," Chesterfield wrote. He wanted his son to learn to act one way while feeling another. He was wholly unconcerned with Philip's integrity; it was his ambition that worried him. "Be serious with the serious, gay with the gay, and trifle with the triflers," he wrote to Philip in a letter. "In assuming these various shapes, endeavor to make each of them seem to sit easy upon you, and even to appear to be your own natural one." He urged Philip to make nice with everyone, to never turn anyone into an enemy: "Perhaps you will say that it is impossible to please everybody. I grant it; but it does not follow that one should not therefore endeavor to please as many as one can." Chesterfield urged Philip to be an equal-opportunity capitulator, to ingratiate himself to everyone, regardless of his or her rank. "You cannot, and I'm sure you do not think yourself superior by nature to the Savoyard who cleans your room or the footman who cleans your shoes," he wrote. The point of treating everyone respectfully, Chesterfield emphasized, wasn't to impress God or in service to some abstract idea like *goodness;* the point, rather, was that anyone could wind up being useful in Philip's rise to prominence. It was strategic to not have enemies. "Be convinced, that there are no persons so insignificant and inconsiderable, but may, some time or other, have it in their power to be of use to you, which they certainly will not if you have shown them contempt." For an aristocrat, Chesterfield was oddly obsessed with his own survival. He showed little concern for his legacy and cared only about the heights he might achieve in his lifetime.

He sent his son tips for picking up women, too. He promised that the key to seduction was flattery, especially with unattractive girls. "Every woman who is not absolutely ugly thinks herself handsome, but not hearing often that she is so, is the more grateful and obliged to the few who tell her so," he wrote. He told Philip to avoid using pretentious words like *namely* and to never tell stories, unless they were short. "Talk often," Chesterfield wrote Philip, "but never long." If Philip ever felt compelled to contradict someone, his father suggested he do so gently, with phrases like "I am not sure" or "I should rather think."

Philip, however, seems to have quietly ignored most of his father's advice. He didn't care about ingratiating himself to Europe's elite or sleeping with dozens of women. He cared about Eugenia. With a father like that, marrying for love must have felt like an act of treason.

One could sum up Chesterfield's advice this way: it's more important to be shrewd than genuine; there's no real value to "being oneself"—a term not then in the lexicon. Chesterfield wanted Philip to win at life, to marry well and earn a prominent appointment. He didn't particularly care if Philip enjoyed the process. "I do not regret the time that I passed in pleasures; they were seasonable; they were the pleasures of youth," Chesterfield wrote. "But knowing them as I do, I know their real value, and how much they are generally overrated." His letters were an instruction manual for a life of great achievement and maybe some joy.

WHEN IT WAS published in 1774, Chesterfield's book of letters was disparaged by the English press. "They teach the morals of a whore, and the manners of a dancing master," Samuel Johnson wrote in his review. Johnson, of course, was nursing a grudge—unlike Chesterfield, he dwelled unabashedly on his feelings. After the review came out, everyone in Britain wanted to read this despicable book. There were never enough copies. This may have been the earliest recorded instance of what we now call "hate-reading," that peculiar exercise of feeling repelled by a book we can't put down—it happens when the words reflect some part of ourselves we prefer to ignore. Chesterfield wasn't Europe's only social climber; many of his readers certainly had their own strategies for getting ahead. But only Chesterfield's methods were published.

Chesterfield was skewered for being superficial and small-minded. Books were meant to be serious and communicate lofty ideas about God, philosophy, and ethics. (Chesterfield had implored Philip not to waste his time reading "unnecessary" books—like novels and travelogues.) Chesterfield's letters, meanwhile, were about hygiene and small talk. Across the Western world, empires were being overthrown and democratic societies erected in their place, and Chesterfield was focused on securing his son a sinecure as a midlevel bureaucrat.

The book reached America a year later, in 1775, and readers there were similarly disgusted. "The utile is so studiously blended with the vile," wrote Mercy Otis Warren, a political activist from Massachusetts, in an op-ed in *Boston Magazine*. Warren's teenage son had become obsessed with Chesterfield's letters, and she feared what he was learning from them. "I have no quarrel with the graces," she wrote. "I love the Douceurs of civility, the placid manners l'amiable. But I love better that frankness and sincerity that bespeak a soul above dissimulation; that genuine, resolute, manly fortitude." She conceded that Chesterfield had some practical suggestions for getting one's way, but she didn't want to raise a son who made efficacy his guiding light. She wanted to raise a son who meant what he said, who stood for something larger than his own success.

Abigail and John Adams were also repulsed by Chesterfield's letters. John Adams described them as being "stained with libertine Morals and base Principles." Abigail urged her younger brother not to follow Chesterfield's advice and to flatter a woman only when he meant it. She told her brother that most women had a nose for dishonesty and preferred a man who demonstrated a "purity of sentiment" over a sweet-talker.

The letters may have been morally "stained," but they were also a fun read—witty, blunt, a little crass. Chesterfield's cosmopolitanism, his many glamorous friends across Europe, his talk of meeting kings and attending balls and the distinctive allure of French women must have seemed exotic and exciting to someone like Mercy Otis

Warren's teenage son. But it wasn't the book itself that Warren objected to; she didn't call for it to be burned or anything so extreme. She worried what would happen if people *followed* Chesterfield's advice, what would come of America if it was largely inhabited by opportunists.

The backlash had as much to do with the contents of the book as the author's nationality: it was the beginning of the Revolution, and many Americans were automatically disdainful of anything British, including Chesterfield and his guide to social maneuvering. Taking a stance against Chesterfield's letters was a way to ally oneself with the American cause.

But some American parents adored Chesterfield. They, too, were worried about raising sons who could fend for themselves. They treated his letters like a secret trove of wisdom they'd happened upon and didn't care if their author was British. "No man can be accomplished in mind or body without their perusal," wrote one southern father, a few years after Chesterfield's book came out, in a letter to his son. Other letters from the time show that parents recited Chesterfield when encouraging or disciplining their children; they'd cite him when they wanted to underscore the importance of clean nails or the humiliation of a misspelled word, or to emphasize the severity of some seemingly minor social infraction. "I know of a man of quality who never recovered from the ridicule of having spelled wholesome without the 'w,'" Chesterfield once wrote Philip, as many American parents reminded their own teenage children. Now everyone in America had access to a father like Chesterfield—distant and calculating, but also knowing and crafty. He was a man who knew how to get ahead by being poised and complimentary, and going with the flow.

On April 16, 1787, as Alexander Hamilton and others were calling for the ratification of the Constitution, America's first professionally produced play opened in New York. It was a five-act comedy by Royall Tyler called *The Contrast*, and it focused on the rivalry between two men, Billy Dimple and Colonel Manly, who had fallen in love with the same woman. Manly, as his surname would imply, is brave and virtuous, a former military officer who'd fought against the British. Dimple is an Anglophile and dandy who had just returned from a stint in England and "was now metamorphosed into a flippant, pallid, polite beau, who devotes the morning to his toilet, reads a few pages of Chesterfield's letters, and then minces out to put the infamous principles in practice on every woman he meets," as one character explains. This being a comedy, Manly gets the girl. Even in his humiliation, Dimple smugly reminds the audience of his superiority, of "the contrast between a gentleman who has read Chesterfield and received the polish of Europe and an unpolished, untraveled American." Manly ends the play by telling the audience that Dimple's moves may work on European girls, but American women were different. "Probity, virtue, honor, though they should have not have received the polish of Europe, will secure to an honest American the good graces of his fair countrywomen." In America, in other words, sincerity mattered more than style. And Chesterfield had become synonymous with all the vapid formality that Americans had fought to free themselves from.

I HAVE WONDERED how advice books inherited such a bad rap, why they tend to fall squarely in the category of things you read when no one is watching. Maybe at one point, consulting advice was indication of sacrilege, that you were turning to texts other than the Bible for instructions on how to live. Seeking advice is an admission of cluelessness, and no one likes to appear naïve.

Reading Chesterfield, I thought about how seeking advice is also an admission of selfishness. We look to advice to better ourselves, for simple tricks that will help us get our way—the kind of tactical wisdom that Chesterfield offered his son. Advice, as a genre, rarely concerns itself with morality; it only pertains to the material world and the practical considerations for thriving there—companionship,

money, power. Seeking advice is an admission of superficiality. Chesterfield is one of the earliest examples in this long tradition of morally
ambiguous reading, of books that seek to strengthen some of our
least noble instincts.

While advice-givers tend to be distinctly unconcerned with
morals, many have instigated explosive ethical debates, Chesterfield being among the first. He introduced an ethical question that
Americans continue to grapple with: Is it okay to say one thing while
believing another? Or to put it in another way: What's more important, honesty or politeness?

Lionel Trilling, the literary critic, picked up this question in
1972 when he published *Sincerity and Authenticity*, in which he de-
fines two distinct terms that he believed Americans had conflated.
He describes sincerity as the "congruence between avowal and actual feeling." A sincere work of literature is one in which the author seeks to convey exactly what she's thinking—your comfort be
damned. Authenticity, meanwhile, is a matter of personal integrity:
you know when you're being authentic, even if other people don't. It's
a virtue that puts little stock in what other people think and instead
emphasizes determination and self-awareness.

Using this parlance, Chesterfield urged his son to be authentic
but never sincere. He wanted his son to be purposeful when he
chose to imitate someone. "I would much rather have the assent of
your reason to my advice than the submission of your will to my authority. This, I will persuade myself, will happen," he wrote Philip.
He hoped that Philip would learn to calibrate his behavior in service of his goals. But sincerity, to Chesterfield, was for chumps. He
instructed his son to never share his true feelings or thoughts, to
never appear vulnerable or emotional. There is no need for sincerity
if you have no self to begin with. And Chesterfield had no self, only
a résumé.

When Alexis de Tocqueville, the diplomat and political scientist, visited America in 1831, he was surprised, touched even,

by how earnest Americans were, writing in his book *Democracy in America* that Americans were "frequently more sincere" than the French. Americans tend to think its preferable if our greetings and gifts reflect our individual feelings and tastes rather than uphold an arbitrary custom. It's an American value to eschew what's expected, to challenge the status quo. There's a cult philosophical movement known as "radical honesty," which first came to prominence in 2007, that advises people be completely honest at all times, even if you hate the food your host spent ten hours preparing or you want to sleep with your best friend's wife. Most people would not go that far, but earnestness is a part of American culture—we want our politicians to be honest, we created Taylor Swift, and the point of most children's movies is to "be yourself," no matter what anyone says.

Being oneself is crucial to political and social progress—institutions only change when individuals persistently make their discomfort known and take issue when their employer or school or local museum interferes with their ability to be themselves, their pursuit of sincerity. At the same time, most people would agree that there are certain instances when it's unpleasant, disrespectful even, to "be yourself." Your true self may be most comfortable barefoot, but your neighbor on the cross-country flight would likely prefer that you suppress that urge for the next six hours. Public spaces operate on the premise that visitors will sacrifice their personal preferences to public rules. "For most people, 'be yourself' is actually terrible advice," wrote Adam Grant, a professor at the Wharton School at the University of Pennsylvania, in a 2016 op-ed in the *New York Times*. "Nobody wants to see your true self. We all have thoughts and feelings that we believe are fundamental to our lives, but that are better left unspoken." It's not natural to lower your voice when you're angry or to eat with a fork and knife. But civilization is unnatural by definition and relies on etiquette to function. Turning the music down, wearing a suit to a wedding, writing a thank-you card may seem annoying or even dishonest. But sometimes one has to be a bit dishonest in pursuit of a bigger goal. If you were being completely sincere, you'd tell your boss how much you hate her, but then you'd get fired and derail the nonprofit you work for. You returned the creepy motivational poster your great aunt bought you for Christmas, but you sent a thank-you card anyway because a small lie is better than a lifetime of bad blood.

In *Democracy in America*, Tocqueville notes another difference between America and France: "Americans of all ages, all conditions, all minds constantly unite." Lines between social classes were more porous in America than in Europe. When George Washington was elected president, he insisted that he be addressed as "Mr. President" rather than the more obsequious honorifics suggested by his staff, like "His Serene Highness," "His Magistracy," and "His Elective Magisty." It was a minor detail, but an important one, that leveled the relationship between the president and his citizens. In 1857, the author Samuel Wells wrote a pocket guide on manners called *How to Behave*. Wells was inspired to write the book because he felt the country needed a "truly American and republican school of politeness." European manners, he thought, were too elaborate, stiff, and exacting; America needed a guide that spoke to its egalitarian mission. Wells believed that of all the social guides that had ever been written, Chesterfield's was the nearest to a "republican school." He includes a chapter of "Maxims by Lord Chesterfield."

Chesterfield wanted Philip to be able to fit in anywhere. He believed that with some basic observational skills, anyone could blend in at the fanciest of balls. He was certain that being well-mannered was as simple as being gracious and open-minded. "Take, rather than give, the tone of the company you are in," Chesterfield wrote Philip. Chesterfield's advice was meant to help Philip bridge cultural and linguistic divisions. He recognized that manners, anywhere, weren't that hard to learn. He was the precedent for the many manuals published in the decades since aimed at business-men fearful of committing a social faux pas while working abroad. Chesterfield believed that any two people, if so inclined and with a bit of preparation, could get along well enough. You could shed your identity if it got in the way; you could imitate or flatter your way to acceptance.

THREE

Funny Business

Benjamin Franklin

IN 1732, BEFORE BENJAMIN FRANKLIN EXPERIMENTED with electricity or went to England to conduct diplomatic negotiations, he published a book of aphorisms called *Poor Richard's Almanack*. Each line contained some practical kernel of advice, like: "Diligence is the mother of good luck" or "Early to bed and early to rise makes a man healthy, wealthy, and wise." Many of them rhymed. The maxims directed people to be practical and grateful, with reminders like, "Fish and visitors stink in three days" or "Genius without education is like silver in the mine." They were nagging refrains that, if ever said aloud, would be met with an impatient, "I know that already" groan. Which is why Franklin chose to write not just under a different name but with a wholly different identity. His alter ego was Richard Saunders, or "Poor Richard," a farmer with a folksy manner, an unsatisfied wife, and morbid hobbies: he is determined to use weather patterns to predict the deaths of his friends and rivals.

The premise of the almanac was a simple joke: advice from a man who had no right to be giving it. A significant portion of his annual almanac was on the subject of money; Richard stressed the importance of being frugal, of never living beyond one's means. ("A Penny saved is Twopence clear.") Of course, "Poor Richard" is not the best moniker for a financial wizard. But that was the joke! The almanac included proverbs on love and marriage. ("Where there's marriage without love, there will be love without marriage.") In one preface, Richard disparages his wife, Bridget, for being chatty and wasteful, for buying a petticoat they couldn't afford, and for developing a pretentious taste for expensive tea. They come across as being among the last couples one would turn to for marriage advice.

While Franklin was writing *Poor Richard's Almanack*, he was also the editor and publisher of the *Pennsylvania Gazette* (where he invented the still-popular font **Franklin Gothic**) and a member of various civic associations. So why, amid all his serious responsibilities, did he want to spend his time on a somewhat goofy book? Franklin was reckless and unfocused with his ambition, a perennial multitasker, always doing dozens of things at once. But he was too righteous, too puritanical, to partake in things he didn't believe in, and he believed that "good" books offered more than entertainment. "No Piece can properly be called good, and well written, which is void of any Tendency to benefit the Reader, either by improving his Virtue or his Knowledge," he once wrote. Franklin wanted readers of *Poor Richard's Almanack* to come for the joke but stay for the pithy, quotable wisdom. He wanted to reduce the human experience into a textbook, a how-to guide for moral living. He seemed to believe that America needed a book like *Poor Richard's Almanack,* and many Americans appeared to agree with him. Between 1733 and 1758, Franklin published his almanac every year, and each edition sold upward of ten thousand copies—more than the Bible. Franklin recognized his opportunity: "Observing that it was generally read, scarce any neighborhood in the province being without it, I consider'd it as a proper vehicle for conveying instruction among the common people, who bought scarcely any other book."

UNLIKE POOR RICHARD, Benjamin Franklin had every right to be giving advice. His father, Josiah, was a candle and soap maker who had come to America from England when he was twenty-five. Benjamin, the youngest of six children, was a top student in primary school, but Josiah didn't have the money to pay for more schooling. He was ten when he dropped out.

He continued his studies independently. He was a voracious reader, and he'd assign himself essays and force himself to write two or three drafts. He never had any intention of publishing these pieces, but he wanted the practice. He liked to compare the drafts and pick a favorite. He forced himself to practice his penmanship and to translate prose into verse and verse into prose, to broaden his capacity for both forms. All of his favorite writers worked at *The Spectator*, a London daily, and Franklin committed their best sentences to memory. One of those writers was Joseph Addison and one of those sentences was this: "I shall endeavor to enliven Morality with Wit, and to temper Wit with Morality." It was a mantra that permeated all of Franklin's later writings, but most especially the almanacs. As a writer, Franklin sought to dispense medicine that went down easy, to dress up broccoli as dessert.

After Franklin dropped out of school, he apprenticed himself to his older brother James, who was the printer and publisher of the *New-England Courant*, the only independent paper in the colonies. The apprenticeship was a nine-year commitment, which felt like a lifetime sentence. Though famous for his self-discipline, Franklin had a fanciful side. He liked to read travel journals and had, he wrote, "a hankering for the sea." James was tough on his younger brother, assigning him all the most grueling, repetitive tasks, keeping him long hours, and refusing to let him write. Benjamin didn't want to wait nine years to start his career as a writer. (He'd be twenty-one by then.) So he taught himself how to disguise his handwriting—all those self-inflicted penmanship exercises were useful after all—and he started submitting articles to the *Courant* under various pseudonyms.

The first character Franklin developed was Silence Dogood, a prudish widow from rural Massachusetts. She wrote personal essays about falling in love and editorials about religion, class, and education. For a long time, James never made much of the fact that Dogood shared many of the same interests as his younger brother. Benjamin was resentful of his former classmates who had the money to continue with school, especially those who went to Harvard. One of Dogood's early pieces rips into Harvard for its elitism, for educating privileged, undeserving children and then retroactively designating them geniuses: "The most part of those who were traveling thither were little better than dunces or blockheads." Another of Dogood's pieces argues that the government should be free from religious influence: "A Man compounded of Law and Gospel, is able to cheat a whole Country with his Religion, and then destroy them under *Colour of Law*: And here the Clergy are in great Danger of being deceiv'd, and the People of being deceiv'd by the Clergy, until the Monster arrives to such Power and Wealth, that he is out of the reach of both, and can oppress the People without their own blind Assistance." After James wrote a similar piece, he was told by local authorities that they'd need to approve every issue of the *Courant* in advance. Dogood's story didn't mince words but was somehow considered less controversial. Ben took note of this: anything written by a dowdy older woman was unlikely to be perceived as a threat.

In September of 1723, about five years into his apprenticeship, Franklin broke his contract and ran away, making his way to Philadelphia. (It was while working for his older brother, he later wrote, that he developed an "aversion to arbitrary power.") He founded his own paper, the *Gazette*, and created several new pseudonyms, including Martha Careful and Caelia Shortface. Writing and thinking as a woman was an exercise in empathy, a chance to see the world from another perspective—much like any of his self-administered courses. It was also a way of rehearsing his ideas before committing his name to them.

By then, Franklin wasn't using pseudonyms because he wanted to conceal his identity. Rather, he understood that the messenger determined the message, that an article about abortion had intrinsically higher stakes if it came from a woman than if it came from a man. And, like any good publisher, he knew that stakes sold papers and could change the way people think. He took a pseudonym if he thought it made things more interesting. When his competitor, the *American Mercury*, published a short piece about abortion, he sent two letters to the editor, one from Caelia Shortface and the other from Martha Careful, imploring the *Mercury* to never mention the subject again. (The unofficial policy on abortion in the colonies was don't ask, don't tell.) "If he Publish any more of that kind," wrote Martha Careful, "my sister Molly and my Self, with some others, are Resolved to run the Hazard of taking him by the Beard, at the next Place we meet him, and make an Example of him for his Immodesty." Franklin was interested in creating a totalizing, immersive experience for the reader, a perfect pairing of text and author. "It is observed, that the Generality of People, now a days, are unwilling either to commend or dispraise what they read, until they are in some measure informed who or what the Author of it is, whether he be *poor* or *rich*, *old* or *young*, a *Schollar* or a *Leather Apron Man*," he wrote at the time. He was a practical shape-shifter who tried to maximize the wit and the impact of his work by adjusting the character of its author. He never worried that people would find this tactic dishonorable. He assumed readers understood that every author, to one degree or another, was playing a part. And Franklin had the imagination and ambition to play many. He wrote his newspaper's advice column, "The Casuist," and on weeks when there weren't any interesting letters to respond to, he wrote those as well. He set the tone of the advice column: even when contending with serious matters, like mourning or heartbreak, it should be wry and playful. One time, he wrote a letter from the perspective of a man whose wife had cheated on him with their neighbor. The man was heartbroken, but rather than ruminate, he thought he'd proposition his neighbor's wife for some revenge sex. "The Casuist" told him to "return not evil for evil, but repay evil with good." For Franklin, every story, even the scandalous ones, had a moral in the end.

———

FRANKLIN WROTE CRIME stories and gossip items—after all, he had newspapers to sell. In his spare time, he wrote lectures about virtue. He was determined to attain "moral perfection." He composed a comprehensive list of every virtue, as if they were dog breeds or car models or Pantone colors, and set out to collect them all. He came up with thirteen and defined each in a sentence or two:

Temperance, Eat not to dullness; drink not to elevation.

Silence, Speak not but what may benefit others or yourself; avoid trifling conversation.

Order, Let all your things have their places; let each part of your business have its time.

Resolution, Resolve to perform what you ought; perform without fail what you resolve.

Frugality, Make no expense but to do good to others or yourself; i.e., waste nothing.

Industry, Lose no time; be always employ'd in something useful; cut off all unnecessary actions.

Sincerity, Use no hurtful deceit; think innocently and justly, and, if you speak, speak accordingly.

Justice, Wrong none by doing injuries, or omitting the benefits that are your duty.

Moderation, Avoid extremes; forbear resenting injuries so much as you think they deserve.

Cleanliness, Tolerate no uncleanliness in body, clothes, or habitation.

Tranquility, Be not disturbed at trifles, or at accidents common or unavoidable.

Chastity, Rarely use venery but for health or offspring, never to dullness, weakness, or the injury of your own or another's peace or reputation.

Humility, Imitate Jesus and Socrates.

Franklin tested and graded himself on each virtue, every day. "I made a little book, in which I allotted a page for each of the virtues. I rul'd each page with red ink, so as to have seven columns, one for each day of the week, marking each column with a letter for the day. I cross'd these columns with thirteen red lines, marking the beginning of each line with the first letter of one of the virtues, on which line, and in its proper column, I might mark, by a little black spot, every fault I found upon examination to have been committed respecting that virtue upon that day." Order, he found, was the virtue that most challenged him. He had never been especially organized, and as much as he tried to keep his papers in their proper place and follow a daily work routine, he could never quite muster the self-discipline. He did not list curiosity as one of his fourteen virtues, though he probably should have. He was impatient with anyone who lacked the drive to learn. "We are all born ignorant, but one must work hard to remain stupid," Franklin is credited with saying.

When Franklin was growing up, all the popular guidebooks were written by preachers. Cotton Mather, one popular preacher, wrote four hundred such books, but there was one in particular that Franklin had read and reread as a boy, *Bonifacius: Essays to Do Good*. The book so inspired him that as an adult, Franklin wrote a letter of thanks to Mather's surviving son. "If I have been a useful citizen, the public owes the advantage of it to that book."

Franklin's family was Presbyterian, but by the time he was twenty or so, he'd stopped attending Sunday services. He believed in a Supreme Being, but he believed in free will more. He was no ideologue; his nearest thing to a worldview was that anything could be improved thorough observation and study. The Ten Commandments, in a way, were far easier to follow than Franklin's list of virtues.

The Commandments provided a clear list of things a good person should and shouldn't do, while for Franklin, goodness was an endless gradient—one could always acquire more of it.

Franklin was too practical, too of-this-world, to sell his advice as the key to a peaceful afterlife. He couldn't promise acceptance to Heaven, or that Heaven existed at all. Franklin believed, rather, that the only way to convince people to behave themselves was to convince them of the tangible and immediate benefits of doing so. Franklin promoted his thirteen virtues as tricks to finding satisfaction on earth. He sold industry as the key to success, temperance as the key to a long life, and sincerity as the key to happiness. Like Chesterfield, Franklin's advice was tactical. He did not expect people to chase moral goodness for its own sake—not everyone aspired to be priestly. But while Chesterfield cared only about himself and his son, Franklin believed that an industrious, frugal populace, behaving in their own best interest, was the most effective way to build a stronger society. Self-improvement, in Franklin's view, was never selfish. When a person applied himself to becoming more virtuous, society became slightly more virtuous, too.

For the most part, Franklin's virtues were not substantially different than the advice Mather provided in his books. They both encouraged modesty, hard work, and cautiousness. But Franklin wanted his advice to *feel* different than a preacher's guide. He wanted to find a new, more user-friendly format for dispensing wisdom.

Writing as Poor Richard distinguished Franklin's book from the self-serious volumes written by Mather and others like him. Humor, Franklin discovered, was an effective means of proselytizing, a way to turn prescriptive advice into pleasurable reading. People loved Poor Richard. Clergy members purchased extra copies to distribute among their parishioners. Franklin's message echoed that of their Sunday sermons, but readers could enjoy the sly wit and the strange disclosures about Poor Richard's sad life. Franklin knew that the best way to grab people's attention was to make them laugh or stroke their ego. Poor Richard did both, inviting readers to laugh on his behalf. As Poor Richard said, "He is a fool who cannot conceal his wisdom."

~

MANY FAMOUS ADVICE-GIVERS have walked the line between earnestness and satire, a line thinner than one might think. In the 1950s, the *Economist* published a regular column on management by C. Northcote Parkinson, a naval historian. It was intended as a satirical column that would poke fun at large, unnecessary bureaucracies. "Work expands so as to fill the time available for its completion," he wrote. "There need be little or no relationship between the work to be done and the size of the staff to which it may be assigned." He wrote about "commitology"—the study of committees. The committee, he wrote, "takes root and grows, it flowers, wilts, and dies, scattering the seed from which other committees will bloom in their turn." Parkinson's deadpan humor was interpreted as solemn wisdom, and soon enough, he was billed a genuine expert on efficiency. Parkinson went along with it; he lectured on how companies might streamline their operations, making up management theories as he went along. In the 1970s, Michael Korda, a senior editor at Simon and Schuster, wrote a book called *Power!: How to Get It, How to Use It*. Korda, inspired by Parkinson, had written a satirical guide to acquiring power. "The more elaborate and expensive pieces of office machinery are seldom power symbols—merely knowing how to use them or even where they are, indicates a low power rating," he wrote. He wrote that ocean blue was the ultimate "power color" and advised low-level workers to acquire the keys to file cabinets and supply rooms so that their colleagues would come to depend on them. As soon as the book came out, Korda was whisked onto the self-help circuit. In New York, there was a noted rush on blue suits and blue office furnishings. Korda's follow-up book, *Success!*, was written in that same sardonic tone, and again, readers interpreted it as straightforward advice.

Satire offered cover, safety. These were confident people, but they recognized that it was absurd to proclaim themselves experts in subjects as broad and far-reaching as power and success. They had no professional degree in these topics. There was nothing in particular about them that gave them a superior knowledge of human experience; they had guessed their way to prominence. A touch of sarcasm was one way to acknowledge the inherent bizarreness of their role.

Franklin may have felt that Poor Richard was more qualified to dispense advice than he was. In 1730, Franklin married Deborah Read, largely because he was impressed by her frugality—which is the romantic equivalent of praising a film for being short. They had a child, a daughter, but their marriage was largely long-distance. Franklin spent eighteen years of their forty-four-year relationship in Europe, tending to some urgent diplomatic matter. He had a number of affairs, some of them epistolary, some of them consummated. Franklin, for all his obsession with moral perfection, had a tolerant perspective on affairs. Poor Richard offers no opinion about activities that take place within the privacy of the home. He's lax on masturbation and adulterous thoughts. Franklin never waded into the nebulous territory of intentions. He was too practical, too civically oriented, to care about anything aside from discernible, public actions. Poor Richard has no dictums about the way one should feel; his sayings only apply to how one behaves.

Franklin wrote an essay, under his own name, called "Old Mistresses Apologue," in which he urges a younger friend to find a wife. "Marriage," he wrote, "is the most natural State of Man, and therefore the State in which you are most likely to find solid Happiness." But should his friend commit to the bachelor's life, Franklin advises that he only have affairs with older women: they are smarter, more discreet, and eternally grateful for the attention. Like all of Franklin's advice, the essay teeters on the edge between sarcasm and earnest guidance. It's a tone of infinite flexibility and demonstrates a certain cowardice. Anything said or written in this liminal, permissive space can be excused later on with a quick "Kidding!"

⌒‿⌒

ADVICE, STEREOTYPICALLY, IS meant for the individual seeking a competitive advantage in business or love. But not Franklin's
almanacs. They compiled values he wanted all Americans to embrace. He set out to write a moral playbook for a new, more perfect
society. Philadelphia was the second-most populous city in the colonies, after Boston. But unlike Boston, which was ruled by Puritan
elders, Philadelphia permitted the practice of all religions, and the
city was splintered into three separate communities—the Quakers,
the Germans, and the "Scots-Irish"—and there was little in the way
of a centralized government. "A saying here: Pennsylvania is heaven
for farmers, paradise for artisans, and hell for officials and preachers," a visitor from London reported. Franklin offered advice that
applied to everyone, regardless of religion or national origin. He
seemed to want all of America to behave in accordance with Poor
Richard's maxims; he thought the country would be most successful
if everyone was polite and hardworking. "Some thought [the alma-
nac] had its share of influence in producing that growing plenty of
money which was observable for several years after its publications,"
Franklin notes in his autobiography.

In recent years, educators and parents have focused on teaching
their kids to have "grit," or resilience—a trait, much like Franklin's notion of "resolution," that allows people to set and achieve
their goals and overcome inevitable setbacks. Educators agree that
these "non-cognitive" skills are as important, if not more important, than traditional academic subjects, like algebra and chemistry.
But they've found that they're far harder to teach. "For all our talk
about non-cognitive skills, nobody has yet found a reliable way to
teach kids to be grittier and more resilient," writes Paul Tough, the
author of *How Children Succeed*. Franklin grappled with that very
same question: How do you teach people values, rather than skills?
Richard Saunders was the best he came up with, though he never
pretended it was a perfect solution, or that anyone actually listened.

In the final edition of the almanac, there's a speech written from the perspective of a character named Father Abraham, a crotchety, wise old man who urges his listeners to be frugal and avoid debt. Franklin writes that those in attendance "heard it, and approved the doctrine, and immediately practiced the contrary." He seemed to expect the readers of his almanacs to do the same.

Franklin was more of an Anglophile than the other Founding Fathers, late to join the revolutionary cause, and too old to fight in the war. (He was nearly seventy years old when the war began.) He was never a revolutionary; he was a pragmatist. Near the end of his life, he began to speak out against slavery. He thought slavery was a moral perversion that should be policed and outlawed—"an atrocious debasement of human nature that its very extirpation, if not performed with solicitous care, may sometimes open a source of serious evils." He made a practical case for abolition: "The unhappy man, who has long been treated as a brute animal, too frequently sinks beneath the common standard of the human species. The galling chains, that bind his body, do also fetter his intellectual faculties, and impair the social affections of his heart." Slaves, he argued, could contribute a great deal to society if given the chance. He couldn't say whether resisting slavery would guarantee entry to Heaven. But he could promise that it would improve life on earth.

FOUR

American Guru

William Alcott

On May 15, 1850, dozens of people gathered at Clinton Hall, at the corner of Astor Place and 8th Street in Manhattan, to discuss the future of vegetarianism in America. It was one of the first national conventions for American vegetarians, and its main attraction was Sylvester Graham. Graham, a Presbyterian minister, had inspired a whole lifestyle movement. His thousands of followers referred to themselves "Grahamites" and lived in urban communes where they cooked meatless meals, slept on hard mattresses, and took only cold baths, as Graham, their guru, instructed. They made their own crackers from a combination of white and wheat flour—"Graham crackers"—and abstained from alcohol and spices. People mocked the Grahamites as a humorless cult; journalists referred to Graham and his health regimen as "dietetic charlatanry." The other prominent figures of the vegetarian movement were middling researchers or preachers with a passion for healthy eating. They wanted to reform the American diet and regulate the meat industry, and many of them considered Graham a giant distraction. But he was the distraction that drew crowds. They needed him.

After several days of lectures and discussions, the group assembled at Clinton Hall decided to form an official organization: the American Vegetarian Society. They drew up a constitution with fourteen guiding principles, such as "Flesh-eating is the key-stone to a wide-spread arch of superfluous wants" and "Cruelty, in any form, for the mere purpose of procuring unnecessary food, or to gratify depraved appetites, is obnoxious to the pure human soul."

They also held elections for AVS's inaugural president and vice presidents. Graham, the group's only celebrity, was an obvious choice for president and seemed a shoo-in. But Graham didn't win—he was named of the organization's nine vice presidents. He lost to a middle-aged physician named William Alcott.

Alcott was a prolific author of diet books and published a vegetarian magazine. He was more staid than Graham, and more practical. *Charismatic* was not a word anyone would use to describe him. A predilection for cult leadership was never in his blood. He was mild-mannered and erudite, determined to prove through his voluminous writing that vegetarians were healthier and lived longer than omnivores. But Alcott possessed something that Graham did not: a medical degree. Alcott had the pedigree to legitimize the AVS's going theories about the benefits of a vegetarian diet. The medical field was still primitive; Alcott was fairly certain that the digestive system was located in the left shoulder. But his degree lent him a certain authority that Graham lacked.

Near the end of the conference, Alcott addressed his electorate for the first time. He was a long-winded speaker and not an especially electric one. At one point in his speech, he recited an exhaustive list of prominent vegetarians: "I will also refer to some of the philosophers, such as Porphyry, who, though he wrote against Christianity, was a sober, intellectual, and mighty man, and such were many others, who were substantially, essentially, and truly vegetarian." It was clear he saw vegetarianism as something more than a diet; it was a community, a lifestyle, a movement. And Alcott intended to take it mainstream. Together, he told the crowd, they'd make "everybody . . . understand that we are something more than grass eaters."

～⚬～

ALCOTT WAS BORN in 1798 in a farming community near New Haven, Connecticut. His father was a farmer who specialized in growing flax. He couldn't afford to send William to school and kept him busy on the farm. Alcott was a severe young man with a lanky build and a bulbous, off-center nose. In his books, he comes across as an indoor creature, poorly suited for farm life, whose favorite pastime is reading the Bible.

When William was growing up, no one in his family ever went to the doctor, even when they were ill. There were only a few licensed doctors in Connecticut, and the Alcotts didn't trust them. When they were sick, they visited traditional healers and midwives or concocted their own remedies at home. As a child, William heard rumors that doctors cut up dead bodies and studied their insides, something he felt only a heartless maniac could do.

In the early 1800s, a number of states, including Connecticut, New York, Ohio, and Massachusetts, began to crack down on midwives and homeopathic healers by passing laws that imposed fines on unlicensed physicians. In 1821, for instance, when Connecticut passed the country's first law restricting abortion, the intent was not to outlaw the procedure but to regulate the traditional healers and midwives who tended to perform them. The larger goal was to centralize the practice of medicine, so that all health-care providers held the same accreditations. Until then, healing had been more of an art form than a skill set. Material knowledge mattered less than a capacity to put people at ease, an instinct for the right question, and boatloads of empathy—qualities we now refer to as "bedside manner."

The standardization of medicine was intended to improve the overall quality of treatment. But, for years, it had the opposite effect.

At the beginning, medical schools were degree factories where aspiring physicians attended lectures by professors who knew little
more than they did. The schools were functionally autonomous,
connected to established universities by name only; they could admit
whomever they pleased, and professors divvied tuition fees among
themselves. "The creation of the type was the fertile source of un-
foreseen harm to medical education and to medical practice," writes
Abraham Flexner, who was responsible for reforming medical education in the twentieth century. "The schools were essentially private
ventures, money-making in spirit and object." There were no labs;
most schools lacked the resources for the dissections that had so disturbed Alcott. Early medical school was one long, largely inaccurate
lecture in anatomy.

What medical school did offer was a professional path for young
men who lacked an undergraduate degree—none was required at
the time—and wanted to secure a more respected position in society. Yale Medical School, which was founded in 1810, was one of
the first medical schools in the country. And, in 1822, at the age of
twenty-four, Alcott enrolled. He was desperate to get off his father's
farm. Medicine was more academic than farming, but like farming,
it required a certain faith in natural processes, an understanding that
seeds sprout, flowers bloom, and the body can heal from a cold on its
own and that humans should only intervene when necessary.

Alcott completed medical school in 1825. About a year later, he
developed an undiagnosed lung disorder that left him bedridden.
He could hardly breathe and spent months hallucinating, unable to
move. No one could figure out what was wrong with him. Doctors
prescribed medicine, but nothing worked. He spent long days in bed
praying, preparing to die.

But after about year, Alcott recovered as suddenly as he'd fallen
ill. He came to the conclusion that it was his appeals to God that
had saved him. Medicine, he determined, was pointless. His recov-
ery, he wrote, "renewed my declaration of independence with regard

to those earthly props on which I had so long been wont to lean, and of dependence on God, and on his natural and moral enactments."

Alcott's convalescence changed him. He gave up meat, as he believed the Bible instructed, and swore off modern medicine. He had no interest in working as a physician anymore; he couldn't bring himself to peddle what he now saw as nonsense. He'd come to believe that health and spirituality were inextricably linked, that devotion to God was the surest path to longevity.

So Alcott became a kind of preacher, performing lectures across the country about spirituality and wellness. He wrote books, dozens of them. He started writing in the early 1830s, and within a span of thirty years, he'd published more than forty. He wrote about nutrition, as well as bathing, hygiene, and household cleanliness. He wrote a guidebook for men, *A Young Man's Guide,* and one for women, *A Young Women's Book of Health,* and one for new mothers. He advised new mothers to breastfeed, to dress their infants in clean flannel—not cotton—and to keep their children out of the dirt. "The strange belief that 'dirt is healthy' has much influence on the daily practice of thousands who are ignorant of the human structure, and the laws that govern and regulate the animal economy," Alcott wrote. "It is not the dirt which promotes their health, but their active exercise in the open air; the advantages of which are more than sufficient to compensate for the injury which they sustain from the dirt." Although Alcott had a fraught relationship to the medical profession, he stood on his credentials to justify his dietary theories. His book *The Vegetable Diet* bore the subtitle, "As Sanctioned by Medical Men." The book is a compilation of profiles of healthy vegetarians, most of them doctors and many of them unnamed. "A physician of some eminence, now residing in Philadelphia, has been heard to say that it was his decided opinion that mankind would live longest and be healthiest and happiest on mere bread and water," he wrote. "Prof R. D. Mussey, of Hanover, New Hampshire, whose science and skill as a surgeon and physician are well known and attested all over New

England, has for many years taught, both directly and indirectly, in his public lectures, that man is naturally a fruit and vegetable eater." Despite his skepticism toward medicine, his books were predicated on the idea that doctors knew more than the rest of us and it was wise to follow their advice on all matters of health. Alcott personally advised that people abstain from meat as well as green cucumbers, grapes, tomatoes, and peppers. Tomatoes, in particular, he'd found were "quite insoluble and unwholesome."

Alcott's most ambitious book, *The Laws of Health*, was a collection of two thousand practices for a healthy life. It included exercises to strengthen the body as well as spiritual recommendations. "If the infirmities of age come upon us, it is because we have disobeyed, either intentionally or ignorantly, the Divine Laws," he wrote. All of Alcott's more physiological recommendations are designed to strengthen his readers' connection with God. Cleanliness, he wrote, abates the spread of certain diseases and promotes mental clarity, but more importantly, it supports God's vision for the way people ought to live. Alcott wrote several vegetarian cookbooks, and in each, he argues that a vegetarian diet strengthens the immune system and promotes higher energy and better sleep, but most importantly, it enables communion with God. He often quotes 1 Corinthians 10:31: "Whether you eat, or drink, or whatever you do, do it all to the glory of God." His advice is meant to improve one's life on earth and guarantee entry to heaven; he offers the key to both a good life and a good death.

Eating meat, he warns readers, leads to rheumatism, constant headaches, canker sores, and tooth decay. It also indicates a dangerous lack of impulse control. "There is no slavery in this world like the slavery of a man to his appetite," he said. "Let man but abstain from the use of the flesh and fish, and the slavery of one man to another cannot long exist."

Alcott believed that vegetarianism and abolitionism were ideologically linked. Abstaining from animal products was a way to boycott slave labor, he argued, but on an individual level, a vegetarian was more empathetic than someone whose stomach was "crammed with animal abominations," as one abolitionist phrased it. The AVS worked closely with various abolitionist groups. William Lloyd Garrison's abolitionist magazine, *The Liberator*, printed supportive articles about the American Vegetarian Society and advertised their annual conferences.

The American vegetarian movement's earliest leaders were British activists who arrived in Philadelphia in the 1820s with the hopes of starting a new Christian sect centered on the importance of meatless eating. According to the historian Adam Shprintzen, until the Civil War "the vegetarian movement saw the diet as a catalyst for a total reform ideology, including abolitionism, women's suffrage, pacifism, and economic equality." It was less concerned with the health of the individual dieter than that of the society she resided in. It was nutritional advice that conformed to the same patterns as etiquette manuals from the early nineteenth century; the authors, generally, were less concerned about giving readers tips for impressing their party guests and more concerned about establishing social guideposts so that everyone felt comfortable. Samuel Wells, who published *How to Behave* in 1856, defined politeness as the "spontaneous recognition of human solidarity."

After the Civil War, Shprintzen writes, the promise of vegetarianism shifted to "creating healthy, vital bodies best prepared to advance socially and economically." Graham, in this regard, was ahead of his time. He was less politically motivated than Alcott, promising his followers longevity and optimal health. His followers were supposed to keep their windows open, bathe every morning, dry off briskly, and sing cheerfully to themselves as they readied themselves for the day. He thought sex should be had, at most, once a month, and he forbade masturbation.

Alcott was more idealistic—his ultimate goal was to end slavery. And his version of vegetarianism was more accessible and less regimented than Grahamism, something anyone with a passing interest could try. The word *cultish* is often hurled at "lifestyle" movements.

It applies to Grahamism, a diet followed in homage to an idol. But Alcott cared more about vegetarianism than his own celebrity. He provided something more straightforward and impersonal—one could follow Alcott's recommendations without ever knowing who Alcott was. His books are mainly composed of quotes from other people. He wasn't merely being retiring, he was being strategic: he believed in crowdsourcing, that the only way to drive people toward vegetarianism was to demonstrate the diet's popularity among a plurality of people and "medicine men," to show that everyone was doing it.

LOOKING AT THE quantity of new nutritional advice today, one might think that eating is a fairly recent phenomenon. Every few months, it seems, there's a new dieting fad, each promising a healthier, better life. Some diets are centered around particular food groups, while others are based on the diets of other cultures. When I was growing up in New York in the 1990s, my mom was convinced that a Mediterranean diet, heavy on olive oil, whole grains, and fish, was the healthiest way to eat. More recently, my parents have been convinced that red meat and butter—foods we avoided my entire childhood—are good for you. In the 1920s, there was the Inuit diet craze, where people ate raw fish and caribou at home. In 1950, Gaylord Hauser's book *Look Younger, Live Longer*, which sold out three printings within a year, listed five "wonder foods" that promised lifelong health and beauty: powdered brewer's yeast, powdered skim milk, yogurt, wheat germ, and blackstrap molasses. In the 1960s, Japanese-inspired macrobiotic food, heavy on pickled vegetables and whole grains, was considered the paragon of healthy eating. In the 1990s, Dr. Robert Atkins encouraged people to abstain from whole grains and eat more bacon. Today, you can choose the Paleo diet, heavy on meat, or the raw food diet, which eschews consuming anything that's been cooked;

or you could become a juicer, someone who thinks vegetables are best when liquefied.

Each of these diets has a devoted following, with its own gurus and jargon, and offers the kind of moral clarity hard to find outside of religious contexts. They may speak of "grass-fed" meat and Michael Pollan, or "bulletproof" coffee and Dave Asprey, but they are each chasing optimum health, however they've come to define it. In the 1980s, Nathan Pritkin, a well-known vegetarian, and Robert Atkins, the creator of the Atkins diet, were frequently booked on the same television show. Atkins was an egomaniac, out to create his own fame—why else would he name his diet after himself? Pritkin, in turn, was Alcott's successor, a moralistic bore who encouraged restraint without scientific justification. It made for good television; there was always yelling. It pitted one vision of health against another and made the simplest imaginable question—What's healthy?—unbearably complex. Everything was healthy. Nothing was healthy. No one seemed to know.

Vegetarianism is still in wide circulation, as is its more stringent cousin, veganism, which forbids the consumption of all animal by-products. Unlike the other diets I mentioned above, vegetarianism has a political orientation; people become vegetarians for reasons other than their personal health and fitness. They may object to violence against animals or have concerns about ecological preservation, water shortages, or global warming.

Alcott found a balance between the practical and grandiose. Vegetarianism, he insisted, wasn't just good for you, it was good for society. He and the other members of the AVS sought to bring Christian values into American kitchens, to revive Americans from the indolent, thoughtless slumber they felt heavy meat consumption had induced en masse. Spreading vegetarianism, the group felt, was a moral imperative, the key to ending slavery and reorienting American culture toward the values on which it was founded.

But the AVS also had basic, material concerns about meat consumption. Though meat could be preserved or cured, it quickly spoiled, and home refrigeration units had not yet been invented. In 1906, the writer Upton Sinclair published a novel set in the Chicago stockyards, *The Jungle,* and though the book was categorized as fiction, it shed a light on the unsanitary practices at large slaughterhouses, where owners purposely repackaged spoiled, diseased meats and sold them to customers. That year, largely in response to Sinclair's book, President Theodore Roosevelt signed a bill giving the previously powerless Food and Drug Administration the authority to regulate the agricultural industry. But for all of Graham's and Alcott's working lives, meat was an unknown quantity and its widespread consumption presented a legitimate public health issue.

But that didn't stop nineteenth-century Americans from eating meat. They ate tons of it, far more than we do now. According to one researcher, Americans in 1850 were consuming, on average, 175 pounds of meat a year, as compared to the 100 pounds of meat a year Americans eat today. (That number includes chicken, which nineteenth-century Americans ate sparingly.) Nineteenth-century Americans ate bears, raccoons, opossums, hares, wild turkeys, ducks, grouse, and pheasant. It took months of sweaty labor to grow fruits, vegetables, and grains and the product was unsatisfying and the work could easily be undone by an unexpected rainstorm. Meat, meanwhile, was everywhere. In some cases, even falling from the sky. The Eskimo curlew, a long-necked bird that's since gone extinct, would grow so fat that it would fall from the air and burst on the ground—New Englanders called them "doughbirds." After visiting America, Charles Dickens noted with surprise that "breakfast would have been no breakfast" without a steak cooked in butter.

I have poured through the American diet crazes over the last two hundred years looking for commonalities. Vegetables, everyone admits, are a healthy choice, as long as they aren't deep-fried. So is eating slowly, and in moderation. Everything else is up for debate.

Diets don't, however, emerge out of thin air. Each nutrition craze is an attempt to course-correct a new pattern in American public health. The Mediterranean diet, for instance, emerged because of widespread concerns about high cholesterol and heart disease; the turn against carbohydrates is a response to the unknown consequences of eating too many processed foods. The American Vegetarian Society was, in part, responding to the lack of health regulations at slaughterhouses.

But all of these diets have one thing in common; they each expand far beyond nutrition. They are spearheaded by doctors who behave like preachers. They provide a lifestyle, methods for sharing one's "journey" with others, a sense of belonging. Few people seemed to care that Robert Atkins was a licensed physician or that he temporarily lost his license in the early nineties. (He administered an experimental cancer treatment and the patient had a bad reaction that involved blurry vision and numbness in one leg.) Atkins offered more than good health; he offered a *definition* of health, tenets to eat and live by.

⁓

GRAHAM WASN'T SUPPOSED to die young. But he did, at fifty-seven, for unknown reasons. The AVS was still a nascent organization, and its members feared that they'd never recover from the humiliation of Graham's early death. Their guru had promised longevity and failed to achieve it himself; everyone would see them as hypocrites.

Alcott and his colleagues tried to control the damage. In October 1851, a month after Graham's passing, they released a statement in the *American Vegetarian and Health Journal*, their official newsletter. Graham had been overworked for years, they wrote in his death announcement, and had been feeling ill for some time. "The immediate cause of his decease," according to their statement, was a "warm bath" prescribed by Graham's doctor. They never expounded upon the risks of bathing but still blamed the incompetent doctor. They mentioned that Graham suffered from chronic health issues, like anxiety and insomnia—which, they made sure to clarify, were wholly unrelated to his diet.

A year later, the AVS was still making excuses for Graham's untimely death. In September 1852, Alcott wrote an unkind piece about Graham, his "undue anxiety," and his addiction to his own unhappiness. The moral of Graham's death, Alcott concluded, was to reduce stress and worry—not to consume meat.

Alcott died a few years later, in 1859. He was sixty years old. Few people outside of the vegetarian community knew who Alcott was, so there was no real risk that people would notice the minor hypocrisy of his death—he too had promised followers that vegetarians had exceptionally long lifespans—and no chance that the movement would die with him.

There are now vegetarian options in the most unexpected places and at every fast-food chain. Alcott should largely be credited for this. He normalized meatless eating by staying out of the way. I can't speak to whether vegetarianism is healthy. But as Alcott realized, it offers something that other diets cannot: an identity. One can *be* a vegetarian, while most other diets are something one can *do*. He recognized that a diet wasn't merely how one ate, but how one lived.

part two

As a Friend

They had caught a glimpse of themselves in a mirror, a mirror
placed at a turning point where they had expected to see
daylight and freedom, and though each of them, individually,
was far from believing himself perfect, all had counted on the
virtues of others to rescue them from themselves.

—Mary McCarthy, *The Oasis*

EVERY YEAR, AROUND DECEMBER, GOOGLE PUBLISHES
a list of its most frequently asked questions. Many of them are factual questions, clarifying a new trend or a term that's been cycling
through the news. "What is the electoral college?" is a popular question during election years. "What's Pokémon GO?" was trending
at the end of 2016. There are also sticky emotional questions and
hypochondriacal questions, like "How to tell if he likes you" or "Is
the five-second rule real?" or "How do I know if I have Zika?"

What are we looking for when we Google these questions? An
informed opinion? A Reddit post by someone who's had Zika? An

article from a science journal? A quiz? Are Google searches simply a socially acceptable way of talking to ourselves, as we've become so closely tethered to our various internet-connected devices that these machines seem like extensions of our brains?

Maybe we're looking for someone—anyone, really—to say that everything is okay. To tell you that you're probably not sick from the popcorn you just ate off the floor, and that you don't have Zika, and he probably likes you back—and if not, who needs him?

What do we want when we ask for advice? Sometimes it's straightforward: an answer. We want to know how to dress for a first job interview, or how to prepare a résumé, or if meat is bad for you—which, as I mentioned in the previous chapter, is still up for debate. But sometimes we're looking for empathy, for someone to acknowledge our pain and confusion, for a simple, satisfying "That sounds awful" or "I'm sorry that happened." Other times, we're looking for encouragement, for an antidote to our own self-doubt, for a peppy "Of course it's going to be fine!" or a convincing "You can do it!"

The advice-givers in this chapter were generous purveyors of either empathy or encouragement, and sometimes both. They offered advice in the traditional sense; they were not without theories about the right way to comport oneself at home and at work, among one's in-laws, and at a "function," as they'd say. But dispensing these theories was not their primary service: they were all in the business of putting people at ease. They were attentive friends, sympathetic and boosterish, and unintimidated by the darkest strains of emotional pain.

They all came to prominence in the twentieth century and, in many ways, were reacting against the emotional dogmatism of the Victorian era, when feelings were monitored like napalm. Women were never to display anger—one popular advice book from 1847 states that an "enraged woman" was "one of the most disgusting sites in nature." Women, certain women anyway, *were* allowed to be nervous. Upper-class women were encouraged to have nervous breakdowns in public. "It is considered natural and almost laudable to break down under all conceivable varieties of strain—a winter dissipation, a houseful of servants, a quarrel with a female friend," noted Dr. Mary Putnam Jacobi, a specialist in women's health in 1895. Their servants, however, were supposed to be resilient and hearty, able to "endure effort, exposure, and hardship," according to one guidebook.

By the early twentieth century, there was a generalized sense that feelings were bad for your health and that most people functioned best without them. A 1909 article in the *Saturday Evening Post* warned that emotions like fear, anger, or excitement could do irrevocable damage to one's internal organs: "By the time an emotion has fairly got us in its grip . . . the blood supply of half the organs in our body has then powerfully altered, and often completely reversed." The advice-givers in this section offered spaces where it was okay to express one's feelings, spaces where that was the entire point.

Depending on whom you ask, empathy is an instinct, a skill, a virtue, or a sin. I have commended my dog's instinct for empathy; he's a retriever-shepherd mix, hyperactive by nature, but I can tell that he knows when I'm sick or had a rough day by his gladness to curl up beside me on the bed. Empathy is taught in kindergarten and at medical school. Some say that empathy is the catalyst of altruism: we donate our coats because we empathize with how painful and difficult it must be to survive winter without one; we drop off meals for new parents because we empathize with how overwhelmed and busy they are. Paul Bloom, a psychologist at Harvard, argues that empathy is, in fact, a well-disguised sin, that it drives people to make detrimental choices in the name of kindness when they'd have a greater impact if they detached from their feelings and acted rationally—they could help fifty families survive the winter rather than one.

Whatever one's theories on empathy, the people in this chapter overflow with it. Dorothy Dix was an advice columnist at the turn of the twentieth century who became famous for absorbing people's pain. The twin sisters who wrote "Dear Abby" and "Ann Landers," two of the most popular advice columns in American history, sympathized with readers who were unprepared for the cultural upheaval of the 1960s. Mildred Newman was a celebrated psychoanalyst and author in the 1970s who earned fifty dollars a session—a hefty price at the time—for treating her clients' problems as if they were her own.

Dale Carnegie, the author of the famed 1939 book *How to Win Friends and Influence People,* did not traffic in empathy but in encouragement—empathy's rowdy, more easygoing cousin. We seek encouragement when we're on the verge of taking a risk, when we're itching to ask for a raise, move to a new city, or try a new recipe for dinner. There's no predicting the future—the chicken could turn out to be terrible. But encouragement is license to give it a shot.

Carnegie, who started his career as a public-speaking instructor, had a certain genius for making people try, for making them braver. His actual advice on public speaking is vague and unconvincing. It's the empty, unknowing platitudes—assurances like "You can do it!" and "It's going to be fine!"—that people adored and apparently needed, that kept them coming back for more.

FIVE

Sob Sister

Dorothy Dix

IN 1890, TWO SOCIOLOGISTS SET OUT TO STUDY WHAT it was like to live in Middle America at the turn of the century. They embedded in Muncie, Indiana, a city of thirty thousand people, but refer to it in their fieldwork as "Middletown," both to emphasize its averageness and to preserve their subjects' anonymity. The sociologists, a married couple named Robert Straighton Lynd and Helen Merrell Lynd, were interested in how Americans structured their lives, if they lived in nuclear families, brought their children to church, and owned their homes. They were curious about everyday choices and how they were made: Was a teenage daughter allowed to date? Did she play any sports after school? What did families eat for dinner, and how much time did they spend on the telephone?

The Lynds struggled to find an end to their study. They published the first half of the Middletown studies in 1929 and the second half in 1939. They learned that most "Middletown" residents wanted their children to go to college but disdained teachers and academia. They found that most women worked as housewives and considered having children a moral obligation; that most families owned their homes and went to church every Sunday. The Lynds also discovered that the "most potent single agency" of "shaping the habits of thought" was not the local pastor, the mayor, or even the president. It was Dorothy Dix's advice columns.

"Dorothy Dix Talks" was written by Elizabeth Gilmer and ran from 1896 to 1950. At its height, it was read by sixty million people every week and appeared in 273 newspapers across America, Europe, Mexico, and Latin America. Her photo was plastered on buses across Europe.

Gilmer had dark hair, a mild smile, and pained, pert eyes. She was petite, less than five feet tall—a "half-portion sort of person," as she put it. She walked with a subtle but unmistakable limp and was so soft-spoken that her voice sounded like it was reverberating through a seashell. She was mousy and, on first appearance, fragile and demure, a walking embodiment of emotional pain. She was an approachable advice columnist because she made it seem as if there was little pain in this world she hadn't personally encountered.

"As I look back upon my life I see it as a battlefield strewn with the wrecks of dead dreams and broken hopes and shattered illusions—a battle in which I have always fought with the odds tremendously against me, and which has left me scarred and bruised and maimed and old before my time. Yet I have no pity for myself," she once wrote. "It is only the women whose eyes have been washed clear with tears who get the broad vision that makes them little sisters to all the world."

Gilmer had suffered, but she wasn't weak. She was less America's little sister than its worldly, resilient aunt. She had three writing careers at a time when few women had one—in addition to being an advice columnist, she was a crime reporter and a theater critic. In her columns, she conveys the distinct impression of having seen it all. As a reporter, her specialty was tear-jerking profiles of women who'd encountered violence, who'd lost a loved one or were forced to commit murder in self-defense. "I have been the confidante of the women who keep brothels and the girls in them. I have sat in prison cells and listened to the heart stories of murderesses," Gilmer once wrote in a column. "There is no joy or sorrow that can tear at the human heart that I do not know. All of this has given me knowledge and an understanding of human nature that no young girl or woman who has led just a home life could have."

She was undistracted, almost unmoved, by hardship. Her advice, typically, was to dry your tears and move along. She didn't try to fix anyone's problems. She listened. Pain, she'd found, was a fundamental part of life, especially for women. She advised her readers to adjust quickly to life's disappointments. In her experience, there was no point to lingering on a problem, because another one would come soon enough.

ELIZABETH MERIWETHER WAS born in 1861 in Woodstock, Tennessee, a farming community on the Kentucky border. The Civil War had left her parents land rich but cash poor. She grew up shooting guns, riding horses, tracking animals, and wandering the trails of her family's abandoned cotton plantation. Her mother died when she was young, and she was raised by her father, William Douglas Meriwether, who was often distracted by his family's ailing fortune.

Elizabeth attended an all-girls school that was less an institute for learning than a source of unofficial aid for the daughters of fallen Confederate heroes. "Teachers were the Miss Annas and the Miss Marys, whose claims to their positions lay, at least in part, in the fact that Papa had died a hero under General Bragg or in the Mississippi campaign," according to her biographer Harnett T. Kane. She didn't learn much there, but her family's decaying mansion had an extensive library that included the complete works of Dickens and Shakespeare. She devoured every volume. She wrote a short story and won a local writing competition and fantasized about writing professionally one day.

When she was twenty-one, she became engaged to George Gilmer, her stepmother's brother. Her father was thrilled: Gilmer was tall and handsome and had some money saved away. He was a catch, especially for a girl like his daughter. He was an adventurer, ten years older than Elizabeth, who had traveled all across America and worked in Indian Territory and who regaled her with stories of Buffalo Bill Cody, warpaths, and raids. Elizabeth was skeptical of him—she couldn't tell if any of his stories were true—but her younger sister was about to get married and she didn't want to be the only daughter left in the house. "The marriage was not my idea," she later told friends. "I don't suppose I ever felt toward him as they thought I did, or should have felt."

After they married, George and Elizabeth Gilmer traveled around Tennessee and Alabama, looking for work. George had ambitions to open his own business, first a hardware company, then a chemical firm. But nothing ever panned out. He'd start a job, work for a few weeks, decide he couldn't bear it, and quit. Then they'd move to the next town over, where George would accept a new job and the pattern would repeat itself. He was a delicate man, often undone by what were then called "moods."

A few years into their marriage, George stopped working altogether and it fell to Elizabeth to pay their rent. She was, by then, making some money from writing. She submitted to essay competitions and wrote occasionally for the *New Orleans Picayune*. But that brought them hardly enough money to eat. Some weeks, they ate chocolate éclairs for breakfast, lunch, and dinner—they were cheap, at least, and filling.

When Elizabeth was thirty-two, she returned home to Woodstock, Tennessee, for a visit. She and George had been married for ten years and she was undernourished, her arms like "matches with skin on them." She spent her days lying in her childhood bed and staring up at the ceiling, unable to move. Her father decided she needed a vacation and sent her to a resort on the Mississippi coast to relax for a few weeks.

At the resort, there was an older woman in the cabin next to hers who was also vacationing alone. Elizabeth, lonely or curious, struck up a conversation. They talked about inane neighborly things, like the weather and the shore birds, and then, gradually, about other things, like the marriage Elizabeth was escaping. The older woman eventually introduced herself as Eliza Jane Nicholson, the owner of the *New Orleans Picayune*. Elizabeth summoned the nerve to bring her writing samples. "Why God, child, you can write!" Nicholson said. By the end of the trip, Elizabeth had a staff position waiting for her at the paper.

Elizabeth started at the *Picayune* in 1894. She was a tireless reporter, always volunteering for additional assignments. During the week, she wrote obituaries and covered local crime; on weekends, she assisted the editor of the paper's literary supplement. By night, she studied the thesaurus and the dictionary and read and reread the columns she admired, committing them to memory. She was so overextended that she was known to sprint from one department to the other, but she appeared cheerful even in her frenzy. "She's the kind they speak of around editorial rooms as 'a damn good newspaperman,'" a colleague later said.

About a year into her job at the *Picayune,* one of the top editors at the paper determined that they needed more columns that catered to women readers and appointed Elizabeth to spearhead one. Her first step was a trip to the library to research the competition. Most major papers published columns on women's issues; they provided recipes, gossip items, and tips on landing a husband and home decor. The authors all had catchy, alliterative names, like Fanny Fern, Jenny June, or Catharine Cole. But the tone of these columns tended to be syrupy and mawkish, filled with false cheer. (Fanny Fern is credited with coining the phrase "The way to a man's heart is through his stomach.") Elizabeth decided that her column would be different. She would be honest with her readers, even if meant occasionally dour copy.

"It came to me that everything in the world had been written about women and for women, except the truth. They had been celebrated as angels. They had been pitied as martyrs," she'd later write. "It was time for them to shake themselves up and get busy at being practical." In her column, spades would be called spades; problems would never be dressed down. She would urge women to mind their finances, to embrace their independence, to be realistic and cunning. But she didn't want to break with every tradition, like the alliterative pen name. She had always loved the name Dorothy. And Dix had been the surname of her favorite housekeeper growing up. So that was it: Dorothy Dix. Her editor approved.

Dorothy Dix was first revealed to *Picayune* readers in the winter of 1895. The initial name for the column was "Sunday Salad." Her editors assumed that it'd be a fitting title for a column about women's issues.

Dix published the occasional recipe, but from the start, she devoted her column to personal essays about gender, marriage, ethics, and religion. In an early column, she reflected on a sermon she'd heard at church the week prior. The pastor "told how women ought never to leave the sacred precincts of home and how when she went out in the world to battle with men for money, she unsexed herself and killed the chivalry every man cherished for his ideal of womanhood." The sermon infuriated her. "I wanted to ask him if it was nobler to stay in the sacred precincts of home and starve, or be the object of grudging charity than it was to earn an honest, independent living." She urged this pastor, and the reader, to reconsider the very definition of chivalry. "The chivalry that prompts a man to give his women employees reasonable hours and fair wages, and that shows them invariable courtesy, may not be as romantic and picturesque as that which sent a good knight into the list with his lady's gloves on his helmet, but it's a good deal more to the point nowadays."

Her advice was thoroughly modern and, apparently, exactly what women wanted to hear. Readers huddled outside the *Picayune*'s office hoping to meet her. And, when it became clear that the column appealed to men as well as women, Gilmer's editors renamed it "Dorothy Dix Talks."

George did not exactly rejoice at his wife's success. After they had settled in New Orleans, he took another stab at starting his own business, as a turpentine distiller. Elizabeth gave him the money he needed to start a new company, and though it eventually took off, his success did little to lessen his depression. When the *Picayune* held social events, he'd silently nurse his whiskey while his wife gossiped with colleagues. He resented it when people in New Orleans referred to him as "Mr. Dix." Her colleagues wondered why such a charming, sensitive woman like Elizabeth had ever married him. Friends urged her to file for divorce, but she was old-fashioned when it came to marriage and intended to keep her vows. There was little research or dialogue about mental illness in the early twentieth century, and though it was socially acceptable for women to have bouts with depression, to be feeble and bedridden for no discernible reason, men were supposed to be steelier. No historian or biographer has given George a retroactive diagnosis. But Elizabeth was an unusually compassionate person—she was compassionate for a living. And perhaps she knew, somehow, that George suffered from untreatable pain beyond his control, even if there was no name for it.

"MY HUSBAND IS a brute. He mistreats me. He has affairs with other women. He wants to be rid of me," wrote one of Dix's correspondents in 1902. Gilmer received up to a thousand such letters a day.

"My heart bleeds for you," Dorothy Dix replied. "But will you be any better off if you are divorced? A beast of a husband is no worse than the wolf at the door. Alimony is difficult to collect. It is hard to make a living."

This was typical Dix response, equal parts sympathy and tough love. Women wrote to her about their abusive husbands, their unwanted pregnancies, their loveless marriages, their dissatisfaction with domestic life. None of it roused Dix; she appears to have accepted that powerlessness and despair were facts of a woman's life.

She discouraged her readers from wallowing and urged that they buck up and make the most of what they have.

In the beginning, Gilmer privately responded to as many letters as she could but rarely published these exchanges. In 1901, after accepting a contract with Hearst to publish a column every weekday, she printed letters and her replies three days a week. For the other two days, she wrote columns that would be classified today as pop psychology but which she referred to as "sermonettes." She gave them ambitious titles, like "Are You Good Company to Yourself?," "Keeping Young," and "Our Lives Are What We Make of Them." Her single most popular column over the course of her fifty-six-year career was called "Dictates for a Happy Life." It was published and republished many dozens of times. It includes this kernel of advice: "Make up your mind to be happy. If you are ever to be happy, it must start now, today." Another sour but resilient Dix mantra: "I stood yesterday. I can stand today. And I will not permit myself to think about what happens tomorrow." There was no conceivable incident, in her view, that permitted someone to remain sorrowful for long. And she'd heard it all: death of a child, infertility, every variety of heartbreak.

In the preindustrial era, men and women had shared economic and domestic responsibilities. Since men were thought to be the more rational sex, it was often their responsibility to oversee their children's moral and religious education while their wives produced and sold items to contribute to the family's income. It was in the mid to late 1800s that gender roles sharpened and women were relegated to the home. At the turn of the century, there was a boom of boys groups, like the Boys Brigades, the Boones, and the Boy Scouts of America, that encouraged young men to take pride in their gender.

When Gilmer began writing at the turn of the twentieth century, married women could not own property or keep a separate bank account. Single women who needed to earn their own living could be stenographers, bookkeepers, teachers, nurses, or telephone operators, and not much else. Women could not serve on juries or hold public office, and they were not allowed to vote. Most married women could not access birth control without their husband's written permission. Divorce laws were stringent, except in so-called divorce havens in Indiana, Utah, or the Dakotas, where wealthy couples from the East Coast would decamp for six months or so, depending on residency requirements, to officially dissolve their miserable unions. Law enforcement usually refrained from intervening in incidents of domestic conflict, even when there was a clear indication of violence. (Until the mid-1970s, there was no such thing as marital rape. Rape was defined nationwide as nonconsensual sex between non-married partners.) Abortion was illegal, so many women took the risk of a back-alley procedure. Between 1930 and 1939, an estimated seventeen thousand women died each year from botched abortions.

Dix's correspondents seem legitimately confused about their circumstances. They don't understand how they're meant to keep living with a husband they hate or why they can't enter professions that interest them. They are aware of the rules but baffled by them. Dix urges all women, married and single, to develop skills and learn a trade, so they can support themselves if they have to, but mostly to stave off boredom. "I want to urge you girls, with all the earnestness of which I am capable, to psychoanalyze yourselves and try to find out what talents and aptitudes nature bestowed upon you, and to go to some school where you can develop your gift."

Gilmer was a suffragist and made no attempt to mask her feminist beliefs. She once wrote a column called "The Ordinary Woman" that urged readers to attribute greater value to domestic work. "Women . . . are toiling over cooking-stoves, slaving at sewing-machines, pinching and economizing to educate and cultivate their children. . . . The Ordinary Woman is the real heroine of life," she wrote. She urged couples not to "degrade marriage into a kind of vaudeville show, where the wife is doing a continuous performance, and the husband is an audience of one, who may get bored at any moment and get up and leave." She received many letters from women who struggled to find a date, let alone a husband. She instructed them to find jobs they loved and devote themselves to their careers. At a time when more than 80 percent of college-educated women were married, she reminded single women that there was an alternative and that being a bachelorette in perpetuity was not something to mourn. "If the business girl will look around at her married friends she will see that most of them look older than she does; that few of them are as well-dressed or can afford the amusements she enjoys. And she will discover that the husband who remains a gallant lover after three or four years of married life is about as rare as hens' teeth," she wrote.

In one column, she suggested offhandedly that husbands begin paying their wives. Another time, she urged a woman with an ungrateful husband to go on strike until he came to appreciate her contributions to their household. "Let him come home and find no dinner because the cook has struck for wages. Let him find beds unmade, the floors unswept. Let him find that he hasn't a clean collar or a clean shirt," she wrote. She was quick to point out that hosting, entertaining, and primping weren't frivolous activities; they were forms of labor, too. Dix published these columns more than fifty years before Silvia Federici wrote her seminal feminist text, *Wages Against Housework,* in which she calls for wives to be paid a salary. As Federici wrote, "If we take wages for housework as a political perspective, we can see that struggling for it is going to produce a revolution in our lives and in our social power as women. It is also clear that if we think we do not 'need' that money, it is because we have accepted the particular forms of prostitution of body and mind by which we get the money to hide that need."

Gilmer, however, did not present herself as a revolutionary. She was far too cynical to advocate, or even imagine, far-reaching social change. She accepted that women were screwed and made herself available to hear their complaints. She urged her readers to treat marriage as a practical arrangement, to drop any romantic fantasies about finding a soul mate. Marriage, she reminded her readers, provided stability—nothing more. There was no joy in it. Wives shouldn't expect much from their husbands aside from the roof over their head. During their Middletown research, the Lynds found that most American adults treated "romance in marriage as something which, like their religion, must be believed in to hold society together." Dix was one of those rare public figures to acknowledge that marriage was not always as dreamy as it seemed.

In part, Gilmer preached practicality to women because she had little faith in men. She saw them as perpetual children, indolent and impatient, seeking wives who doted on them like mothers. Men, she wrote, preferred unremarkable women. Women who had humor, brains, or beauty made men feel unsettled; they made it difficult for a man to appear extraordinary, and even the most ordinary man saw himself as anything but. "Men prefer mediocrity in women," Dix wrote.

> They like a girl to be so-so, but not too much so, if you get what I mean. They prefer the pretty girl to the beauty. You couldn't invite Venus into your kitchen. Same way about brains. If I had a daughter, I should pray Heaven to make her neither a Dumb Dora nor a highbrow college graduate, but to bestow on her a good, moderate, serviceable amount of gray matter that would enable her to understand what men are talking about without ever being tempted to make any wise-cracks herself. In that way I should assure her, not only of being able to marry well, but always to keep her husband.

She received many dozens of letters from women who dreaded pampering themselves for a night out with their husbands. Dix empathized. She saw primping as yet another burden of womanhood, tedious and tiring. "There is no other right that women envy so persistently and entirely and sincerely, as the right to be as ugly as nature made them, and to look as old as they really are," she wrote. But she urged her readers to primp anyway: that's what their husbands wanted, and did they have a better way to survive?

~~~~~~~~~

ALL SORTS OF people sought Dorothy Dix's counsel: a teenage boy who couldn't tell if a girl he liked liked him back; a man whose seven-year-old son had died in car accident; a widow who'd fallen madly in love with her son-in-law and wanted to run away with him. (Dix came down hard on her: "Flight from him, not with him, is your only salvation and the only way to save your daughter's home and marriage and yourself a lot of grief, and your son-in-law from making a laughingstock of himself.") She received numerous suicide notes; she always responded. No question was too heavy, or too light. She heard from girls and women who wanted her opinion on what to wear or how to do their makeup. People sought her ethical counsel on open-ended questions, such as if gossip could ever be an influence for good or if there were any benefits to aging.

She wrote a weekly column for fifty-six years. In that period, America survived two world wars and the Great Depression, invented the atomic bomb, and gave women the right to vote. Women began working outside the home in greater numbers, especially during wartime, and still wrote to Dix with their tales of abuse, neglect, and frustration.

Gilmer did not believe in equality, or at least she thought it too unrealistic, but she believed in sisterhood. She figured that there wasn't much women could do about their unfortunate circumstances, aside from giving one another the space to complain. She referred to herself, proudly, as a "sob sister" and was certain that most women needed a sob sister, a shoulder to cry on. Husbands, in her experience, were useless on that front.

In her column, Gilmer did not advocate for the relaxation of divorce laws or access to birth control. She had the most public platform of any woman writer working at the turn of the century. And one might argue that she could have used her column to encourage social progress. She knew Susan B. Anthony, but they're rarely grouped together. Gilmer has largely been omitted from the history of suffrage movement; she's been deemed too defeatist and conservative. Gilmer was not one for protests, but she gave women a space where they could commiserate with other women about the banality of their misery and called attention to many of the same issues raised by Betty Friedan decades later—the tedium of housework, a commonsense desire for financial independence, and the slow-burning misery of being stuck in a life one didn't choose.

Here's one story that Dix liked to tell: She was leaving her New Orleans home one afternoon. As she opened the door, an older woman barged inside.

"You remember telling me I ought to give him time to get tired of her?"

"Yes," she replied, though she hadn't a clue which letter the woman was referring to. She had received countless letters about adulterous husbands.

"He did. But now it's another woman. And I'm going to kill her."

"Why her?" Elizabeth asked, trying to remain calm. "Why don't you kill him?"

She invited the woman to sit for tea and convinced her not to murder her husband or his mistress. But Dix's instinct to blame the husband rather than the girlfriend is indicative of Dix's variety of feminism. She never suggested that women were blameless—she believed that everyone bore responsibility for their own happiness. But she had found that women's struggles were not treated with the severity and empathy they deserved and felt that women needed some slack, especially from one another.

The last Dix column came out in April 1949. She died a year later, at the age of ninety. She had continued to do other journalism work on top of the column, writing theater reviews and gritty multipart crime series. She wrote about her travels through Hawaii and Japan. But it was the column that drained her and kept her up at night. "It took me a dozen years to realize the enormous responsibility people thrust upon me," she later wrote. Her books and crime series were more prestigious, but the column—half a century of persistent emotional labor—was the real work.

SIX

Happy Thoughts

Dale Carnegie

> Men must necessarily be the active agents of their own
> well-being and well-doing; and . . . however much the
> wise and good may owe to others, they themselves must
> in the very nature of things be their own best helpers.
>
> —Samuel Smiles, *Self Help*

SOME YEARS AGO, I WROTE AN ARTICLE ABOUT EX-
convicts trying to start their own businesses and turn their lives
around. There were seven of them, and each had read *How to Win
Friends and Influence People* when they got out of prison. The book,
written by Dale Carnegie and published in 1936, remains one of
the best-selling business books of all time. It has reportedly been
purchased more than thirty million times. One of the men, who'd
served twenty years for a jewelry heist and read a lot of self-help, told
me that Carnegie's book was the only thing he'd found that made it
seem possible to start over.

Before he wrote the book, Carnegie taught public-speaking
classes at the YMCA and he eventually started his own school,

the Dale Carnegie Center for Excellence, in 1912. With the book's success, the school expanded, and it now has branches in ninety countries and in all fifty states. It offers a variety of courses, like "Confident, Assertive, and in Charge," "How to Communicate with Diplomacy and Tact," and "How to Win Friends and Influence (Business) People." Warren Buffett, the billionaire and investment banker, attended Carnegie's school and credits it for his success. "In my office, you will not see the degree I have from the University of Nebraska, or the master's degree I have from Columbia University, but you'll see the certificate I got from the Dale Carnegie course," Buffett told a documentary film crew. The courses usually cost upward of $1,500, but the schools regularly host free sessions for potential students, and I decided to go to one. I could imagine how optimism, with practice, could be learned, but what I couldn't picture, and wanted to see for myself, was how it might be taught.

The Manhattan branch of the Dale Carnegie Institute is housed in a basement of an Upper East Side high-rise. When I arrived, two women in dark suits cheerfully handed me a name tag. Names were important to Dale Carnegie. Several of the success stories in his book are about people whose achievements can largely be attributed to their gift for remembering people's names. Carnegie was certain that if you repeated someone's name, a lot, they would invariably begin to like you, that a name said repeatedly was like a love spell. "Remember that a person's name is to that person the sweetest and most important sound in any language," he wrote.

I was directed to Classroom B, a windowless room with worn gray carpeting. There were twenty or so students sitting in folding chairs, white name tags adhered to their button-down shirts, obedient and eager.

I had read *How to Win Friends and Influence People* for the first time a few weeks prior. I'd struggled to finish it. Carnegie's thinking is as predictable as a golden retriever who leaves a tennis ball at your feet. His great epiphany is that when you are nice to people, they are more likely to be nice back. My kindergarten teacher had covered similar ground.

Most of the other students were men, and most of them wore suits. Many had come with colleagues, forming corporate cliques. There was a crew from Citibank, one from Chase, and one from the drugstore Duane Reade. They all seemed to have read Carnegie's book. Not everyone had found it revelatory, but they blamed the medium rather than Carnegie's methodology: they thought a class might be a better way to absorb Carnegie's philosophy—after all, school had been Carnegie's original method of evangelism. One of the men sitting near me worked in the accounting department at the bank HSBC. He smelled like air freshener, and he wore a suit with no tie. At work, he explained, his cubicle neighbors worked in different departments and he had little reason to speak with them. He'd become so accustomed to communicating by email or chat that he felt he needed a refresher in basic conversation. He said this in such an offhanded way that made me think he knew other people with a similar predicament at work, which made sense and also made me sad.

The man sitting next to me had shaggy hair and a friendly face. He was a musician, a singer-songwriter, who supported himself as a real estate broker. He'd been losing clients over the past few years. He'd found that people preferred browsing listings online for free to interacting with an agent for money. He had been trying to plan his next career move and came across an online flyer for a free Dale Carnegie class. "Free," he repeated, as though it explained everything. He had always worked for himself. "I never thought of myself as a natural leader," he told me. "It's kind of amazing that you can just learn to be one."

Our instructor was a middle-aged woman in a dark pantsuit with a sturdy, windproof bob. She congratulated us for being there. "Everyone here works for a company, or wants to work for a company," she said. Everyone's name tag listed their employer. (Mine read: "Book.")

The Carnegie school assumes that everyone aspires to work at a corporation with clear hierarchies and ladders to climb. The flyer that the musician/realtor found online had said that the class was intended for "employees at all levels in a corporation who seek to maximize their performance, become stronger leaders and add more value to the organization." The class, and Carnegie's book, is designed for a particular kind of striver, one struggling to get noticed by higher-ups. It is intended, in other words, for a kind of workplace, and worker, that may not exist for much longer. But when Carnegie began peddling his particular brand of optimism during the Great Depression, a stable corporate job was the ultimate dream, and his readers were willing to sacrifice anything for it.

DALE CARNEGEY (AND yes, that's spelled correctly) was born in 1888 in Maryville, a small town in northwest Missouri. His parents were farmers and it was Dale's job to milk the cows each morning before school. The Carnegeys grew their own fruits and vegetables, butchered and smoked their own pigs, and traded their eggs and milk for coffee and sugar. They scraped by, barely. Dale hated farmwork and spent his childhood trying to finagle his way out of it. "The work I loathed was churning the cream into butter, cleaning out the hen house, cutting weeds, and milking cows. Above all else, I hated to chop wood. I despised it so bitterly that we would never have any firewood stored up in advance," he wrote, according to his biographer Steven Watts.

When he was sixteen, the family moved to Warrensburg, in southeast Missouri. There was a university there, the State Normal School, where tuition was free. It was primarily a teachers' college, but they offered courses in a variety of disciplines, like biology, philosophy, and religion. He enrolled as soon as his family arrived in town; he planned to become a teacher one day. During his first year, Dale had a massive growth spurt and outgrew all of his clothes, and his parents didn't have the money to buy him new ones. He looked ridiculous with his long limbs and broad, half-moon ears. Girls ignored him; they tended to go for the athletes, the confident, brawny types. But Dale noticed that the school's top debaters, even the scrawny ones, had decent luck with women. With nothing to lose, he joined one of the school's literary fraternities, which hosted public-speaking tournaments on campus.

He bombed his first competition. "I was so crushed, so beaten, so despondent, that I literally thought of suicide!" he'd recall years later. "Sounds silly? Not when you are seventeen or eighteen and suffering from an inferiority complex!"

He practiced obsessively. He'd recite famous speeches as he milked the cows and rode his horse to school. It paid off: in his third year of college, he won the school's debate championship. He was elected student body vice president and was invited to deliver sermons at churches around Warrensburg. He even got his first girlfriend.

His mother hoped he'd become a missionary or a preacher. But instead, Dale became a salesman—he didn't want to be poor, like his parents. He traveled across the Midwest selling home education courses to ranchers. He had a knack for sales and soon moved onto more lucrative wares, like bacon, soap, and lard.

By twenty-three, he'd saved enough money to move to New York and enroll in drama school. He didn't want to be an actor, per se, but he thought he could be a public speaker, reciting stories and poems before crowds. His dream was to join the Chautauqua lecture circuit, an ensemble road show of public intellectuals and storytellers who performed in makeshift tents across America. Its speakers included pastors, poets, and actors. Their most coveted speaker was William Jennings Bryan, a two-time candidate for president; crowds were wild for his essay on temperance. Most of their speakers had one or two hit speeches they returned to again and again, for years. It was a potentially lucrative career, but Dale's family didn't approve. His mother believed that only heathens performed on stage. "It is far nobler work than selling meat," he assured her.

In 1911, he enrolled in the American Academy of Dramatic Arts, considered one of the most prestigious theater schools in the country, where he learned, among other things, how to imitate a chair. He tried out for various theater productions but could never land a part. He began teaching public-speaking classes at the YMCA so he could stay solvent until his theater career took off. He developed a reputation as a masterful teacher, and the classes took up more and more of his time. Thousands of students signed up to take "Effective Speaking and Human Relations" with Dale Carnegey. He helped salesmen perfect their pitch, businessmen steady their nerves before a big presentation; he taught his students how to summon courage when they were nervous and feign confidence when they were sick with terror. He could train anyone to liberate themselves from shyness. He was heralded as a magician, one who could turn an awkward loaf into a charmer or coach a wallflower into the spotlight. He became an expert on communication and management, even though he'd never been a manager. He had spent his career gigging, cobbling together an income between teaching, lecturing, and writing. His daily life resembled that of an adjunct professor circa 2018. He had no knowledge of what it was like to commute to the same office to do the same job day after day and year after year. Everything he knew about corporate life was based on what his students told him. And yet he became a world-renowned expert in achieving corporate success.

His course grew in popularity. He was invited to teach in Newark and Baltimore. In 1915, he collected his lectures and notes into a book: *Public Speaking: A Practical Course for Businessmen.*

Later that year he registered for the draft, but he was ineligible for active duty because he was missing the top of his left index finger— from an accident as a child—and he was assigned to an administrative post at a Long Island military base. After the war, he accepted a job as a business manager for a theater troupe. While on tour through

Europe, he met Lolita Baucaire, a German actress with unlikely claims to royalty. They married in 1921 and settled in Paris, where they lived on the royalties for his first book and Carnegey worked on a novel that he never published. (They divorced in 1931.) When he returned to New York in 1926 to resume his public-speaking classes, he changed his last name to Carnegie. He thought the new spelling made his name easier to remember. (And by then, he'd already developed his theory about the importance of a memorable name.) It was a name that most people already knew, as it belonged to one of the country's richest families. An editor from Simon and Schuster encouraged him to write a book about "the art of getting along with people" that would include a collection of his public-speaking lessons as well as new materials. It was Carnegie who came up with the book's title: *How to Win Friends and Influence People.*

WHEN *HOW TO Win Friends and Influence People* was published in 1936, unemployment in America was at 16.9 percent. It was the tail end of the Great Depression and virtually no one was hiring. Those with jobs were frantic to hold on to them, and Carnegie's book, a manual in people-pleasing, included some sound advice for those trying not to get fired. Among the first lessons of *How to Win Friends and Influence People* is don't "criticize, condemn, or complain." He has six rules for getting people to like you, and they all encourage flattery and pleasantries. Rule #1: "Become genuinely interested in other people." Rule #2: "Smile!" He has twelve additional rules for "winning people to your way of thinking" through acquiescence. Rule #1: "The only way to get the best of an argument is to avoid it." Rule #7: "Let the other person feel that the idea is his or hers." There are several rules that encourage some variation of "lavish praise" or "honest and sincere appreciation." Carnegie advised that people aspire to be—to borrow Chesterfield's favorite adjective—"easy," that they learn to blend.

Carnegie's book is a compendium of case studies of great men and their achievements, men like Benjamin Franklin, Abraham Lincoln, and Lloyd George, Great Britain's prime minister during World War I. He writes that true leaders tread softly. They ask questions and never bark orders; they heap praise upon their employees and never dwell on their mistakes; they are self-effacing and encouraging and never imperious or cruel. They are authoritative but gentle. His book argues that kindness, stereotypically considered a liability in the workplace, is actually an asset. Carnegie had found that men were socialized to think that being brutish, loud, and somewhat awful was the only way to demonstrate readiness for power. Offices functioned like one perpetual rush session, like laboratories of aggressive showmanship. He encourages his readers to be sensitive and tactful. He argues that politeness is the most effective tactic for getting ahead. "Why, I wonder, don't we use the same common sense when trying to change people that we use when trying to change dogs? Why don't we use meat instead of a whip? Why don't we use praise instead of condemnation?" he writes.

While Carnegie writes about great men, his book is largely intended for their employees. And although Carnegie's advice was applicable to the fearful employees of the Great Depression, the book does not read as if it was written during a difficult or dire moment. It is a happy book. "Dale Carnegie sells people what most of them desperately need," said the *Saturday Evening Post* in a 1937 profile. "He sells them hope." Much of that can be attributed to Carnegie's zippy prose. ("Skeptical? Well, I like skeptical people.") He offers no prognosis of the economy, no dour, grandfatherly reminders about it being "hard out there." He seems to have no awareness of how hard it really was.

Carnegie was not the first person to evangelize about the power of optimism. In the mid-1800s, a group of psychologists, philosophers, and religious leaders formed what they called the school of New Thought. They believed in the power of "mind-cures," in the efficacy of determination and grit. William James, a psychologist, popularized the ideas of the New Thought movement and wrote of the "all-saving power of healthy-minded attitudes." He argued that if you mustered your mental powers and stayed focused, you could achieve anything—wealth, social success, popularity. Positivity could even heal a cold. Human cognition, James and his colleagues argued, was the universe's ultimate causal force; it could override God and nature.

Carnegie often cites James in his books and lessons. (In *How to Win Friends and Influence People*, he describes James as "one of the most distinguished psychologists and philosophers America has ever produced.") "You don't feel like smiling? Then what? Two things. First, force yourself to smile. If you are alone, force yourself to whistle or hum a tune or sing. Act as if you were already happy, and that will tend to make you happy," Carnegie writes. He is citing one of James's theories that our facial expressions determine as well as indicate our moods. Carnegie instructs his readers to ask questions even if they have none, to listen when they're bored, and to bring cheer to any room they enter. Carnegie believed that our actions dictate our thoughts, that we can train ourselves to be happier, smarter, and more productive by behaving as if those things were already true. If managers treated their employees as if they were competent, they would *become* competent. If employees treated their managers as if they were wise and compassionate, they would stop behaving like tyrants. "If you want to improve a person in a certain aspect, act as though that particular trait was already one of his outstanding characteristics," Carnegie writes. Another rule: "Give the other person a fine reputation to live up to." All anyone wants, Carnegie writes, is to feel appreciated. Carnegie believed that if you're generous with your perceptions of others, you can have all the friends and influence in the world.

The cult of positive thinking has outlived Carnegie. The most prominent example is probably *The Secret*, Rhonda Byrne's self-help philosophy, which claims that one can will an outcome into existence simply by wanting it badly enough. "The Benefits of Optimism Are

Real" read a recent headline for an *Atlantic* article that summarized the latest psychological research on positive thinking. Ruminating and venting, the article finds, have no tangible benefits, but cheerful resilience pays dividends.

There is, however, another school of behavioral psychologists who believe that too much optimism makes you soft. It can zap your motivation—if you're certain that life will turn out as you hope, then you don't have the same hunger to try. Gabrielle Oettingen, a psychologist at New York University, studied a group of women enrolled in a weight-reduction program and found that it was the pessimists who lost the most weight. "Dreaming about the future calms you down, measurably reducing systolic blood pressure, but it also can drain you of the energy you need to take action in pursuit of your goals," Oettingen concluded.

Many have questioned Carnegie's theory about the necessity of kindness in the workplace. In the 1970s, one of the best-selling business advice books was Robert Ringer's *Winning Through Intimidation*, which argues that confidence and assertiveness are the keys to success and encourages readers to treat each of their colleagues as if they were rivals in a death match. Today's business advice catered to women is, essentially, reverse Carnegie. Carnegie evangelized about the importance of listening. (Another rule: "Be a good listener. Encourage others to talk about themselves.") But studies show that men interrupt their female colleagues with far greater frequency than their female colleagues interrupt them, and Sheryl Sandberg and other ambassadors of female ambition urge women who want to climb the corporate ladder to speak up. Likewise, Carnegie encouraged his readers to be perpetually deferential: "The unvarnished truth is that almost all the people you meet feel themselves superior to you in some way, and a sure way to their hearts is to let them realize in some subtle way that you recognize their importance." Yet Sandberg, among others, advises women to develop their confidence and guard themselves from men who take credit for their ideas.

There are other ways in which Carnegie's advice seems outdated. By the year 2020, 40 percent of American workers will be freelancers, according to a study conducted by the software company Intuit. That means they'll make their income as Carnegie *did* as opposed to how he *said*, cobbling together their income from different clients and projects. Corporate loyalty is more fleeting today than it was in Carnegie's day. There's been a shift to individual "brands," with employees, at all ranks, trying to create a distinct identity for themselves online. In this new era of heightened individualism, corporations have had to offer new perks and toys to instill company camaraderie. My friends who speak of their jobs as if they're permanent arrangements, who strive for the contemporary equivalent of the gold watch, all work for tech companies. They work on lush campuses where they're served gourmet food, expensive coffee, and craft beer—for free.

But most companies don't make such efforts and most businesses aren't trying to retain their workforce. "Fifty years ago, when you went to business school you were taught that you want a loyal, dedicated, skilled workforce," said Nelson Lichtenstein, director of the Center for the Study of Work, Labor, and Democracy at UC Santa Barbara, told the *Los Angeles Times*. "Today, if you go to business school, they tell you [you] don't want a permanent workforce. That's considered new standard operating procedure. It reflects a real shift in power."

Carnegie treated the employee-employer relationship as a sacred, symbiotic bond. His advice made sense when our jobs were as binding as marriage, but does it bear any relevance in today's service economy, where work is structured more like a string of one-night stands?

IN 1859, THE author Samuel Smiles published a book called *Self-Help*. (It's the first known use of the term.) In it, he explains that perseverance is the key to success. Accomplished people work harder than regular people. Success is anyone's for the taking. All you have to do was drill down—get up earlier, stay up later, and apply yourself.

Carnegie applied this same ethos to popularity. Anyone can be popular if they smile a lot and perfect the art of the compliment. All self-help, Carnegie included, promises that the world isn't rigged. That no dream is too big. That we can re-create ourselves to be prettier, smarter, more productive, and more likable. Self-help recasts personality traits as skills. It posits that anything can be learned.

Carnegie's theories on how to inspire workplace loyalty do not apply to the burgeoning freelance labor market. But his ideas about the importance of emotional intelligence are, perhaps, more apt than ever. Jobs are changing; careers that don't exist today will be in demand a decade from now. The modern, post-Fordism worker has to be easy to work with and open to change. Automation will replace many jobs in the decades to come, but emotional labor, jobs centered on the "fine art of getting along with people," to quote *How to Win Friends and Influence People,* will never go away.

In the class, we memorized each other's names and practiced enunciating our own. We learned a very complicated "visual mnemonic" to help us memorize Carnegie's principles for success. It involved an elaborate Rube Goldberg that started with a bouquet of flowers and a golden *v* and ended with red headphones on a microphone stand. I forgot it within seconds. Our instructor peppered her lecture with moralistic maxims like, "You have two ears and one mouth for a reason."

For the last exercise of the night, we wrote down our goals and shared them with a partner. The realtor/musician wanted to record more songs. I wanted to finish my book and do more overseas reporting. Then we had to make a list of everything we were going to change about *ourselves* to accomplish those goals. That was the real goal. We could all be more industrious, more tenacious, more direct. All we had to do was try.

SEVEN

Everything Changes

Dear Abby and Ann Landers

ESTHER PAULINE FRIEDMAN AND PAULINE ESTHER Friedman were born on July 4, 1918, in Sioux City, Iowa. Esther Pauline was born first, by seventeen minutes. They were identical twins, and from when they were toddlers until they were married, Eppie and Popo, as they were known, shared a bed and slept with their arms wrapped around each other. They took all the same classes, had all the same friends. In junior high, a teacher recommended that they be placed in different classrooms and the girls cried to the principal that "they'd rather die."

But by the time they reached middle age, the sisters were estranged. They were married by then and had changed their names to Esther Lederer and Pauline Phillips, though they were both better known by their pen names: Ann Landers and Abigail Van Buren— or "Dear Abby."

For more than three decades, the sisters were the two most popular advice columnists in the country, collectively filling Dorothy Dix's shoes. In 1955, Eppie beat out dozens of other aspiring advice columnists to write the "Ann Landers" column at the *Chicago Sun-Times,* which was then syndicated in more than thirty

97

papers. A few months later, Popo browbeat the editors at the *San Francisco Chronicle* into letting her start an advice column of her own. Within the decade, "Dear Abby" was the most widely syndicated column in America. At their height, the sisters appeared in 1,600 papers combined.

They were basically the only two syndicated advice columnists in the 1960s, which meant that their only competition was one another. It grew vicious between them. Popo undersold "Dear Abby" to the *Sioux City Journal* so she would be the sister their hometown read and remembered. Eppie went from three to seven columns a week, so the papers that carried her column couldn't run her sister's on off days. Popo mocked her sister's nose job in *Life* magazine. "She now speculates aloud that Ann revealed certain Freudian flaws of character by going through with the operation," writes the reporter. In that same article, Eppie describes her sister as being "like the kid who beats a dog until somebody looks, and then starts petting it."

They gave advice when Elvis Presley released "Heartbreak Hotel," his first major hit. They gave advice when Martin Luther King delivered his "I Have a Dream" speech and led a peace march from Selma to Montgomery. They gave advice when American stores began carrying miniskirts, when *Rolling Stone* published its first issue, and when hundreds of thousands of hippies converged in Woodstock, New York, for a music festival. They gave advice when the Supreme Court legalized abortion. They gave advice when President Nixon was impeached, when the Berlin Wall fell, and when President Clinton was discovered to be having an affair with a twenty-two-year-old intern.

It was in the sixties, though, when the sisters rose to prominence. In their columns, they pined for simpler days when husbands never strayed, women saved themselves for marriage, and every child was raised in a stable nuclear family. There never really was such a time: At the turn of the twentieth century, the divorce rate in America was already the highest in the world. A 1939 study found that two-thirds of women born after 1910 had premarital sex. In the 1940s, almost 10 percent of children grew up in a household without either parent. (By the 1990s, this rate had halved.) According to the historian Stephanie Coontz, the fifties marked the first time in a hundred years that the age for marriage and motherhood fell and divorce rates declined. The social uprisings of the sixties and seventies that so upset the twins were reactions to this historical anomaly.

The twins had frilly taste. They were the embarrassing aunts you loved but sometimes couldn't stand. But even *they* evolved. They could be slow to accept change, but they got there eventually. They changed their minds on interracial marriage, interfaith marriages, and divorce. In doing so, they normalized the idea of social progress. Because if Ann and Abby could adjust to modern times, then so could anyone.

FOR THEIR FIRST twenty years on the planet, the twin sisters wore matching outfits and lived matching lives. Their days were as identical as their genes. They'd go on double dates together and swap pairs midway through the evening. Boys could never tell which sister was which. But if you squinted, you might notice that Eppie's cheeks were punctured with thin dimples while Popo's were not, that Popo was shapelier and that her nose was a smidge longer.

Morton Phillips noticed. He was a student at the University of Minnesota who met the twins at a fraternity party shortly before their twentieth birthday. He had an uncanny ability to tell the twins apart. And it was Popo he liked. Phillips was moderate in almost every way: he was a political moderate, a moderate student, of moderate height. The exception was his immoderate wealth. He was the heir to a massive liquor fortune and his family was among the richest in the Midwest.

The twins' parents, Abe and Becky, were delighted when Phillips proposed. Eppie was already engaged by then, to a law student from a prominent Sioux City family. Abe worked in real estate and

owned a vaudeville theater where the twin sisters sometimes performed duets on their violins; Becky stayed at home with their five
children. It was tail end of the Great Depression, and now the Fried-
mans could rest assured that their twin daughters would be fine.

The sisters went shopping for wedding veils at Sioux City's biggest department store—they'd always planned to have a double
wedding and wear matching gowns. The clerk who assisted them
was a tall, dark-haired man around their age who had the nerve to
ask Eppie out. His name was Jules Lederer, and Eppie broke off her
engagement after their first date. Lederer was a chain-smoking high
school dropout, but he was charming and funny and Eppie loved
him. They had a short engagement so she and Popo could go ahead
with the double wedding.

On July 4, 1939, their twenty-first birthday, Eppie and Popo
married Jules and Morton at the only synagogue in Sioux City. After
the wedding, Popo and Morton took a honeymoon through Canada; Eppie and Jules had planned to come along, but they couldn't
afford to travel further than Chicago. The Phillipses settled in Eau
Claire, Wisconsin, where Morton worked as an executive for one of
his family's companies. The Lederers moved eight times in eleven
years, from Sioux City to Los Angeles to Chicago, picking up and
leaving whenever Jules found a job that paid ten dollars more a week.
Eventually Morton got Jules a position in the sales department at
Presto, a kitchen appliance manufacturer owned by his family, and
the Lederers moved to Eau Claire as well. The couples lived on opposite sides of town; the Phillipses had a stately mansion, with enough
spare bedrooms to accommodate their hired help, while the Lederers
found a compact house that Eppie nicknamed "Peanut Place."

In 1954, Jules was offered a job in Chicago as the president of a
company that manufactured ballpoint pens. He and Eppie moved
to the city that year along with their fourteen-year-old daughter, Margo. Popo reportedly told neighbors that it was Eppie who
wanted out of Eau Claire because she was tired of being upstaged by
her twin. "She couldn't stand it," she said.

But Jules's new job in Chicago paid far better than his job in Eau Claire, and the Lederers were able to buy an apartment on Lake Shore Drive with views of Lake Michigan and enroll Margo in private school. Jules was often on the road or working late, and Eppie, then thirty-seven, was bored. She had a family friend at the *Chicago Sun-Times* and called him one day to see if Ann Landers, their advice columnist, happened to be looking for an assistant. It so happened that Ruth Crowley, the columnist behind "Ann Landers" and a registered nurse, had died unexpectedly at few months before (she was forty-eight) and the paper was seeking a replacement. Eppie decided to apply. The family friend warned her not to get her hopes up—all the other applicants were professional journalists.

The application was a blind writing test, responding to three letters. They concerned interfaith marriages, psychosomatic hives, and a conflict with a neighbor over walnuts—if they fell from your neighbor's tree onto *your* side of the yard, weren't you entitled to keep them? Eppie didn't own a typewriter, so she rented one. The paper hired a company to administer psychological profiles on the top candidates, and Eppie showed a higher level of aggressiveness than anyone they'd ever tested.

Eppie submitted her test and tried to put it out of her head. Some days later, the phone rang. "Good morning, Ann Landers!" the man on the line said. The job was hers. They offered her eighty-seven dollars a week, which seemed astronomical to her. She'd never received a salary before.

Eppie's first instinct was to panic. She was a college dropout who had never written anything for publication beyond the school paper, and now she'd have to write something for a national audience three days a week. She'd never even held a job before. She arrived at the *Sun-Times* newsroom to find five thousand letters on her desk that needed her reply.

Her second instinct was to call Popo, at least according to Popo's version of events. Eppie said that her sister begged to write the column with her and she didn't see the harm. Popo said that they crafted all the early columns together, with the exception of those she wrote alone. "I provided the sharp answers," Popo said. "My stuff was published and it looked awfully good in print."

A few months into her tenure, Eppie's editors ended her collaboration with her sister. The letters were being sent to the *Sun-Times* in confidence, and it was unethical to share with them with anyone outside the paper. They mustered the budget to hire Eppie two assistants. (At the height of her career, she'd have thirteen assistants at a time.) She painted the walls of her office bubblegum pink and settled in.

Popo missed working on the column. "I loved writing those letters," she said. "I was ecstatically happy and having a ball!" She felt angry with her sister for not crediting her properly. "Eppie should have given me credit, but she didn't, and I understand her wanting to forget."

Popo, Morton, and their two children had moved to Hillsborough, outside San Francisco, where Morton was running one of his family's distributorships. Eighty-five days after Eppie published the first Ann Landers column, Popo cold-called the *San Francisco Chronicle*. She was invited in for a meeting. She was given a writing test and, not long after, had an advice column of her own. She agreed to write for free, so long she held the copyright to her new pen name: Abigail Van Buren. Eppie stopped calling not long after the column launched.

"Twin Lovelorn Advisers Torn Asunder by Success" read a headline in *Life* magazine in 1958. Popo told *Life* that Eppie had always been jealous of her. She'd been jealous of her as a child when Popo won the spot of first violin in the school orchestra. She was jealous when she married Morton—it had been Eppie who'd fantasized about marrying a millionaire. Now, she was jealous of Popo's professional success. Popo mentioned that a she kept a copy of *The Hostile Mind* on her bedside table; the book was a primer on the origins of human hostility and provided insight into her twin sister's afflicted brain. In response, Eppie directed all of her off-the-charts aggression toward beating her sister. "She was mad because her column wasn't in some paper in Aardvark, Arkansas," Marshall Field V, whose family owned the *Sun-Times*, told the journalist Carol Felsenthal. "She was only in 400 papers, and her sister was in 401."

B<small>Y</small> 1965, <small>A</small> decade after they both launched their columns, Popo's Dear Abby was carried in 700 newspapers while Eppie's Ann Landers was carried in 638. Dear Abby was winning. Her margin of victory was especially impressive considering that Ann Landers had an early lead—by the time Eppie took over the franchise, it was already carried in thirty papers. Popo had accomplished Dear Abby's rise all on her own.

Dear Abby's trademark was her snappy one-liners: "Three strikes and a man is out, no matter how good his pitches," she told Three-Time Loser, a woman wondering whether she should get back together with her ex-husband. "Snoring is the sweetest music this side of heaven. Ask any widow," she told a woman whose husband was keeping her up at night. Both sisters wrote with mock impatience, reminding their readers that their problems weren't nearly as earth-shattering as they seemed to believe, but Abby's responses were more biting. One woman wrote Abby because she feared she'd drunk too much on her twenty-first birthday. "I had three martinis. During dinner, we split a bottle of wine. After dinner we had two brandies. Did I do wrong?" Dear Abby's reply: "Probably." She wasn't always so harsh. She had a way of offering gentle but unsentimental encouragement, as when a male nurse wrote to her in 1974 asking why God had chosen to punish him with a male body. "Nature sometimes makes biological blunders, as is the case when one's body does not conform with his (or her) natural feelings," she wrote. "You are not alone. Don't feel guilty. One cannot help what he feels."

Ann Landers was more moralistic and more serious than her sister. One woman wrote to Ann Landers because she wanted advice about how to raise her daughter, whom she described as the "home-liest child I had ever seen."

"The growing up years are going to be very hard on this pa-thetic child. Please tell me how to face the future cheerfully," she wrote.

"The pathetic one in the family is you," Ann Landers replied. "Get some counseling, mother. You've got a geranium in your cranium."

The sisters also had different relationships to their personas. Eppie never went by Ann Landers in her personal life, while Popo always introduced herself as Dear Abby or Abigail Van Buren (a habit that she passed down to her daughter Jeanne Phillips, who took over the column in 2002 and says "Hello, this is Dear Abby" when she picks up the phone).

But their columns functioned in the exact same way. After they published a letter, readers would chime in, contradicting or elabo-rating on the original column. There were long trains of conversa-tions about snoring husbands and how to act around your husband's new wife. Readers would write in with factual corrections and both columnists would reprint these replies, unedited. One woman, for instance, wrote to Ann Landers with some statistics she'd read about the prevalence of automobile accidents among teenagers. She reprinted another reader's essay, without comment, about the value of strong sibling relationships.

Over time, their readers returned to the columns not just for Ab-by's and Ann's advice but to hear from one another. According to a study by David Gudelunas, a professor at Fairfield University, when Eppie started the column, 91 percent of letters contained a question; by the 1990s, only 34 percent of letters did. By then, most people were writing her to share advice of their own. The columns offered opportunities for readers to see their names in print and anonymous venues for sharing information—much like a comments section on a website. They were the predecessor to anonymous chat rooms. Many wrote to them with the kind of easily sated curiosities that we now only reveal to Google, with questions like, "What is the difference between a mule, a jackass and a donkey?" or "Is there anything in insecticides that could excite a man?"

The twins gave similar, if not identical, advice. In the 1960s, Abby objected to married women working outside the home: "In America, one out of every four wives work. Is this good? I doubt it. Call me old-fashioned, but I think it unwise for a married woman to hold down a full-time job outside her home. She's already got one in her home!" A wife who worked, Abby argued, threatened her marriage and neglected her children. (Her children were already teenagers, she'd remind readers, when she started writing the column.) She believed there was natural order to marriage and that husbands and wives should respect their rightful places. "The female, whether conscious of her needs or not, is really content only with a husband who projects masculinity and authority," she wrote. Being a wife was a full-time job, even when there were no children. She was obliged to maintain her appearance and home, to entertain her husband, his business associates, and friends. "Marriage isn't a 50-50 proposition. It's more like 80-20 and the little woman is at the long end of the arithmetic," Abby wrote. She opposed divorce—even when the marriage was loveless, sexless, and miserable for both parties, even when the husband was an alcoholic, a philanderer, a workaholic, or abusive. She once advised a woman whose husband had given her two black eyes to give the marriage another shot. "I contend that there are no two people in the world who cannot live together in reasonable harmony if they really try," she wrote.

Ann Landers agreed. She felt there was nothing that a wife couldn't learn to tolerate and that a distracted husband, a boring husband, an unloving husband were all better than no husband at all. "I do not believe that a woman should live with a man who abuses her," Ann Landers wrote in 1960. "In such cases, I recommend separate roofs and child support. That is not the same as divorce. In my book, marriage is forever." These views were standard for the time—it was the "golden age of marriage." By 1958, the divorce rate was half of what it was in 1947 and there was a general sense that divorce was an emergency measure, never the logical conclusion of a romantic disentanglement. No-fault divorce, which allows a couple to legally separate without proof of wrongdoing, only became widely available in the early 1980s. Eppie had a habit of showboating her wifeliness. Rather than her own initials, she had "Jules' Wife" sewn into the label of her mink coat and blue mink stole. For their thirtieth wedding anniversary, she wrote a loving letter to Jules in place of a normal column, listing all the things she admired about him, like his work ethic and his tenacity. "I consider it a privilege to be the wife of this beautiful guy who took on the world with a tenth-grade education and a hole in his sock," she wrote. She always wrote under the byline Ann Landers, but for this column she was "Mrs. Jules Lederer."

Their readers came from every corner of America: some of them were doctors, wealthy businessmen, and politicians; others were barely scraping by. But one thing they shared, as the late sixties hit, was fear. Everything was changing. Their sons were gay; everyone seemed to be getting divorced. Their friends and cousins were coming home with boyfriends and girlfriends of different religions and different races. They wanted to know what Ann and Abby made of interracial couples and hippies and premarital sex. Ann and Abby, for the most part, remained aloof and practical. The position of an advice columnist, as they both defined it, was an inherently centrist one. It was their job to be dispassionate, to base their advice on social averages. "Do not agree to engage in any practice you consider frightening, abnormal, or weird," Abby once advised a reader. The Friedman sisters were not moral heroes. They lacked Dorothy Dix's empathy. "I'm sorry" was not in their vocabulary. They could be intolerant and cruel and mocked people in distress—Abby especially. But they never cast themselves as ethicists. They weren't interested in what was right; they were interested in what was normal. They saw themselves as the keepers of the social curve. Their advice was a reminder of what was expected of their readers: to buck up, respect their commitments, not be weird. Abby preached acceptance—of your gay daughter or your cross-dressing brother—partly because forgiveness was more efficient than the alternative. She seemed to think that emotions were a waste of time. Eppie was similar. Her response to conflict was to either "dismiss it or rationalize it," as one friend told Carol Felsenthal. By the late 1960s, Abby was a vocal supporter of Planned Parenthood, but she considered this less a political position than a demonstration of good sense. When a reader asked in 1969 how a "lovely, brilliant girl like you ever [got] taken in by Planned Parenthood," Abby replied: "I read the figures on population explosion, and saw pictures of thousands of starving children born of parents who did not want them and could not feed them." Birth control had been legal for four years by then. If something was officially legal, then it was time for Abby and Ann to show their support, even if it still made them uneasy. Ann, privately, appeared disturbed by the idea of interracial and interfaith marriage—"I always say stick to your own kind," she told a black colleague at the *Sun-Times* in the nineties. But she never wrote anything that brazen in her column, especially after 1967, when the Supreme Court struck down laws prohibiting interracial marriage in *Loving v. Virginia*. "Our daughter who is in law school told us last night that she wants to announce her engagement to a black medical student," began one letter to Ann Landers in 1973. "We are not prejudiced people, Ann. In fact, we are the most liberal people in our social circle. . . . But having a black son-in-law is another matter." Ann Landers told Indiana Parents that she sympathized with them, but "whether you like it or not, this is the direction in which the world is moving."

Their columns could be glib, but they took their responsibilities seriously. They always offered a clear course of action, even if it was only directing the reader to look up a local therapist in the yellow pages. "I view it as one of journalism's great challenges, a unique opportunity to spotlight ignorance, fear, and stupidity," Eppie once wrote. "I pray that I am equal to the task." Eppie took her column so seriously that she would call up sources like Supreme Court justice William O. Douglas to settle a minor dispute among neighbors. "She had a Rolodex to kill for," as Felsenthal once said. (Queen

Elizabeth once stopped by, with little warning, for lunch and didn't seem to mind that all Eppie had to feed her was salami.) In the 1960s, when many parents were fearful that their teenage children were being seduced by cult leaders, Popo invited a religious scholar to write a guest column about the merits of skepticism.

Both sisters preferred to voice the majority opinion, but there were a few issues about which they felt strongly. Dear Abby was progressive on gay rights. A popular genre of "Dear Abby" letters come from parents who suspect that their son or daughter is gay. In 1975, she received a letter from one such mother who feared that her daughter, a college student, was about to destroy her life. "Why do you assume that her sexual preference will necessarily 'ruin' her life? If you love her, accept her as she is and let her know it," Abby wrote. In 1971, she told a reader who was apprehensive about a wedding invitation from a gay couple that everyone had the right to celebrate their commitment.

In 1962, a man wrote an impassioned letter to Ann Landers explaining why he felt men had a right to spank their wives. It was perfectly legal, he reasoned. (In the early sixties, wife spanking was legal in most states, but not all.) "Women are not as smart as men and they need guidance," he wrote. "A good, hard spanking is the most effective method of correcting small faults before they turn into big ones." He signed it "The Boss." Ann Landers didn't care if spanking your wife was legal; it was wrong. "If more men tried it, there would be fewer men in this country," she wrote, which was the closest she ever came to issuing a physical threat. In response to a letter about teaching boys to shoot guns, Ann Landers skipped the question entirely and used her column to advocate for stronger gun laws. "What is needed is a strong federal gun law. The state laws aren't working," she wrote. She included a chart showing handgun deaths by country—in 1980, there were more than ten thousand in America and less than fifty in all the other countries listed. "These recent figures are enough to make an American hide his head in shame."

IN 1975, AFTER thirty-six years together, Jules informed Eppie that he wanted a divorce. He'd met another woman in London. Eppie was busy with her column and speaking engagements; he had started a car rental company that required constant travel. They'd grown apart. Jules had bought them a weekend house in Michigan, hoping that they'd go there and cut off from the rest of the world, but Eppie found the house too remote and drafty. "A nice idea, a weekend place, but not particularly useful. Since neither one of them liked to relax, they didn't need a special house to do it in," wrote Margo, their daughter. Jules fell into a routine on business trips in which he'd drink too much and smoke too much, and he wasn't able to stop when he returned home. Eppie, who never drank and lectured those who did, didn't notice that Jules was drunk before lunch until his secretary pointed it out.

Eppie broke the news in an "Ann Landers" column. "The lady with all the answers does not know the answer to this one." She closed with four inches of blank space as a "memorial to one of the world's best marriages that didn't make it to the finish line." She confessed that after Jules asked for the divorce, she went out to buy him underwear, socks, and groceries. He had no experience, she reasoned, buying these things himself, and she could not break the habit of taking care of him. "The ultimate liberated woman, she played the game—the old-fashioned one—in which she never acknowledged the degree to which her life was her own," Margo wrote.

For decades, Ann had counseled readers who felt uneasy about the ever-changing rules around gender, work, and sex. Why was a woman returning to work when her daughter was less than six months old? Why would a young boy want to try on a dress? Ann Landers had reminded her readers that change, though intimidating and even horrifying, was inevitable. She told them to accept that their seventeen-year-old daughter wanted to go on birth control, that their cousin was in love with a Jew, or—as the case may be—that their husband of three decades wanted a divorce. She was placed in the humbling position of needing her own advice, forced to recognize that change happened, whether you wanted it to or not. Eppie received more than thirty thousand letters of condolence about her divorce; her readers were like old friends by then, and they knew that a divorce was not what Ann Landers would have wanted.

Eppie and Popo's opinions about divorce and premarital sex loosened as the eighties approached. They had more tolerance for women working outside the home; they had to come to accept interfaith marriage and men with long hair. "I've gone through a gradual process of loosening my views as my children become adults, and they and their friends taught me that maybe I was a little out of step," Popo once said. "I will change my mind," Eppie said during a lecture she gave at Harvard. "I don't think that damages my credibility."

But some things didn't change. In 1981, a few months after the release of her book *The Best of Dear Abby*, Popo did an interview with *Ladies' Home Journal* and said she pitied Eppie for having spent her whole life in second place. "Her husband worked for mine. I drove a luxury car; she drove a lower-priced model. And that had to hurt. Look, she needs a lot of reinforcement," she said. She mocked Eppie for getting a face-lift. "I'm quite opposed to chopping myself up, but it was her right. Why not? When you cry a lot. It's got to show." She was sixty-three years old and as catty as ever. Popo later said that she was misquoted. Eppie didn't believe her but forgave her anyway. They had been back on speaking terms for a number of years by then, and Eppie, it seems, wasn't in the mood to fight.

Eppie decided to be permissive and set her bar low, just as she would advise her readers. *Get over it*, she would have written if someone had asked for her advice about a brutal sibling rivalry. *She's still your sister*. It wasn't *wrong* to hate your sister, but despising a relative that much was inconvenient and odd, and wouldn't it be more pleasant if everyone let it go?

EIGHT

Indulgence Is a Virtue

Mildred Newman

Every day, once a day, give yourself a present.
Don't plan it, don't wait for it, just let it happen.
It could be a new shirt at the men's store, a catnap in
your office chair, or two cups of good hot black coffee.

—Dale Cooper, *Twin Peaks*

SIGMUND FREUD'S FIRST AND LAST VISIT TO AMERICA was in September 1909. He found the country revolting and later described it as a "giant mistake." He thought its people were anti-intellectual and greedy and that his American colleagues had adulterated his psychoanalytic methods.

Freud had famously discovered a cure for mental illnesses like anxiety, hysteria, and depression—the so-called talking cure. His patients would come to his office four to five days a week, lay on his couch, and think aloud for an hour or more. Freud, meanwhile, would sit behind the patient, so as not to be noticed. For the process to work, the analyst had to refrain from offering his opinion. An analyst was not a friend or adviser; he facilitated the patient's connection to her unconscious mind but shared no commentary on her daily life. He interpreted her dreams but stated no opinion on whether the man she was thinking about was worth a second date. Freud appeared to be dogmatic about how psychoanalysis could be practiced and had no tolerance for criticism. He severed ties with colleagues who disagreed with him.

Although Freud didn't trust his American colleagues, they were among his most eager and obedient disciples. (It was the Europeans who were more skeptical.) Americans practiced psychoanalysis with greater orthodoxy than Freud himself. As a clinician, Freud dismissed many of his own rules. He modified the length and frequency of sessions according to his mood; he gave advice, shared personal information, and allowed his dog to roam the room during sessions. He meddled in his patients' lives. In 1922, Freud encouraged one of his patients, the psychiatrist Horace Frink, to leave his wife and marry an heiress named Anjelika Bjur. Frink was gay, and Freud reasoned that that he was better off repressed and rich than repressed and poor. (This wasn't a selfless act. Freud also assumed, correctly, that once they were married, Bjur would fund psychoanalytic research.) One of Freud's students, the Hungarian analyst Sandor Ferencezi, was known to take patients onto his lap and shower them with kisses. Ferencezi argued that his patients needed affection and warmth—"humanness," as he called it. Freud requested that Ferencezi tone down his humanness but never disciplined him further.

American analysts, generally, were as diffident as Freud instructed. And until the late 1950s, psychoanalysis was America's most popular form of therapy and was considered the highest standard of psychological care; "analysis" was virtually synonymous with psychological treatment. (There's a line in *West Side Story*, the 1957 musical, where a young gang member sings to a police officer, "Officer Krupke, you're really a square. This boy don't need a judge, he need an analyst's care!") By the end of the decade, more psychologists were practicing behavioral therapy, a more practical school of counseling less focused on sifting through the past than on helping patients develop the social and self-soothing skills they need to get through the day.

In the 1960s and '70s, Americans became more curious about therapy, and more curious about themselves. There appeared to be many more ways to live than people had been aware of: Men could grow their hair long; women could attend law school. Couples could control the size of their families. The establishment of the Peace Corps in 1961 gave more young people the opportunity to see the world, and drugs gave them access to a whole other dimension of reality. People—especially young, white, middle-class people—had more choices in this brave new world. Choices they needed help making.

This need was met with a proliferation of therapies designed to assist people with these choices, to help them determine what they *truly* wanted. Behavioral therapy grew more popular. But there were also group seminars, like Arica or EST, that promised more self-knowledge and less psychic pain. There were therapies that were purely physical, that disposed of talking altogether and treated movement as the best means of self-discovery, like Reichian therapy, acupuncture, and Rolfing, an intentionally painful form of massage.

Traditional talk therapy was still popular. But analysis was more clinical than consulting a guru or taking a group seminar at Esalen, a retreat in Big Sur, California, where there were hot tubs, delicious food, and many potential sexual partners. Psychotherapy, by comparison, didn't seem very fun. Unless one had a therapist like Mildred Newman.

BEFORE SHE WAS a Freudian analyst, Mildred Newman studied modern dance and worked as a (clothed) artist's model. She was born in New York, in East Harlem, in 1920. Her parents were Russian immigrants and spoke Yiddish at home. She was a gifted student and graduated high school when she was fifteen. After college, she received her master's in psychology at Hunter College, in New York, and studied at the National Psychological Association for Psychoanalysis. She was a disciple of Theodor Reik, who was in turn a disciple of Freud.

In the mid-1950s, Newman opened a private practice in Greenwich Village, a neighborhood in downtown Manhattan popular with artist types. Her first celebrity client was Paula Prentiss, a comedic actress with a gravelly voice that made her sound like she had just woken up. When Prentiss started seeing Newman, she'd recently been released from a psychiatric facility. She had started inpatient treatment after an episode during the shooting of Woody Allen's *What's New, Pussycat?* in which she'd climbed onto ceiling rafters, dangled by one hand, and threatened to let go. A crew member had rescued her.

Prentiss gushed about Newman to everyone she met on the set of *Catch-22*, and before the film wrapped, her costar, Anthony Perkins, her director, Mike Nichols, and Nora Ephron, who was writing a story about the making of the film for the *New York Times,* had all scheduled appointments. After meeting Newman, they all became evangelists. On the set of *Play It as It Lays,* an adaptation of the Joan Didion novel, Perkins distributed homemade pamphlets of Newman's maxims, inspiring his director, Frank Perry, to give her a call. The referral mill continued to spawn: the playwright Neil Simon, the director Joel Schumacher, and the gossip columnist Liz Smith all became clients. They all spoke of Newman with a reverence that recalls druggy teenagers at their first music festival.

In 1977, *Interview* magazine published a conversation between Schumacher and Smith. "I think the world is divided between people who have had analysis and people who haven't," Schumacher said. "Honestly, Lizzie, I don't know how people live without it." Newman, he said, had changed his life. "Just like in show businesses, or any other business, there are stars and she's definitely a star." "Well, you know I agree with you about that," Smith replied.

Newman looked like a star. She wore caftans and red lipstick. She was as friendly and affectionate as a favorite family pet but possessed the airy dignity of a ballerina at curtain call. "She was a person who made everyone feel special. If she went to a store, the person at that store felt special," said her son Neal Newman, a psychologist in Ohio. "Every person who spoke at her funeral, they all kidded that they were her favorite."

Newman was not a traditional American psychoanalyst. She did not intellectualize her clients' problems—she solved them. "It's not a doctor-patient relationship. She is a friend. Sometimes when I'm feeling bad she'll call—she'll know when I'm in trouble. It's like osmosis. She's always available," said the film critic Rex Reed, another former patient. Newman was more available than the average psychoanalyst, more *involved*. She gladly fielded calls from her patients' book or film agents if they were inflicting too much stress on them. Newman and her patients had meals together, took vacations together; she visited them on set and invited them to her summer home in Woodstock to unwind over long weekends. Her husband, Bernard Berkowitz, was a therapist, too—they shared a practice and sometimes saw patients together. They believed that patients benefited from getting two perspectives, from "binocular vision," as Newman phrased it. Nora Ephron "was either talking about Mildred and Bernie, as she called them, or she was with Mildred," said Ephron's friend Marie Brenner.

In Ephron's autobiographical novel, *Heartburn*, the main character, Rachel, is a pregnant cookbook writer who learns that her husband is having an affair. (The story is based on the dissolution of Ephron's marriage to the journalist Carl Bernstein.) In her distress, Rachel leans on her therapist, Vera Maxwell, who is Newman by a different name. Vera wears the signature caftans and red lipstick. She's warm and flamboyant. "She's very direct," Rachel says, "she's not one of those shrinks who sit there impassively and says, 'Mmmmhmm' every so often." Vera overshares; she speaks candidly about her marriage. "Vera says that the sex she has with

Niccolo is as good after twenty years of marriage as it was at the beginning." Vera often has to interrupt a session to take a call from a client having a breakdown at a film festival. She tells confusing jokes that might make more sense in their original Yiddish and has a trove of hard-to-follow fables that she categorizes by subject matter. There's the "one about the man from Minsk" and one about "the kreplach"—a meat-filled dumpling. The jokes hit and miss in equal frequency.

When Rachel wakes up from an emergency cesarean, Vera is sitting by her hospital bed. "Vera looked at me and her eyes filled with tears. She does this sometimes, especially when I am being hateful and difficult; she responds by having all the feelings I'm refusing to have." Vera is the greatest friend in the universe, compassionate and attentive. The empathy she offers is of the highest professional grade.

Newman was a gifted coddler: she could coddle her clients without their ever realizing it. "Some people help you and you feel like they did it all. My mother didn't take away from the person that they were running their own life," Neal Newman said. For those who no longer had time for friendships, or found that all their friendships had been corrupted by fame, Newman was glad to fill in.

⌒⌣⌒

IN THE 1970S, Newman charged fifty dollars for a fifty-minute session. For those who couldn't afford her friendship at that price, she published a book, *How to Be Your Own Best Friend*, in 1971. (The pamphlet that Perkins distributed on set was an early, private draft, available only to clients and acquaintances.) Berkowitz, though listed as a coauthor, was more sous-chef than a copilot. "I think that, with a little help from me, she really should be credited for the self-help deluge that happened," Berkowitz later said. "She inspired people, opened them up to a more fulfilled life." The hardcover cost $4.95. The paperback was $1.50. It sold millions of copies, and in 1975, Newman published a second book, *How to Be Awake and Alive*. Both books present Newman's famed fables in their convoluted entirety. Here's "the kreplach story":

> There was a young boy who had a kreplach phobia. Every time he would see kreplach, he would scream. His screams were so upsetting to his mother that she took him to a therapist, who said, "Oh this is a very simple problem. Take him home and make kreplach from beginning to end and let him follow each step, and then he won't scream anymore."
>
> So the mother did just that. She started with the flour, and said, "Are you afraid of this?" And the little boy said, "No!"
>
> Then she rolled the flour and showed him the dough, and said, "Are you afraid of this?" And again he said, "No!"
>
> Then she showed him the chopped meat and said, "Do you know what this is?" He said, "Yes!" And she said, "Are you frightened of this?" He said, "No!"
>
> Then she put the meat in the dough, and still he wasn't frightened, but when she made the corners and put it altogether, he shrieked, "Kreplach!" and was very frightened.

In the book, Newman connects this allegory to a young woman who dates broke, troubled men and breaks it off as soon as she's coached them to be healthy and successful. The stories are all this vague and her interpretations equally hard to follow. That was the intention. "They wrote it as a projective device, so that each person can get what they needed from it," said Neal, Newman's son. Newman and Berkowitz weren't interested in typifying personalities or mechanizing the therapeutic process. They were evangelists of self-help, in the most literal sense, and the stories were offered as open-ended tools for readers to use as they wished.

The books are compilations of vague and encouraging nostrums, pressing readers to trust their instincts and forgive their faults. Newman was a believer in self-gratification, that a person's foremost responsibility was to herself. "People worry about pollution. But the harm we do ourselves is a lot more dangerous to the environment," they wrote. "Doing what makes you feel good about yourself is really the opposite of self-indulgence. It doesn't mean gratifying an isolated part of you; it means satisfying your whole self."

She advocated, unapologetically, for pleasure. There was nothing inherently worthy about asceticism. Anything too challenging or painful should be skipped. "When we use our will power to achieve goals that do not spring out of us, but which we set for the sake of pleasing others or to fulfill a fantasy about who we are, we create a kind of monster," they wrote. "We have all met people who are held together by sheer will power; the effort's enormous, but the result is hardly worth it." They encouraged readers to set achievable goals and to forgive themselves if they failed to accomplish them. "Don't judge yourself at all; accept yourself and move on from there."

Anthony Perkins identified as gay when he became Newman's patient but was too ashamed to have a relationship with a man. Newman pushed him to try dating women. She wasn't homophobic, she insisted, but being gay seemed hard and she wanted Perkins, and all her patients, to lead simple, joyous lives. "She would say to me, 'It's not that I want you to spend less time by yourself in monosexual isolation. But wouldn't you want to make the choice to do that rather than it being the only thing you *can* do?'" Perkins recalled. She wanted him to experience sexual pleasure—she was an ambassador for pleasure in all forms. Perkins ended up marrying a woman fifteen years younger than him and crediting Newman for saving his life. "I owe the second half of my life to the years I spent in Newman's office," he said. "It would be errant dishonesty to put it any other way."

Newman, like the good Freudian she was, treated the unconscious as the holy grail, to be probed and mined for secrets. But she had also found that excavating the unconscious could be laborious and painful, and there was no guarantee of immediate benefits. Her clients were impatient—the other trendy American therapies promised a fast fix. Newman, despite her psychoanalytic training, felt that she owed her clients the gratification of visible results. Her tactic for appeasing the unconscious mind was a steadfast regimen of pleasure. The unconscious, she'd found, liked to be indulged.

⁓

"CREATIVE PEOPLE HAVE got to spend a certain amount of time in self obsession," Woody Allen told Stephen Faber and Marc Green, the authors of *Hollywood on the Couch*. "Psychoanalysis and psychotherapy deal with those very things that the artist is concerned with, his feelings about his life, his feelings about himself. For an artist, what's so terrible to spend an hour in the day, to lie on the couch and just talk freely about your deepest feelings on any subject? It's dramatic and fascinating. And as you can face certain problems with a larger view, a more generous view, with more grasp of them and perspective of them, you have a chance to have a larger view of your writing."

There's nothing so terrible about this, except that not everyone can afford therapy. In a recent survey of mentally ill young adults who have not sought treatment, nearly half said that they'd gladly seek professional help if it weren't so expensive. The other half of people surveyed either were too ashamed to enter therapy or were confident they'd find a way to heal on their own. There's an app for almost everything, and there are a fleet of apps designed to ease social anxiety, practice mindfulness, and encourage positive thinking. There are also, of course, books, websites, and old episodes of *Oprah* to screen on YouTube—all free, or at least cheaper than therapy. I have one friend who was suffering from depression, didn't have insurance, and bought a cognitive behavioral workbook on Amazon—she swears by it.

Newman's books democratized therapy. She recognized that the goals of psychoanalysis weren't high-brow or extreme, that everyone—not just creative people or those with a severe mental illness—could use some encouragement and that such encouragement could come as easily from a book as from an analyst. American mythology

privileges scrappiness over pedigree and self-reliance over profes-
sionalism, and Newman correctly predicted that many thousands of
Americans who would never pay for an appointment would gladly
purchase a book at $1.50.

She also recognized that if famous people talked publicly about
how much they loved therapy, hordes of Americans would be lured
to give it a try. The early 1970s were the early years of the celebrity
worship industry, before every diet, gym, and exercise regimen was
endorsed by a famous face and the checkout aisle included a buffet
of tabloids that captured celebrities running errands in their sweatpants. *How to Be Your Own Best Friend*, with its glowing blurbs from
celebrities, was unlike anything else on the shelf. "I want to tell
you that it's magic, but the whole point of the book is that there is
no magic. So instead, let me simply say that I can't live without it,"
wrote Nora Ephron. "I read it twice a day with a glass of water. It
has never failed to uplift me," wrote Neil Simon.

Hollywood had long been enamored with therapy. In 1925, the
producer Samuel Goldwyn supposedly offered Freud a $100,000
consulting deal to help writers and actors capture the emotional
depths of their characters. Judy Garland was an obsessive patient;
Marilyn Monroe was so dependent on her therapist that she purchased a home in Brentwood so she could live closer to him. When
the composer Ira Gershwin and his wife Leonore threw parties at
their home in Beverly Hills, they'd set up eight tables and make
sure that there was a psychiatrist seated at each one—shrinks, they'd
found, were the most popular party guests. Throughout the 1950s,
it was not uncommon for an actor to bring his therapist to set. The
famed acting couch Lee Strasberg and the director Elia Kazan prescribed therapy to any actor experiencing a block and struggling to
connect with a character. In the 1960s and '70s, Hollywood churned
out a series of paeans to psychoanalysis, including the John Huston
biopic *Freud* and the many films featuring Woody Allen as a fret-
ful romantic hero. Joan Didion, writing for the *New York Review
of Books*, thought that Allen ought to be embarrassed by his endless

pursuit of self-knowledge. "This notion of oneself as a kind of continuing career—something to work at, work on, 'make an effort' for and subject to an hour a day of emotional Nautilus training, all in the interest of not of attaining grace but of improving one's 'relationships'—is fairly recent in the world, at least in the world not inhabited by adolescents," Didion wrote. "The message that large numbers of people are getting from *Manhattan* and *Interiors* and *Annie Hall* is that this kind of emotional shopping around is the proper business of life's better students, that adolescence can now extend to middle age."

But therapy in Allen's circles was not merely a practice of endless navel-gazing but offered writers and actors a competitive edge. ("You have a chance to have a larger view of your writing," as Allen said.) The talking cure was considered a kind of sorcery that would enable you write the screenplay or land the part that would change your career forever. (Much like the promises made by the Church of Scientology, which has its own particular draw among Hollywood types.) Through therapy, they could harness their inner talents or even discover talents they didn't know they had.

Today, Hollywood has diversified its therapeutic obsession. I'm writing this from Los Angeles, in a quiet neighborhood on the east side, and there's a yoga studio, a homeopathy office, a natural food store, an acupuncture clinic, and a juice store all within a mile of the apartment where I'm staying. The juice store sells a smoothie with coconut and dates called "Intuitive Energy" and another with apple and strawberries called "Brain Juice." So much in this city carries the promise of an awakening—a spinning class, a salt crystal, a concoction of coconut and dates. Much of LA's "wellness" industry is driven by the same vague sense of competition that drove people to talk therapy a few decades ago, because people in creative industries tend to be vulnerable targets, prone to accepting whatever "help" they can get.

There's an unsubtle suggestion that doing yoga or consuming a concoction of coconut and dates will not only make you feel good but make you a better person. The idea, first articulated by Benjamin Franklin, that all self-improvement is an inherently moral act still influences the many therapeutic businesses in Los Angeles and across the country. I think about this when a yoga teacher instructs me and my classmates to "dedicate" our practice to someone who needs us. Wouldn't it be better, I always think, if we called our loved ones after class?

Newman made no claims of humanitarianism. She administered therapy as an amoral practice. She believed that everyone should be self-centered enough to take time for themselves, not just so they could accelerate their careers or become better parents but to sate their own curiosities. "It does mean being self-centered enough to care for yourself and to take care of yourself," she wrote in *How to Be Your Own Best Friend*. Less than a decade earlier, Abby Van Buren had reminded women that marriage was, by definition, burdensome and laborious and that wives were expected to cater to their husbands' every whim. Newman was prescribing indulgences to these doting wives, encouraging them to treat themselves with the same care they lavished upon their husbands and children. "All the kind and thoughtful things you would do towards a living child, all the loving help you would give that child, you can give yourself." Unlike Dale Carnegie, with his mnemonics and instructions on smiling, Newman's books offer nothing in the way of tangible instructions. She has no diet tips, no appendix with physical exercises, only sugary reminders that you deserve everything. While Dorothy Dix implored readers to be practical, reminding them of life's endless compromises, Newman recommended that they gorge on happiness.

Self-care is everywhere. There are endless methods and configurations of "me time." There's movement therapy, animal therapy, ayurvedic eating. There are leaderless therapeutic communities and woodsy retreats. Newman's theory was that they all worked, that the unconscious doesn't need a couch and a doctor to unveil itself but tenderness, patience, and some undivided attention.

part three

Experts Among Us

Instead of Man Thinking, we have the bookworm. Hence the
book-learned class, who value books, as such; not as related to
nature and the human condition, but as making a sort of Third
Estate with the world and soul. Hence the restorers of readings,
the emendators, the bibliomaniacs of all degrees. This is bad;
this is worse than it seems.

—Ralph Waldo Emerson, *The American Scholar*

IN APRIL 2016, ON THE EVE OF WISCONSIN'S REPUBLI-
can primary, Donald Trump gave a stump speech in a convention
center in La Crosse, Wisconsin, a small city on the state's western
border. Trump was, by then, the Republican front-runner. He had
earned a reputation as a populist rabble-rouser who disdained the
conventional thinking that, to his view, had mired DC in incompe-
tency. But the week before the speech, Trump had, uncharacteris-
tically, embraced some of the trappings of political tradition. He'd
hired a cadre of foreign policy experts, including a former adviser to
Mitt Romney and several decorated servicemen who had completed

tours in Iraq and Afghanistan. In La Crosse, however, Trump doubled down on his disdain for Washington protocol and the individuals it bolstered. "The experts are terrible. Look at the mess we're in
with all these experts that we have. Look at the mess. Look at the
Middle East. If our presidents and our politicians went on vacation
for 365 days a year and went to the beach, we'd be in much better
shape right now in the Middle East."

Since his election, President Trump has demonstrated that his
distrust of experts was not merely campaign chest-thumping. He
has chosen, again and again, to treat political experts as lepers, pre-
ferring cabinet members with little knowledge of the agencies they
are meant to run. He trusts a man with business savvy, a man who
can hold a room, over one with relevant experience.

Trump's perception of experts as pompous and incompetent egg-
heads is nothing new. In 1963, Richard Hofstadter, a historian at
Columbia University, reached the conclusion that Americans had
turned against experts because they were too reliant on them, like
teenagers who resent their parents because they need to borrow the
car. "The complexity of modern life has steadily whittled away the
functions the ordinary citizen can intelligently and comprehendingly
perform for himself," Hofstadter wrote. "In the original American
populistic dream, the omnicompetence of the common man was fundamental and indispensable. It was believed that he could, without
much special preparation, pursue the professions and run the government. Today he knows that he cannot even make his breakfast without using devices, more or less mysterious to him, which expertise
has put at his disposal." This was in 1963, before we carried handheld
devices that can both serve as a kitchen timer and entertain us while
the water boils.

Expertise can be acquired in different ways. You can be an expert
on children's health because you spent six years studying to become
a pediatrician or because you've raised four healthy children. Hofstadter observed that it was the pedigreed expert who was the object

of so much disdain. Americans didn't mind the obsessive hobbyist who'd built all his own kitchen appliances—to continue Hofstadter's metaphor. Self-taught knowledge was still respectable. It was the economists, psychologists, and doctors, the accredited experts, who had been deemed problematic.

Popular advice columns are rarely written by certified experts. The top personal finance gurus are not economists and the top nutritional specialists aren't doctors. People seem to prefer advice-givers whose wisdom seems attainable, who learned from doing. By the twentieth century, American readers were long past the days of the Athenian Society, when any gaggle of men could appoint themselves an "intellectual society" and expect to be taken seriously.

There is something impersonal about getting advice from an expert, from someone who may be recycling the thesis from their dissertation or their academic papers. Experts don't have opinions but *theories*. The appeal of an advice columnist like Dorothy Dix or Ann Landers, who has no degree or official accreditation, is that she is reacting instinctively to the letter at hand, basing her answers on her own lived experience rather than on something she read.

Three of the advice-givers in this section, Sylvia Porter, Benjamin Spock, and Elizabeth Kübler-Ross, began their careers as experts in traditional subject areas—finance, pediatrics, and psychology, respectively. For a variety of reasons—a call to public duty, their own outsized egos—they all sought to break out of scholastic circles and address the greater American public. They were each careful to never come across as stonehearted intellectuals. Porter, a well-informed finance columnist, went so far as to pretend that she didn't know much at all about economics. Spock's popularity can be attributed to his tactic of treating mothers like they already knew what they were doing, and Kübler-Ross made a point to distance herself from the medical field. The final advice-giver in this section, Joan Quigley, was an expert in astrology who spent a decade working in secret for Nancy Reagan. Quigley agreed to these terms but couldn't understand why the Reagans were so ashamed of *her*, even though they clearly had great respect for her areas of expertise. This struck Quigley as unfair and at odds with American values: she felt that experts of all stripes, no matter how peculiar their area of knowledge, should be treated equally.

NINE

Honorary Pants

Sylvia Porter

WHEN SARIANI FELDMAN WAS GROWING UP IN PAT-
chogue, Long Island, her father, a doctor, never allowed her inside
his office. She could watch from the doorway as her older brother
John flipped through their father's books and relaxed on his couch.
"The sun rose and set on my brother John," she later said. "I was
just a little girl." She skipped two grade levels and graduated high
school at sixteen. But this had no effect on the rules surrounding her
father's domain. Women simply could not pass.

The Feldmans were Jewish immigrants from Russia. During
World War I, they invested thirty thousand dollars—everything
they had—in so-called Liberty bonds. These were federal bonds advertised as a safe investment and a demonstration of patriotism: the
money went to support the troops in Europe. But Feldman's father
sold their bonds at the wrong time and lost everything. "Of course,
the Wall Street crowd knew what it was doing and sold the bonds
when prices were high," she later said. Sariani was at Vassar, the
esteemed women's college, when her parents lost their money. She
was working on a novel but decided to put aside fiction and study
economic policy instead.

Sariani would go on to become Sylvia Porter, America's first personal finance columnist. She offered financial advice for more than five decades, from the 1930s to the early 1990s. She broke down complex financial news for general audiences, tackling subjects like foreign bonds, corporate debt, and the national deficit. She did not shy from the details and took pride in translating the densest financial "bafflegab"—her word for financial jargon—into something average readers could understand while they scanned the paper with breakfast.

Porter was a populist hero, an advocate for gender equality, affordable childcare, and consumer protection. "We, the consumers" she'd often write when she critiqued government policy. Porter knew from her own family's experience that the last thing most middle-class families needed was a get-rich-quick scheme, and that most investment opportunities peddled to middle-class families were not worth the risk. She offered detailed instructions on how to contact one's representatives, file a suit in small-claims court, and make demands of a customer service representative. She believed middle-class families needed a financial guardian, someone to translate the bafflegab designed to bankrupt them. Porter provided just that for decades, until it became clear that her readers wanted something else entirely.

SHE GRADUATED FROM Vassar in 1932 and later that year married Reid Porter, a New York banker. She wasn't ready to start a family, and with her heart still set on writing, she decided to put her economics degree to use by covering the stock market as a reporter. She watched DC reporters gobble up whatever the Roosevelt administration said without questioning it and knew she could do better. They'd "jot down whatever they were told, and then they'd go off and write their stories. And they did just that, every day, with no clear idea of the international effects of the news they're reporting," she later said.

She applied for a reporting job at the Associated Press, where an editor told her that the financial news department had never had a woman reporter and never would. All the other agencies or papers she queried had a similar response.

The financial industry was more open-minded. Porter accepted a position at the investment firm Glass and Key a few months after graduation. She became an expert in bonds and global markets while she freelanced on the side. She wrote for industry rags like *American Banker* and the *Commercial and Financial Chronicle* under the moniker S. F. Porter, so no one knew she was a woman.

Her byline caught the attention of an editor at the *New York Post*, and she started writing there in 1935. In her articles, she explained how governments issued bonds to finance large-scale endeavors, like infrastructural projects. She felt that readers should have a basic understanding of the mechanics of government lending and to whom America was indebted. It was a civic-minded effort and made for difficult reading. The first sentence of her first article for the *Post* read, "The real significance of the Dominion of Canada's $76,000,000 21/2 percent loan is that it is a 'feeler'—the first issue in a series of refunding operations to convert the entire Dominion and Provincial debt."

With practice, her writing style loosened and her stories became more legible. She wrote features about corruption on Wall Street and women in the financial industry. The latter was a ten-part series, and each installment profiled a woman who, against all odds, had succeeded in the most male-dominated field in America. Porter concluded that the average woman financier "scorns publicity, seeks refuge behind an initial that hides her sex, [and] battles with men on a basis of accomplishment, rather than personality." She was technically writing about her subjects, but the description applied to her as well: she was still writing under her initials so that readers could assume she was a man.

Porter, at that point, didn't write straightforward advice so much as explanatory journalism about the economy. She wrote one exposé about the practice of "free riding," in which financial insiders would make a down payment on new government-issued bonds and resell them at a premium before paying the full asking price. Secretary of the Treasury Henry Morgenthau immediately called a press conference and demanded that the practice end. He insisted on learning the true identity of S. F. Porter, and when he discovered she was a woman, he sent roses to her office at the *Post*. From then on, Morgenthau consulted Porter on policy points and sought her guidance when pricing new government bonds. In 1940, Morgenthau summoned Porter to Florida for a conference on banking, where the two of them devised the nonfluctuating thirty-year Series E savings bond, which would fund American forces fighting World War II— unlike the Liberty bond, which had bankrupted Porter's family, it protected consumers in the case of a government default.

She kept her gender-neutral byline, but as the years went on, she began to make subtle and then less-subtle hints at her gender. In 1941, after the United States entered World War II, she wrote, "There are certain things we—women—can do to make the adjustment easier." Six months later, she wrote, "The first World War brought women into finance and the second World War is giving us our big chance. From this day on, you will write the story."

Most readers didn't catch on. Porter was flown across the country to deliver keynote addresses at clubs and associations where women weren't even allowed entrance. She preferred to say nothing and shock the organizers when she arrived; she liked to make people squirm a little. In 1942, her editor determined it was time to end the farce. "I believe very definitely that the time has come for us to make capital of the fact that S. F. Porter is a woman writing on financial subjects, rather than trying to disguise Sylvia as an old man with a long, white beard," he wrote in an internal memo.

From then on, her daily column, "S. F. Talks," ran with a headshot. Porter, then thirty, had upswept dark hair, a fair complexion, and a regal, impatient smile. Journalists wrote about her with a slack-jawed awe, as if they'd come upon a rare cockatoo. "A financial editor can be beautiful!" read one headline. She was called "Wall Street's Joan of Arc" and the "glamor girl of finance." "Frumpy, one might guess about a woman writer on economics. Not so. Not so," went one article. Porter embraced the attention; she shared her measurements and makeup tips, donned flashy hats for photo shoots. She talked about her weakness for haute fashion and her love of pink. She came across as tidy and maternal, the perfect doting wife. When there weren't any cameras around, she went back to being the loudmouthed reporter who chain-smoked Kent cigarettes, shouted for coffee as soon as she arrived at the office each morning, and kept a bottle of scotch in her desk drawer.

A few months after Porter's big gender reveal, the directors of the New York Stock Exchange held a meeting to discuss whether she should be allowed on the trading floor. Like her father's home office, it had a strict men-only policy. The floor was a hive of ambition, testosterone, and pit stains. Traders took pride in the grimy chaos of their workplace and felt that having a woman around would sour the mood. After a lengthy debate, the directors decided that Porter was a worthy exception. "Sylvia is one of the boys. We hereby award her honorary pants," they wrote in a resolution, according to her biographer Tracy Lucht.

But it was clear that Porter wasn't one of the boys. Her competitors—all men—were hyperwatchful of her and her column. They pounced on her if she quoted an anonymous source—a standard practice in journalism, but when Porter did so, it was reason enough to go on the radio and accuse her of shoddy work. Her "slip was showing," one of her critics said regarding one of these nonscandals. Porter, in response, played down her brains and played up her femininity. She told reporters that she hardly understood the stock market and jotted down whatever she happened to pick up from her second husband, Sumner Collins, who worked on the business side of the *New York World-American.* (She and Porter had divorced in 1941.) In interviews, she complained about the challenge of balancing a checkbook and scoffed at the idea that she could do her own taxes. She seemed to think that she needed to be more approachable, that Americans preferred to get their financial advice from an old-fashioned wife rather than a bookish wonk who seemed like she began every sentence with the word *actually*.

She still wrote explanatory pieces about bonds, the real estate market, government debt, and inflation for the *New York Post*, where she criticized tax policies that hurt small-business owners and middle-class families. "As we belittle and neglect this class, we belittle and neglect America itself," she once wrote. But more of her time was spent writing for women's magazines like *Vogue* and *Good Housekeeping*, in which she dealt with more everyday matters, skipped the details and bafflegab, and presumed that most women saw static when they read their bank statement. Other financial writers, at the *Wall Street Journal* for instance, catered their guidance to the highfalutin class, who had enough money to take risks. Porter wrote about college savings and household budgets for America's growing middle class, for people who were able to buy a house or attend college on the GI Bill and maybe had a bit left over. She issued warnings about mail-order health insurance plans, encouraging readers to double check whether the insurer was licensed in their state and covered hospital stays. She provided lists of reputable student loan providers. She recommended that her readers schedule regular doctor visits to avoid expensive late-stage treatments and buy shoes that fit because they lasted longer. She offered sample cover letters for health aide jobs and described the markers of a mail-order swindle, like vague testimonials and charging an additional fee for an instruction manual.

This was not the old S. F. Porter, the wonky statistician. This was Sylvia Porter, the condescending matriarch. She developed split personalities. As a women's magazine columnist, she helped readers calculate the cost of their groceries and instructed women on what to do if their husbands died at war—borrow money, buy savings bonds, hold on to their homes. She provided bargain calendars indicating the best months of the year to find deals on certain items. Costume jewelry was cheapest in January; Christmas presents should be purchased "anytime but Christmas." She urged all her female readers to take out a life insurance policy, so they had something to fall back on if something happened to their husbands. "Write down the names of one or two men to whom your husband would wish you to turn for advice and financial counsel if he wasn't here," she advised in *Good Housekeeping.*

She supported women with careers but believed that most women belonged at home. If a woman was not *the best* at what she did, Porter argued, she shouldn't work at all. "There's no reason for being in a man's job," she wrote. She argued that society could do more to assist women who happened to be thriving in men's jobs. She advocated for affordable childcare and hoped more companies would invent easy-to-prepare meals that would make the juggle easier for working mothers.

In 1949, she and her husband adopted a baby girl, Cris Sarah, and shortly after, she wrote a piece lamenting the challenges of finding suitable domestic help and the need for an agency that trained and certified maids. Her editor refused to publish it; according to Lucht, he felt it came across as elitist and out of touch and said he was killing the piece for her own sake. Sylvia Porter, like S. F. Porter, was supposed to be the voice of the middle class, for "Mr. and Mrs. America," as she had once put it. But that was easier to do when she didn't also have to contend with the inherent impossibility of being a woman in public, needing to be glamorous but relatable, authoritative but warm, smart but not too smart—all at the same time.

THERE WERE A number of times when Porter nearly stepped away from her role advising the masses to craft federal policy. She edited several of President John F. Kennedy's speeches. In 1964, she was formally offered a job in the Johnson administration. Johnson was a longtime fan of Porter. He admired her clear prose style, her ability to articulate complicated concepts in terms he understood. "Why can't economists talk straight like Sylvia?" he once asked a room of advisers.

Johnson asked Porter to lead the Export-Import Bank, an agency that promotes the export of American goods and services by insuring foreign purchases. She would have been the first woman to hold the position and one of the highest-ranking women in the administration. She turned him down. According to Lucht, Porter sat on the edge of her bed, phone against her ear, tears rolling down her face, and told President Johnson that she could not neglect her column, even for a few years. She explained to the president that journalism was a tough business and that if she took a hiatus there might not be a column for her to return to; she had worked too hard to take that kind of risk.

She was too devoted to her readers to abandon them for the suits of DC. She had intimate exchanges with them—many of the questions Porter received from her female readers had little to do with finance. They were "is it okay" questions about whether teenagers should work after school and splurging on a summer vacation, questions that were easier to pose to an empathic working mother than a bureaucrat. In 1960, Porter was put on the cover of *Time* magazine, wearing a blue velvet beret and a stately gold choker. She looked elegant, like an accomplished equestrian. She was an aspirational figure, a symbol of everything middle-class American women could accomplish if they worked hard and were cautious with their money. If she took the job at the White House, she'd belong in a wholly different stratosphere. She'd have more access to the individuals who designed economic policy, but would readers still trust her?

Porter, like Benjamin Franklin, was convinced that giving advice was a matter of public interest. She wanted the readers of her column to be able to tell when politicians were lying, when new taxes were not in their favor, when banks were offering them faulty deals. Porter's advice was not of the unyieldingly positive, "you can do it if you try" variety; she never promised to unveil the key to a debt-free life or a quick way to make millions, as many other financial advisers have. She understood middle-class life as an inherently defensive position. She accused large investment firms of misleading and defrauding small investors and explained what readers could do to protect themselves. She urged her readers to boycott overpriced goods, and, every year, she reported on increasing costs of basic household items to show how inflation affected working families.

She liked to remind her readers and the men she debated on the radio that women controlled 70 percent of the nation's wealth, that wives held the purse strings in most households; she believed that banks and lenders ought to treat women with greater respect. (Until 1975, with the passage of Equal Credit Opportunity Act, most banks refused to give unmarried women credit unless they had a male cosignatory.) Porter defended female workers for being as hardworking and capable as men. She refuted the myth that female employees fell ill more frequently and that they quit as soon as they had children. She showed that absenteeism rates were roughly equal among male and female workers and that the average married woman spent twenty-five years of her life at a job.

Porter limited herself to advocating small, realizable changes, all within the existing economic structure. As she saw it, it was her job to help readers survive and even succeed. It was not her job to harp on how unfair things were, even when the government failed to control runaway inflation on food and other necessities or passed tax cuts for large corporations. And sometimes she skipped the stories of corporate malfeasance. She did not report on a paperwork scandal that threatened to shut down several brokerages and firms in the mid-1960s. "If you're going to be an analyst and a columnist on economic life, don't you think you have a responsibility not to bring the whole structure down?" she said in an interview with the *Wall Street Journal*. In that way, she is reminiscent of Dorothy Dix, Ann

Landers, and Dear Abby, with a keen eye for the middle road. She understood that people sought her advice because they were feeling optimistic about their financial future, that they were considering a big leap on a new home or a new car and sought reassurance that everything would work out. It was her job to be a killjoy, to prepare her readers for the worst-case scenario. "The higher the aspirations, the more chance that people will be disappointed," she liked to remind her followers.

CONTEMPORARY FINANCIAL GURUS tend to traffic in personality. They have booming voices, deliver catchy zingers, and make outsized promises. Dave Ramsey, perhaps America's most popular financial guru, quotes Christian proverbs as evidence for his theory that all debt is bad debt: "The borrower is the slave of the lender" (Proverbs 22:7). "Give no sleep to your eyes nor slumber to your eyelids; deliver yourself like a gazelle from the hunter's hand" (Proverbs 6:4–5). He recites these lines on his radio program, *The Dave Ramsey Show,* which supposedly more than thirteen million people listen to each week, and in his presentations at stadiums and mega-churches across the country. He believes student debt is a mistake. Business loans are mistake. Credit cards, if you already made the mistake of acquiring one, should be left in a locked drawer—some of his followers, as a sign of their devotion, have mailed their credit cards to Ramsey's office. He casts himself as his own hardest client: When he first graduated from college, he borrowed too much money to build his real estate empire in Tennessee. He had more than four million dollars' worth of property foreclosed on and declared bankruptcy. In his shame, he turned to scripture and discovered the simplicity of a debt-free life.

Suze Orman, the host of *The Suze Orman Show* on CNBC, has nine best-selling financial advice books, including *The Courage to Be Rich.* Her message is a somber one—don't buy the car, sofa, necklace, designer dog, what-have-you, unless you can afford it in cash. She's the voice of reason, a brash and entertaining splash of cold water to remind viewers they can't necessarily have whatever their heart desires. Orman has a habit of yelling, "Are you kidding?" whenever someone is debating a particularly needless purchase. Like that of Ramsey and many other advice-givers, her own story is a dramatic reversal of luck and fortune: at twenty-nine she was a broke waitress in San Francisco and talked herself into a job at Merrill Lynch. She makes her living (a good one: her net worth is over twenty million dollars) telling her followers to resist the temptations of American consumerism, a message she combines with an acute knowledge of how irresistible certain luxuries can be (she admits to having weaknesses—she prefers to fly private) and vague, pseudo-religious reminders that honesty and charity are rewarded—in cash.

Porter, by contrast, spent her career being frank. She never promised anything other than accurate information. She had no easy tricks to save money or make it rain. She was not interested in her readers' spiritual welfare: her advice was myopically focused on money. Toward the end of her career, she published a spree of books, including *Sylvia Porter's Guide to Health Care, Sylvia Porter's A Home of Your Own,* and *Sylvia Porter's Planning Your Retirement.* She started a magazine: *Sylvia Porter's Personal Finance Magazine.* She was a franchise, a frenetic, outsized celebrity, as ubiquitous as Oprah is today. She wrote a daily column, a weekly column, and a weekly newsletter. The only way to write at that volume was to get others to write for her, and she employed dozens of ghostwriters. The joke among New York journalists in the 1960s was that "half of America reads Sylvia Porter, the other half writes it."

The message was always the same: save whatever you can, spend as little as possible. Her advice in these books was less granular than her early, largely unreadable columns. But, unlike Ramsey or Orman, she never implied that moral behavior would be rewarded financially or that assuming debt was a categorically bad decision. She advised her readers to never owe more than 20 percent of their yearly after-tax income and explained the various tactics collectors used to entrap debtors, such as add-on and acceleration clauses. She encouraged her readers to be wary of banks, corporations, the government, insurance agencies—of anyone who made any kind of promise.

But she realized that readers wanted more than her expertise. They wanted a role model and an assuring friend. She was a better wonk than friend, but she did what she could. She shared her weekly grocery list and her monthly household costs ("I took an early morning golf lesson; called the typewriter repairman to fix my new electric portable; paid the piano tuner for his regular quarterly visit"). America was ready for a female financial columnist, but it wasn't ready for a female financial *expert*. America *still* isn't ready for a financial expert of any sort. We may have careful accountants to help us with our taxes and personal financial advisers. But when it comes to those we listen to on the radio or watch on television, Americans still prefer financial gurus who have managed to eke out a living, despite themselves, to people who had a plan all along. We prefer financial advice-givers who make wealth seem like it's *out there*, waiting to be taken.

TEN

Doctor's Orders

Benjamin Spock

> Perhaps society is past praying for, but there is always hope for the individual human being, if you can catch him young enough.
>
> —George Orwell, "Charles Dickens"

"TRUST YOURSELF," BEGINS DR. BENJAMIN SPOCK'S seminal book, *The Common Sense Book of Baby and Child Care*. "You know more than you think you do." Dr. Spock is, save for Dr. Jekyll and Dr. Watson, the most famous doctor in all English-language literature, and his celebrity was earned entirely on the merit of this one book. *The Common Sense Book*, which came out in 1946, continues in the comforting guise of its opening sentence. Spock was an expert in pediatrics and psychology who essentially told his readers that they didn't need an expert's guidance. "Bringing up your child won't be a complicated job if you take it easy, trust your own instincts, and follow the directions that your doctor gives you," he wrote. "We know for a fact that the natural loving care that kindly parents give their children is a hundred times more valuable than their knowing how to pin a diaper just right or how to make a formula expertly."

His book isn't merely a compilation of trust-yourself platitudes. It's a clinical list of recommendations about everything a new parent needs to know. It covers napping, eating, diaper rashes, toilet training, and tips on things like how to pull a tight sweater over a baby's head (over the back). It's an encyclopedic volume on child raising; sixty-five years after it first came out, it remains among the most celebrated books on child development.

Spock's simple, intuitive advice was radical for its time. The parenting experts who preceded him treated babies like delicate, easily broken stations in a factory line. Mothers were told they shouldn't touch or pick up their babies outside of scheduled feedings, that making a baby laugh would impose a strain on his or her nervous system, that a healthy child should be held to a strict schedule. During pregnancy, expecting mothers were instructed to avoid fearful or negative thoughts so as not to pass them along to their children. "Pregnant mothers should avoid thinking of ugly people, or those marked by any deformity or disease; avoid injury, fright and disease of any kind," instructed one 1920s parenting manual. Such risks made it difficult for pregnant women to justify a trip outside. And once the child was born, mothers had even less freedom, as they were supposed to stand guard over their children like sentinels, never showing too much affection. "Handle the baby as little as possible. Turn it occasionally from side to side, feed it, change it, keep it warm, and let it alone; crying is absolutely essential to the development of good strong lungs. A baby should cry vigorously several times each day," said one parenting manual from 1916. Another book, *Psychological Care of Infant and Child*, published in 1928, warned against the "dangers of too much mother love" and advised mothers to never hug or kiss their sons or allow them to sit on their laps. It's unclear how many young mothers actually followed this advice. (In Mary McCarthy's novel *The Group*, which follows a group of Vassar graduates from the class of 1933, one young mother won't leave the apartment because she's too anxious about missing a feeding.) But the takeaway of most late-nineteenth- and early-twentieth-century child-rearing guides was that maternal instinct alone was not enough to raise a competent child. In 1923, the Rockefeller Foundation invested millions of dollars in "research stations" dedicated to child development, bringing together experts from a variety of disciplines with the hopes of standardizing best practices for parents.

Spock, on the other hand, had a sweet and easy thesis: love really is enough. His book was popular for the same reason that the Beatles, frozen yogurt, and Paul Rudd are popular: it was pleasant and uncomplicated. He believed that regular visits to the doctor and parental affection were all a baby needed.

In his book, Spock is the humblest and most retiring of experts. He sees parenting as an ultimate opportunity to express one's values, whatever those values might be. Spock makes few presumptions of his readers, other than their desire to raise happy and healthy children. His advice is not religious or moralistic; it is, rather, the most anodyne, all-sides-of-the-aisle advice imaginable—careful and clear, without ever infringing on individual choice. And yet, a few decades after the book came out, Spock was yanked into the culture wars, labeled a communist, and blamed for destroying several generations of Americans. But unlike Lord Chesterfield and the many other advice-givers who prompted a national debate on ethics and American values, it was not Spock's advice that so upset his readers. It was him.

BENJAMIN MCLANE SPOCK Jr. was born on May 2, 1903, in New Haven, Connecticut. His father, who worked as a lawyer for a railroad company, was always traveling. "He was grave but just," Spock later wrote. Spock couldn't remember his father ever hugging or kissing him. He was raised largely by his mother, Mildred, who was controlling and often cruel, with homeopathic inclinations that ran counter to common sense and her children's safety. She was such a zealot for open air that she had her six children sleep on a night porch, even in the heart of winter, and founded an "open-air school," housed in a tent in a Yale professor's backyard, that only the Spocks and a few other neighborhood children had the courage to attend. The students had their lessons while sitting under a tarp, even when it was freezing out. Mildred had little patience when her kids complained about the cold. "Oh, you piddling creatures," she'd say. She kept her kids on a strange vegetarian diet in which they were encouraged to eat eggs but forbidden to try bananas until they turned twelve. Mildred spanked her children when they lied and when they did anything she considered disrespectful or lazy. She did not work outside the house and swore off all hobbies so she could focus on her children—she refused to play bridge until her youngest was in college.

The only parenting guides that Mildred kept on her shelf were by Dr. Luther Emmett Holt. Holt, who published several books in the 1890s, instructed mothers to be stern and disciplined with their children. "Instinct and maternal love are too often assumed to be a sufficient guide for a mother," he said. He discouraged mothers from being too sentimental. Children should not have their egos stroked and mothers should not celebrate their children's every act or thought. Instead, Holt encouraged mothers to raise children who were deferential and dedicated, so they'd mature into hardworking and humble adults. He didn't think children should be allowed to remain children for long. He advised mothers to promptly wean their children and potty-train them as soon as they could walk. "Children should be kissed, if at all, upon the cheek or the forehead. But the less of this the better."

Mildred was a diligent follower of Holt's advice. Benny, as his mother called him, was the eldest of six children, and at a young age, he was responsible for changing his siblings' diapers, preparing their bottles, and rocking them to sleep. "Everything centered around the baby and everybody loved the baby," Spock's younger sister, Hiddy, told Spock's biographer Thomas Maier. "Ben got this. It conditioned him from the time of childhood to be fascinated with babies."

Spock was an anxious child, fearful of lions, Italians, and trick-or-treating. When he was sixteen, Benny was shoved off to Philip's Academy, a boarding school in Andover, Massachusetts. Mildred forbade him to attend school dances, concerned that they were too prurient for his impressionable mind. (He didn't have his first kiss until he was seventeen.) When he was accepted at Yale, he asked his mother if he could sign up for a dorm room, but it was out of the question. "Benny, it seems clear that you lost your idealism at Andover," Mildred wrote him in a letter. "When you come back to New Haven to go to Yale next fall, you should live at home to try to recover your ideals."

He met Jane Cheney at a party the summer after his sophomore year. He was drawn to her hushed, whimsical voice and asked her to marry him the first night they met. She laughed. The two of them kept in touch, even after Jane enrolled at Bryn Mawr, a women's college in Pennsylvania, and traveled across Europe with her mother, who had planned the trip with the hopes of finding Jane a rich husband. Spock proposed again three years after they met, and they married in the summer after his first year at Yale medical school. He had decided by then to become a pediatrician; he found anatomy boring but children thrilling. Mildred, to his surprise, did not protest when he told her that he was transferring to Columbia, in New York—two glorious hours away from home.

A year or so later, Jane gave birth prematurely to a three-pound baby, who died two days after he was born. The Spocks never spoke of it again, and Benjamin drowned himself in work. He did an internship in the emergency room at New York Nursery and Child's Hospital. It was 1931, and his patients' lives had all been wrecked by the Depression: they told Spock about their rat-infested apartments, their inability to afford food, and he was struck by how preventable their emergencies were, how all his patients really needed was a safe home and some basic medical information. "Demoralized parents would, for example, bring in their babies suffering from chronic diarrhea from spoiled milk. The parents had no way to refrigerate milk except by putting the bottles out on the windowsill in the winter," he later wrote.

Spock was surprised by how impatient the doctors at the hospital were with children. They would demand, for instance, that their terrified young patients stop sucking their thumbs at once. Spock didn't see why thumb-sucking was such a cause for alarm; kids seemed comforted by it. But Spock was an intern and couldn't object to the *real* doctors' theories. "I went along with the belief that thumb-sucking was bad and that you should interfere as soon as you saw it raising its vicious head," Spock would later tell Maier. "I didn't know enough to take a fierce stance against it."

Spock opened his own pediatric practice after his residency, but he found it difficult to make a living. Most families at the time, needing to save money, only brought their children to the doctor in an emergency, and many young couples weren't having children at all. On top of his practice, Spock accepted a job as a school physician at Brearley, an all-girls private school on New York's Upper East Side, and enrolled at the New York Psychoanalytic Institute. He was interested in psychology, having spent time in the psychiatric ward during his residency, and hoped to eventually marry his psychoanalytic training with his expertise in pediatrics—a professional combination that was still rare at the time. "I conceived the idea that someone going into pediatrics should have psychological training. I already knew in a vague way that parents would be asking about toilet training and thumb sucking and resistance to weaning, about fears, about sibling rivalry. . . . Questions like these had been coming up in the pediatric practice for a long time, but pediatricians just used traditional answers like the one for thumb-sucking: It's a bad habit," he later wrote. Spock had an old-fashioned manner, wearing homburg hats and tailored overcoats, and when he and Jane had a son, Michael, in 1933, they raised him in the old-fashioned way. They followed Holt's methods, just as Spock's mother had with him. Michael was placed on a rigid feeding schedule; his parents ignored his cries at night. Affection was doled out cautiously. When Michael's teacher realized he was dyslexic, his father reacted with tough love. "Don't be a booby," Spock would say if Michael complained about school.

As part of his psychoanalytic training, Spock underwent analysis with Sandor Rado, a disciple of Freud. Rado had no experience treating children, but he'd written an essay, "The Anxious Mother" about the sinister instincts behind overzealous parents. "The more devoted she was in watching over and disciplining him, the more fully—but also, the less noticeably—could she gratify thereby her secret pleasure in aggression," Rado wrote.

Spock's sessions with Rado made him realize that there were other, healthier ways to parent children. The premise of Freud's theories is that all neuroses begin in childhood, that adults spend their lifetimes recovering from their relationships with their parents. Surely, Spock thought, his professors at the Psychoanalytic Institute had theories about ways to raise children to minimize future psychological damage. Rado had theories about what not to do—obsess, hover—but had no instructions about what parents *should* do instead. And none of Spock's professors had anything to say about the more pragmatic aspects of parenting. "When I asked my psychoanalytic mentors and my fellow students at the New York Psychoanalytic Institute how they would suggest parents go about toilet training, they'd shrug their shoulders," Spock wrote. "With their adult patients they were working with impressions left over in the unconscious minds from early childhood, but they had no experience at turning this into positive, practical advice for parents."

Ten years after Spock opened a private practice, an editor at Pocket Books, a paperback publisher, approached Spock about writing a book that combined pediatric information with psychological advice. The editor had asked around for a pediatrician with a background in psychology, and Spock was the only name mentioned.

Spock was reluctant, but the editor assured him that no one expected the book to be any good. "We are only going to charge a quarter and can sell ten thousand copies a year easily," Spock recalled him saying.

Spock was interested in writing a parenting book that made readers feel empowered and excited, and that gave mothers the freedom to leave the house. Mothers were not his chief concern, but Spock reasoned that the best way to raise confident, emotionally stable children was to put them in the care of confident, emotionally stable parents. The takeaway of *The Common Sense Book of Baby and Child Care* is that new parents ought to enjoy themselves and embrace their love for their children. Don't worry, Spock wrote, about regulating a child's sleep and eating schedules. "The main purpose of any schedule is to do right by the baby. But another purpose is to enable the parents to care for him in a way that will conserve their strength and spirit." He cautioned against overthinking. Have fun, he advised, as if he were a middle-school gym teacher, as if he wanted every participant to feel like a winner. The book was a family affair. Jane, Spock's wife, researched and fact-checked it.

The book came out in 1946, shortly after Spock's forty-second birthday, and sold more than half a million copies in its first year. He received thousands of adoring fan letters; his favorites tended to go something like this: "It sounds as if you're talking to me as if you think I'm a sensible person." Spock became a celebrity; he was courted by presidents, name-checked on *I Love Lucy* and *The Dick Van Dyke Show*. The success terrified him at first. "I was scared that the book would be misunderstood," he said, "that somebody, thinking she was following my advice, would do something that would make a child worse, or even kill a child."

In 1945, while he was writing the book, the Spocks had their second son, John. With John, Spock was more relaxed about feedings and schedules; he shunned physical discipline. He encouraged his children to call him "Ben," so they'd feel like equal participants in their household. Still, John was terrified of his father.

"He was a scary person, really scary," John told Maier. "Never anything physical. But always instead with judgment and criticism, with a constant kind of monitoring of behavior." Spock instructed parents to relax and trust their instincts, but he was too self-conscious, too socially conservative, to follow his own advice. "One of the things that pushed me to be strict was my anxiety that my sons should not do anything to give themselves and their family a bad reputation," Spock later wrote. "I do care about what the neighbors think."

<hr />

THE FIRST EDITION of Spock's book used the pronoun *she* to describe the parent and *he* to describe the child; it presumed that child-rearing responsibilities fell primarily to the woman and that parents were more concerned with raising successful sons than successful daughters. "I myself think it's a good sign when a mother confesses that boys are more mysterious to her than girls, in some respects: it means she's very much a woman herself and has respect for the male sex as somewhat different," Spock wrote in 1963. He encouraged fathers to praise their daughters' dresses, hairdos, and baking projects. He advised single mothers raising sons to invent a heroic story about their child's missing father. Spock generally advised against lying to children but felt that this was an exception—every boy needed a male role model.

It's not at all surprising that Spock held these views on gender—they were standard for the time. What's surprising is his insistence on sharing them, how porously he defined his "expertise." After the success of his book, he presumed that Americans craved his advice on *everything*, from international affairs, to ethics, to feminism. In 1970, when he was sixty-seven, he published *Decent and Indecent,* in which he gamely tries to draw the line between right and wrong. (One tepid review praised Spock's "vigorous self-confidence.") "My prime concern is that back at the childhood stage, parents and schools not encourage girls to be competitive with males if that is going to make them dissatisfied with raising children, their most creative job in adulthood," he writes in that book. That year, he also wrote an editorial in *Redbook* in which he expressed his reservations about mothers who worked outside the home. "The more radical feminists today insist that mothers have exactly as much right as fathers do to work full time outside the home." These women, Spock continued, seemed to have forgotten that "babies and young children have needs and rights too." In response to these and other statements, Gloria Steinem described Spock as a "major oppressor of women."

Spock's interest in politics emerged later in life. As a young man, he was a Republican because his father was a Republican and he voted in an absentminded way for Calvin Coolidge. By 1960, he supported John F. Kennedy because he agreed with the candidate's interventionist position on foreign affairs. Spock appeared in a television ad with Jacqueline Kennedy. ("We figured a lot of mothers would vote for Jack if they saw him with Spock," one aide told the *New York Times*.) A few months into his presidency, Kennedy invited the Spocks to a dinner party at the White House as a show of thanks.

In 1964, Spock campaigned for Lyndon Johnson. By then, Spock had changed his mind about the Vietnam War and supported Johnson because he opposed sending American troops abroad. When Johnson reversed course and escalated America's involvement in Vietnam, Spock withdrew his support and joined SANE, the National Committee for a Sane Nuclear Policy. He wrote letters to President Johnson explaining his opposition and attended antiwar rallies in DC.

Spock was then a professor at Case Western Reserve University in Cleveland, where he and Jane had a small social circle. Some years earlier, Jane had a mental breakdown and was institutionalized. After her release, she began drinking and often had three or more cocktails by the time Ben came home from work. Activism presented a welcome relief from all that. Spock became involved in the antiwar movement, speaking at demonstrations and going on television; he was the movement's elder statesman and his participation instilled events with a formality that some found off-putting and patriarchal and others found expansive and helpful. Among the left, he was both adored and disdained, depending on whom one asked. He traveled across the county and rallied with crowds of young adults he'd indirectly helped raise. He marched alongside Martin Luther King in Chicago and New York.

In 1968, he was charged with counseling, aiding, and abetting draft resisters. He wore his trademark three-piece blue suit, the same old Dr. Spock, patrician, polite, and reasonable. (He struggled to maintain his gentlemanly wardrobe on the protest circuit: "I would try to take the worst wrinkles out of my suit by pressing a hot wet washcloth against the elbow and knee wrinkles," he later wrote.) He was a "courtly, old-fashioned figure," according to the *New Yorker* writer who covered the case, and spoke with "an earnest simplicity throughout." He was convicted and sentenced to two years in prison, but the decision was overturned the following year by an appeals court. In the course of his life, Spock was arrested at least ten times for civil disobedience. He noted that it only cost twenty-five dollars to post bail.

Spock insisted that all of his political interests were tied, somehow, to pediatrics. His experience in public hospitals had prompted his belief in universal health care and better public education. When a reporter asked why a pediatrician would have a position on the Vietnam War, Spock replied, "What is the use of physicians like myself trying to help parents to bring up children, healthy and happy, to have them killed in such numbers for a cause that is ignoble?"

In 1971, he was chosen to be the presidential candidate for the People's Party, which wasn't so much a political party as a loose affiliation of leftist groups. His decision to run for president created a rift between him and his friends in the Democratic elite. "Ninety-nine percent of my friends tell me to stop behaving like a fool," Spock told *The New Yorker.* "But why should I worry about them?

They not only don't want to change the world, they don't even want to make money—that's how retired they are." Spock was bored by other people his age. He preferred the shaggy, bell-bottomed hippies he met at rallies to the prissy liberals who had bolstered his career. "I want to be around lively people. I like a restaurant that's boisterous with laughing and talking and arguing," he later wrote.

Spock's new life also alienated his wife, Jane. She felt old and unwelcome among her husband's new friends and missed their bourgeois life, their dinners at the White House, and trips to Europe. She'd slaved over the book, just as much as Spock had, but the social benefits were her only compensation.

The Spocks divorced in 1975, after forty-eight years of marriage. Spock, who was in his early seventies, took up with Mary Morgan, a university administrator in her thirties, and embraced every cliché of a man refusing to accept his twilight years. He bought a sailboat, wore purple shirts, and bragged to his editor about sunbathing in the nude and meditating twice a day. He even wore jeans for the first time. When friends and reporters asked Spock and Morgan about their age difference, she'd reply that "they were both sixteen."

SPOCK'S POLITICAL ACTIVISM changed the way people engaged with his parenting advice. The first person to imply that there were political undertones to Spock's *Common Sense Book* was Norman Vincent Peale. Peale was a conservative pundit of scattered accomplishments who had wiggled his way into politics like the wedding guest neither the bride nor groom can remember inviting. He was often invited on talk shows during John F. Kennedy's presidential campaign and argued that being Catholic rendered Kennedy unfit for office—his loyalty would go to the Vatican over the American people, according to Peale's logic. Peale was a Methodist preacher and the author of *The Power of Positive Thinking*, a pop psychology book that reiterated many of Dale Carnegie's theories, and he had published a pocket book of prayers, with prayers for every emotional, professional, and social occasion. There was a "prayer when facing a decision," a "prayer when making a sales call," a "prayer when worried," and a "prayer for traveling by plane," among many others. Peale argued that Spock was at fault for the aimlessness of America's youth, their obsession with drugs, their narcissism, and their lack of civic pride. He said that Spock had encouraged Americans to raise entitled and needy children. The country, Peale said in a widely publicized 1968 sermon, was "paying the price of two generations that followed the Dr. Spock baby plan of instant gratification of needs."

Peale was friend and adviser to President Nixon, and members of the administration soon joined his anti-Spock brigade. Nixon's vice president, Spiro Agnew, coined the term "Spockmanship" to describe the damage the pediatrician had inflicted on America's young. "Spockmanship" was to blame for the long-bearded twenty-year-old on an endless road trip, or the unmannered Vassar student with unshaven armpits. Spock, Agnew said, had encouraged mothers to be too permissive with their children, and as a result, those children had grown up to be draft dodgers and useless hippies—destructive, irresponsible, and hedonistic. "The thing to be carefully avoided, says our foremost authority on children, is 'bossiness,'" Agnew said. "Who do you suppose is to blame when, 10 years later, that child comes from college and sits down at the table with dirty bare feet and a disorderly face full of hair?" Agnew made an ambitious effort to rename the hippies the "Spock-marked" generation.

Nowhere in his book does Spock encourage parents to let their children run wild. He is not opposed to spanking and urges parents to be firm. "I think that good parents who naturally lean towards strictness should stick to their guns and raise their children that way," he writes. "Parents who incline to an easygoing kind of management . . . can also raise children who are considerate and cooperative, as long as the parents are not afraid to be firm about those matters that do seem important to them." Spock warns against "bossiness" only in the sense that parental authority should be automatic and there shouldn't be much showmanship to it. He encourages parents to exercise basic caution, to immunize their children, dress them in life preservers when they are near water, and store cleaning supplies in hard-to-reach places. He agreed with Sador Rado and cautioned parents against being overprotective. But he believed in rules. There were many enforced in the Spock household: for instance, his children were put to bed at six thirty at night and told not to come downstairs until after seven in the morning. "When I was writing the first edition, between 1943 and 1946, the attitude of a majority of people towards infant feeding, toilet training, and general child management was still fairly strict and inflexible," Spock wrote in the introduction to the second edition of the book, which was published in 1958. "Since then, a great change in attitude has occurred, and nowadays there seems to be more chance of a conscientious parent's getting into trouble with permissiveness than with strictness." He set out to write a nonideological guide to parenting that enabled parents to do whatever they thought best. "I never set out to impose any such grand design on the parents of the world. In fact, it grew increasingly clear to me as I continued to practice that there were *so many experts* with the best of intentions telling parents what to do—that parents' most widespread problem was their own uncertainty, a guilty feeling of 'Maybe I don't know enough,'" Spock wrote in his memoir. He had no overarching theory of discipline, no political agenda. At least not when it came to babies.

IN 1976, SPOCK published a new edition of the book, its fourth, to modernize its position on gender roles. "It is indicative of my sexism that it took me three years of discussions with many patient women before I fully understood the nature of my sexism and felt ready to begin, in 1973, the revision of *Baby and Child Care* that was published in 1976," he later wrote. In the updated edition, he cautions parents against praising little girls solely for their appearance and little boys solely for their accomplishments. He had changed his views on working mothers. "Both parents have an equal right to a career if they want one, and an equal obligation to share in the care of their children," he wrote. For the first time, the instructional drawings included images of black parents as well as white ones.

His politics had little effect on the substance of his parenting advice. Feminism didn't change his thoughts on weaning or feeding schedules. He advocated breastfeeding in 1945, and advocated it again in 1976 and in 1998. Spock changed his advice as medical research advanced: his first edition advised that an infant sleep on her stomach, while the later editions instructed that she be placed on her back. But the basics didn't change: children needed the love of their parents, and parents were instinctually primed to provide it. He never abandoned medicine for punditry. Into his eighties, he wrote a column for *Parenting* magazine and continued to update his book. The 1998 edition includes advice for gay and lesbian parents.

Between 1946 and 1998, the book sold more than forty million copies, its sales second only to the Bible. It's no longer on the bestseller list but remains beloved for its clarity and evenhandedness. A friend of mine who recently had a child received three well-worn copies from relatives. "There's no judgment to it (unlike a lot of other books that seem to have strong opinions about breast feeding, etc) and simply gives the information new (and experienced) parents need," one online reviewer wrote. The word *unbiased* is among the most frequently used words on his book's Amazon page. His advice was popular because it didn't sound like advice.

His critics accused him of hypocrisy, of instructing parents to raise kids they couldn't control. Spock was a hypocrite, though for different reasons. He was the godfather of a certain genre of advice that beckons readers to trust themselves and avoid self-doubt. He told readers that their infants were heartier than they appeared, that it was normal to feel ambivalent about a pregnancy or a newborn, or to lose one's patience with a wailing toddler. He bears responsibility for the deluge of parenting advice literature on "what's okay" and "what's normal" on subjects so basic they wouldn't seem to require an expert's guidance. Parents now read books to be told that *it's normal* for there to be tension with an overzealous grandparent, that *it's okay* to allow your child to cry herself to sleep, or sleep in your bed, or watch television, or play alone. This is the contradiction of Benjamin Spock: he insisted his readers didn't need an expert's guidance but went on to bill himself as the consummate expert, on matters ranging from child discipline to the Vietnam War, and helped create a culture in which new parents crave an expert's guidance on *everything*.

Sylvia Porter offered financial advice with a level of precision one could never expect of a friend. Spock, meanwhile, gave the kind of advice frequently offered by a friend or relative—"You're doing great! Don't worry!"—but set a standard in which such assurances only count when they come from an MD. Porter shared her opinions on fiscal policy and consumer rights but never ventured into, say, international affairs, health, or education; outside the column, she took great pains to emphasize how little she really knew, that she was less an expert than a curious housewife. Spock had an expansive claim to authority. He felt that doctors had a duty to protect the public health of the country, which included preventing teenage boys from being sent to war and ensuring that black children had access to safe schools. In his 1996 book *A Better World for Our Children*, published two years before he died, at the age of ninety-four, Spock bemoaned the unraveling of traditional American values and discussed the finer points of workplace etiquette. (He frowned upon people who wore jeans to work.) In *Common Sense*, Spock said to *listen to yourself*; but, in person, political rallies, and his other books, he turned into the kind of expert who invites eye-rolls, who says, *listen to me*.

ELEVEN

Death's Best Friend

Elisabeth Kübler-Ross

So much about death is unknowable: Cancer or car accident? What happens next? But when Elizabeth Kübler-Ross was thirty-seven years old, she decided that she was going to learn everything there was to know about it. There was no precedent for this course of study. At the time, she was a professor and doctor at the hospital affiliated with University of Chicago, and she began conducting interviews with terminally ill patients. The interviews were open-ended, lasting as long or as short as the patient wanted. The patients talked about their pain, their loneliness, their frustrations with their medical care. They talked about the irksome parts of illness, like urinating into a catheter, and their fear of endless blackness.

"You still want to be a person," said a young nun with late-stage Hodgkin's disease. "All the kind people who pushed the wheelchair just drove me to distraction because they pushed me to where they wanted me to go, not where I wanted to go." Another patient, a middle-aged woman with leukemia, sensed that her doctors were withholding information from her. "They have not told me what they found during the operation," she said. "Why in the world can't

they talk to me? Why can't they tell you before they do certain pro-
cedures? Why don't they let you go to the bathroom before they take
you out of the room, like a thing, not like a person?"

Kübler-Ross collected these interviews in her book *On Death
and Dying: What the Dying Have to Teach Doctors, Nurses, Clergy and
Their Own Families*, which was published in 1969. The book bears
the rigorous obsession of a scientist on the brink of discovery. She
is long-winded and detailed, as interested in the forest as she is
the trees. After thousands of hours of interviews, she reached the
conclusion that the process of dying could be loosely broken into
five stages—denial, anger, bargaining, depression, and acceptance.
Kübler-Ross later said that she never conceived of the stages as linear
or all-encompassing, that the main lesson from the two and a half
years she spent interviewing terminally ill patients was that they
desired to be treated as individuals with complicated and layered
feelings rather than as patients with a fixed set of medical needs.
"It's not a map," said David Kessler, who was a frequent collaborator of Kübler-Ross. "No two people are going to go through the
stages exactly alike." Over the years, as the stages have disseminated
across popular culture, readers have interpreted Kübler-Ross's stages
as complete and successive, a conclusion that reflects less what was
written than a desire among caregivers and doctors for a concrete
process to guide them beyond the brink of uncertainty. The book,
as stated in its subtitle, wasn't intended as medical textbook but as
a project that would inspire more empathy for the dying. "It is simply an account of a new and challenging opportunity to refocus on
the patient as a human being, to learn from him the strengths and
weaknesses of our hospital management," she wrote.

Her relationship with these patients continued long after she
published the book and well past their deaths. The people she interviewed reappeared months and years after their funerals, visiting her at work and at home. She'd see them in the elevator after
lectures, apparitions that spoke to her with the clarity of a pilot
warning about oncoming turbulence. They even left little notes on

her desk. She became interested in life after death, and though she never claimed to have studied the afterlife as she had dying, she claimed to understand it all the same. In the later years of her career, she wrote about the afterlife with the confidence of an anthropologist who had returned from fieldwork. "As soon as your soul leaves the body, you will immediately realize that you can perceive everything happening at the place of the dying," she wrote in *On Life After Death*, published in 1991. "You do not register these events with your earthly consciousness, but rather with a new awareness." Friends and colleagues worried about her, that bearing witness to so much despair had frayed her mind and loosened her grip on reality.

Kübler-Ross heard these rumors. "Many people say: 'Of course Doctor Ross has seen too many dying patients. Now she starts getting a bit funny,'" she wrote. She insisted that that she was fine, better than fine. She was known among friends as the most upbeat, energetic person in the world. Though she was a doctor by training, "at home in laboratories," as she'd written in her journal, she was liberated by the possibilities of nonscientific inquiry. To understand the afterlife, she relied on simulations with psychedelic drugs, consultations with mediums, and loose thought experiments. There was more than one way to be an expert, Kübler-Ross seemed to argue: you could study, or you could simply know.

KÜBLER-ROSS'S MEMOIR, *The Wheel of Life*, reads like a fairy tale. Its villains are cruel and ogre-like, weakened by arrogance; hardships always end in victory; fates are written at birth. "I was destined to work with dying patients," she writes. She comes across, from the beginning, as an inspiring but unreliable narrator.

She was born in Zurich, the first of triplets, and weighed two pounds. The doctor, who considered herself a clairvoyant, looked down at the three babies and predicted that the youngest child, who was six pounds and healthy, would be her mother's favorite; the middle child, who was also born precariously underweight, would "choose a path in the middle." When she looked down at Elisabeth, she said, "You will never have to worry about this one."

And so begins Kübler-Ross's journey, one of a restless, curious woman seeking truth despite the well-meaning men who stand in her way. At six, a teacher asked her to write an essay about what she intended to be when she grew up. When she told her parents about the assignment at dinner that night, her father, a middle manager at an office-supply company, told her that she should plan for a career as his secretary. "No, thank you!" young Elisabeth snapped. That night, she wrote in her journal that she planned to become a physician and an adventurer. "I want to find out the purpose of life."

When she graduated from high school, she moved out of the house and found a job as an apprentice in a chemical lab. A few years later, in 1945, she joined the International Voluntary Service for Peace, a European organization that served as the model for the Peace Corps, and traveled to France, Poland, and Germany rebuilding war-torn villages, handing out food, restoring schoolhouses, and providing basic medical care. It was then she realized that healing had more to do with compassion than it did medicine. "The best thing we gave those people was love and hope," she wrote.

When she returned to Zurich, she borrowed money from her sister and enrolled in a local medical school, where she met Emanuel Ross, an American who had fought in the war and was paying for school through the GI Bill. They married in 1958 and moved to Long Island, where they both found internships at a hospital.

In Long Island, she developed a taste for chewing gum, hamburgers, and sugary cereals. She began to wear pants more often than skirts. But she was appalled by certain social aspects of American culture. At the hospital, she found the doctors indifferent, the children rude, and their mothers complete pushovers. "One day in the children's ward I watched a spoiled brat throw a colossal fit when his mother forgot to bring a toy," she wrote. "What were these American mothers and their children thinking? Didn't they have any values? What good was all that stuff when what a sick child really needed was a parent to hold his hand and talk openly and honestly about life?" In 1959, she was offered an internship in the psychiatric unit at Manhattan State Hospital, where she tended to forty schizophrenic women. They were guinea pigs, she wrote in her memoir, enrolled in an experiment to test the efficacy of new medications and LSD. Her job was to administer these experiments and complete the research logs, but instead, she taught the women independent living skills. They learned to comb their hair, dress themselves, and arrive to appointments on time. She took them on field trips and helped them find jobs and their own apartments. Her program was so successful that she was interviewed for a job running the pharmacological unit at Montefiore, a private hospital. During her interview, the director of Montefiore, whom she describes as having the "personality of a cold fish," tried to show off, asking about her experience treating addicts and neurotics, but only so he could expound on his own expertise. She was not impressed. "Knowledge helps, but knowledge alone is not going to help anybody," she recalled telling him. "If you do not use your head and your heart and your soul, you are not going to help a single human being."

He hired her despite this outburst. But after a few years, she and Manny decided it was time to leave New York. They moved to Colorado for bit, and in 1965, they moved to Chicago along with their two children, Kenneth and Barbara. Manny took a position at Northwestern University in the neuropathology department while she completed a PhD in psychology and joined the psychiatric department at the University of Chicago, where she met her fate. Fate introduced itself, as it often does in fairy tales, with an unexpected knock on the door.

She was in her office at the University of Chicago when four seminary students paid her a visit. They were researching death and dying: they wanted to know how to best serve congregants who had ill loved ones or were ill themselves. They asked if she'd be willing to serve as a liaison between the seminary and the hospital, to coordinate interviews with terminally ill patients. They'd heard that she'd written a paper on the psychology of dying. She hadn't, but she took their mistake as a sign.

Every Monday, she arranged a seminar where a dying patient spoke about his or her experiences to a room of rapt seminary students. The patient spoke before a one-way mirror, with the students observing from the other side. She'd ask the dying patient about how they were feeling and their relationships with their doctors. "Patients weren't shy about expressing their dissatisfaction with their medical care—not the actual physical care, but the lack of compassion, empathy, and understanding," she wrote.

Medical students were invited to attend the seminars, but for a long time, none did. "The physicians have been the most reluctant in joining us in this work," Kübler-Ross noted in *On Death and Dying*. "It may take both courage and humility to sit in a seminar which is attended not only by the nurses, students, and social workers with whom they usually work, but in which they are also exposed to the possibility of hearing a frank opinion about the role they play in the reality or fantasy of their patients." American doctors were so preoccupied with avoiding death that they avoided any discussion of it. "I observed the desperate need of the hospital staff to deny the existence of terminally ill patients on their ward." This was typical for the medical profession at the time. In the early 1970s, years after Kübler-Ross began her research, only about 10 percent of doctors told their patients when they had a terminal condition; until 1980, the American Medical Association considered it a doctor's right not to tell their patients if they had an incurable disease. At Kübler-Ross's hospital, most doctors would inform the patient's family of a fatal diagnosis and allow them to decide what to share with the patient.

According to Peter Stearns, a professor and emotional historian, Americans were demonstrative mourners during the decades after the Civil War, when the bereaved were presumed to be inconsolable. But by the mid-twentieth century, Americans had begun to encourage stoicism in the wake of a loss, with writers describing the painlessness of death and instructing mourners that the only way to survive grief was to ignore it. In the 1930s, the *American Mercury*, a popular magazine, carried the foreboding headline "America Conquers Death" and boasted that "death, which dominates European's thoughts, has been put in its proper place in America." A 1950s etiquette writer named Amy Vanderbilt instructed mourners to keep their feelings to themselves. "We are developing a more positive social attitude towards others, who might find it difficult to function well in the company of an outwardly mourning person," she wrote. Dorothy Dix, Ann Landers, and Dear Abby were a bit more empathic, offering their condolences and acknowledging the necessity of tears, but they also advised mourners to seek out distractions. When a father wrote to Dix about losing his seven-year-old son in a car accident, she recommended that he adopt a young child in need. A widow once wrote to Dear Abby comparing her loneliness "to a cancer, but worse" and Abby sugggested that she seek out volunteer work. "There are lonely people to visit, blind folks to read and write for," she wrote. They nudged their readers out of the house; they saw no purpose in wallowing.

Many of Kübler-Ross's peers at the hospital considered her seminars exploitative and ghoulish and believed it cruel to force sick patients to ruminate on their own deaths. Kübler-Ross, in turn, felt that doctors were failing their patients and behaving irrationally. "I think modern medicine has become like a prophet offering a life free of pain. It is nonsense," she wrote. "Medicine has its limits, a fact not taught in medical school."

"When we look back in time and study old cultures and people, we are impressed that death has always been distasteful to man and will probably always be," Kübler-Ross wrote in *On Death and Dying*. "Man has basically not changed. Death is still a fearful, frightening happening and the fear of death is a universal fear even when we think we have mastered it on many levels." She empathized with doctors who had deep thanatological dread but was disheartened that they were unable to override their fears for the sake of their patients.

⌒‿⌒

WHEN I WAS six, my family took a train to DC for a weekend. My father is an American history buff, and he wanted me to see everything: Arlington National Cemetery, the Washington Monument, the memorials, and government buildings. We saw the red velvet seat at Ford's Theatre where Abraham Lincoln was sitting when he was assassinated and watched soldiers, sturdy as nutcrackers, salute the Tomb of the Unknown Soldier. We were climbing the tall marble steps of the Thomas Jefferson Memorial when it dawned on me: Abraham Lincoln, the anonymous soldier, Thomas Jefferson had all been alive once and now they weren't. They had died, just as I would and my parents would. Because everyone died.

I started to shake, my vision went blurry. Mortality was too much for my six-year-old brain and body to process. I vomited on the steps of Thomas Jefferson Memorial and threw up again on the National Mall. I asked my mom, "Why do buildings get to live while people have to die?" She didn't have an answer. At the hotel, a woman at the front desk offered to send up chicken soup. "Did she catch a bug?" she asked. My parents nodded.

We took the train home the next day. But every night, for weeks, I dreamed that I had entered eternal oblivion, that I would never return to waking life. How could you tell, I asked my mom, if you were sleeping or if you were dead? Again, she didn't have an answer. I don't recall if I told my friends at school about what I'd learned in DC. Some months earlier, my friend Sophie had broken the news that there was no such thing as Santa Claus and two of our friends had cried.

If I did say anything, it never reached the point where class moms were calling to complain about the little nihilist depressing their children, but after weeks of nightmares, my parents decided that something had to be done. They could have made an appointment with our rabbi or sent me to see a psychologist or a doctor. But, instead, they invited Kathy over.

Kathy was a friend of my mom's. She was in her late forties and worked as an art dealer, with a specialty in contemporary paintings. She had studied psychology in college, but her primary credential was that she had that ineffable quality that makes you want to tell her things. She had faded blond hair and cavernous dimples, and she wore a turquoise pendant around her neck.

She started coming over once a week or so. She'd sit with me on the floor of my bedroom and we'd talk about death, and what scared me about it. She didn't have any revelations to share. She told me that it was sad when someone died, especially when it was someone you loved. She told me that death scared her, too. She also said that it'd be tragic if I spent my life so distracted by death that I missed the many joys that came before it.

The nightmares went away and Kathy stopped coming over. Some years later, I asked my parents—why Kathy? Why did they trust her to explain death to their youngest daughter? My mom shrugged. What did anyone else know about death that Kathy didn't? She was as much an expert as anyone.

⁓

DOCTORS LOVED KÜBLER-ROSS'S five stages. The stages gave doctors the capacity to diagnose their dying patients, to target their questions and categorize the evidence: if the patient wasn't depressed, then maybe she was in denial. The stages provided guidance on what to say in impossible circumstances. She had, unwittingly, provided doctors with a system for discussing death like a medical process. Her collaborator, Kessler, told me that on more than one occasion, a medical colleague would stop by while he and Kübler-Ross were writing to seek help with a diagnosis. "They'd be like, 'Elisabeth, what stage are they in?' And she would say, 'It's not about the stages! It's about meeting them where they are!'" She found it laughable how some doctors had the gall to hold an essential organ in their hand but had no capacity for ambiguity.

Friends say Kübler-Ross had a certain genius for meeting people where they were. Here's one story her son, Ken Ross, told me: She was interviewing a patient whose mouth was wired shut, whose speech was limited to grunts. None of the other doctors or nurses could understand her, only Kübler-Ross. When the interview was complete, she instructed a wide-eyed physician to bring up an apple from the cafeteria. He pointed out that the patient wouldn't be able to eat it and Kübler-Ross ignored him. She had left the patient's hospital room by the time he returned, apple in hand. The patient broke to tears. The doctor brought her paper and pen so she could explain. She wrote that she'd spent her life as teacher and had told Kübler-Ross that she missed receiving apples from her students.

Kübler-Ross loved doing the interviews, but they exhausted her. She had to cut herself off after four hours. She was not an impartial observer of the dying. She was convinced that people close to death accessed a frequency of consciousness and a capacity for kindness that no one else could. "What you learn from dying patients, you can pass on to your children and to your neighbors," she wrote. She believed that there was no such thing as a premature death, that people died as soon as they'd learned everything they needed to know, and that her dying patients were closer to enlightenment than anyone else she knew. "For me, death is a graduation," she liked to say.

Kübler-Ross believed that every dying patient passed through all five stages but could repeat a phase or experience two or more at the same time. Even denial and acceptance, two directly opposing ideas, could occur simultaneously. "Even the most accepting, the most realistic patients left the possibility open for some cure," she wrote in *On Death and Dying*. There were other feelings, like guilt and regret, that weren't stages, exactly, but companions throughout the process. She wrote of patients who felt guilty for burdening their family members or leaving children behind, and who regretted the years wasted away at work or in front of the television, as if there were no such thing as time.

Kübler-Ross later applied the same five stages to the process of grieving. And, as with dying, she never meant to imply that grief was contained to just five feelings, or that the stages were linear, like levels in a Nintendo game. "They were never meant to tuck messy emotions into neat packages. They are responses to loss that many people have, but there is not a typical response to loss, as there is no typical loss. Our grief is as individual as our lives," she wrote in *On Grief and Grieving*, which she cowrote with Kessler in 2005.

Since 1969, when *On Death and Dying* was published, researchers have pounced on Kübler-Ross's stages for being inaccurate or incomplete and have critiqued her theories for being the product of "highly subjective data gathering," criticisms that Kübler-Ross would likely agree with.

—————

IN 1972, AT the age of forty-two, Kübler-Ross lost her patience altogether with clinical settings. She was frustrated by the way her research had been misinterpreted by her medical colleagues and decided to devote herself full-time to her traveling seminar, "Life, Death, and Transition." It was a weeklong series that included an eclectic mix of exercises "geared towards helping people overcome the tears and anger in their lives." The workshops, which she held everywhere from California to Indiana, involved silent prayers and ritual fires where participants discarded their unwanted feelings and participated in exercises designed to release anger by punching a mattress or snapping a short rubber hose. There were assigned periods for wailing and screaming—she'd found that "active expulsion" of one's feelings was more effective than talking. "Sometimes it pays not to think with your head as much as with your instinct," she wrote. Larry Lincoln, now the director of Tucson Medical Center's hospice program, attended his first workshop in 1983 and went on to lead her workshops all around the country. He said that a third of participants were dying or experiencing "acute grief," another third were medical or caregiving professionals, and the final third were there to seek "psycho-spiritual growth." He fell into the final two categories. He had everything he'd ever wanted: a wonderful marriage, two children, a successful private practice as an infectious disease specialist. But he was burned out and miserable, working fourteen hours a day or more, and incapable of stopping, until he went to the workshop and learned to process the feelings he'd been hiding from himself. "She created a safe space for people to release feelings. It seems simple, but it was really a great talent she had," he told me.

She was on the road more often than she was at home. Her son Ken told me that she'd come home on weekends, cook meals and dessert for the entire week, and leave again. He was a teenager at the time, and he'd sometimes tag along to a weekend conference so he could see his mom. Her name was on the cover of *People* and *Playboy*, and she became the kind of celebrity who was sometimes stopped by strangers on the street. One time, while in Virginia, Kübler-Ross met a fan who invited her over. She reluctantly accepted and followed the woman into her house and then into her living room, where the woman gestured at a photograph on the coffee table. "At first glance, the picture was merely a pretty flower, but then I looked closer and saw that the flower was being used as a perch by a creature with a small body, face, and wings." She turned to the woman and asked, "It's a fairy, isn't it?"

"At this time in my life, I was open to anything and everything," Kübler-Ross writes in her memoir. She was open to a magical element, to living among fairies and ghosts. She wanted to learn everything about the most wholly unknowable thing in the world—the afterlife. (Her husband tried to thwart her explorations, and they divorced in the late 1970s. He's one of the well-intended male villains in her memoir.) There'd been theories posited for centuries, passed down from gods, about reincarnation and heaven, but there was no way to prove or disprove them. Many of the patients she'd interviewed had had near-death experiences, and she asked them to describe what they remembered from the seconds or minutes they spent without breathing. For most, the memories were vivid. They described exiting their bodies and looming above the room with complete panoramic vision, noticing how the doctors nervously tugged at their gloves. They convened briefly with God and met the Virgin Mary, who told them that it wasn't their time yet. Kübler-Ross conducted séances, collaborated with mediums, and moved to the mountains of Escondido, California, where she established a retreat center for the ill and grieving. There, she lived among ghosts. There were Willie, Aenka, Salem, Pedro, and Mario. Her medical colleagues were disheartened by her turn away from science, especially after a medium she trusted named Jay Barham was accused of disguising himself as an "afterlife entity" and forcing himself on grieving widows at her retreats. (He was never charged because of a lack of evidence.) "For years, I have been stalked by a bad reputation," she wrote in her memoir. Larry Lincoln was refused admitting privileges at several East Coast hospitals when administrators learned of his association with Kübler-Ross. "She was emboldened by that kind of controversy," he said. "She never spent time trying to convince the medical community that her work was valid. She was too busy."

She became certain that death was nothing to fear, that it befell each individual at the right time, that it was painless and joyful. "It is no longer a matter of belief, but rather a matter of knowing," she wrote in *On Life After Death*. "After seeing the light, you will experience for the first time what man could have been. . . . In this presence, which many compare with Christ or God, with love or light, you will come to know that all your life on earth was nothing but a school that you had to go through in order to pass certain tests and learn certain lessons." In some ways, her ideas about the afterlife resembled those in the New Testament, though in her version, there was no punishment or suffering, only joy. "She found it frustrating and ridiculously hypocritical, all these doctors who went to church because they believe in God but called her a quack," said Ken, her son. There was, however, a finality to death in the New Testament, whereas she was uncomfortable with the phrase "near-death experience" because it presumed that death existed at all. She liked to say that "there was no such thing as death," though she never elaborated on what happened instead. In a roundabout way, she'd developed a mindset similar to that of the doctors she used to mock back in Chicago, who'd been unable to contend with ambiguity. She subscribed to a rosier sort of denial, refusing to acknowledge the possibility that death was anything other than glorious. This is why tens of thousands of people flocked to her seminars and why many more read her books: she transformed the most brutal thing about living—its unavoidable ending—into something mystical, pleasant even. Though she had no definitive take on what actually happened in death, she had an unusual level of certainty about how one should *feel* about death. To her, there was no heaven or hell, just an easy gladness to be home.

IN 1972, KÜBLER-ROSS testified before the Senate's Special Committee on Aging in a hearing called "Death with Dignity." It had been seven years since President Lyndon Johnson created Medicare, a government program that subsidizes the health-care costs for the elderly, and in that time, government spending on nursing home care had more than doubled. "Medicare puts entirely too much emphasis upon institutionalization of patients, thereby increasing costs of treatment and anxiety among patients," explained Senator Frank Church, a Democrat from Idaho and a member of the aging committee, in his opening statement. They were seeking humane and affordable alternatives to hospitalization.

"We live in a very particular death-denying society," Kübler-Ross told the senators. "We isolate both the dying and the old, and it serves a purpose. They are reminders of our own mortality." She made two recommendations. The first was to train medical students to care for the dying, to make the needs of the elderly and terminally ill as fundamental to medical education as cell biology or anatomy. As it stood, care for the dying fell to nurses, who were underpaid, overworked, and underprepared. (Kübler-Ross also advocated that these nurses have their hours reduced; the work, she said, was too exhausting to sustain eight to ten hours a day.) The second was to develop outpatient programs for the terminally ill, so that patients could spend their last days at home among loved ones. There was already a hospital in London that provided such services, which she pointed to as a potential model.

Two years after the hearing, a nursing professor at Yale, along with two doctors and a chaplain, founded America's first hospice program in Branford, Connecticut. It had no physical facility; all of its doctors and nurses were dispatched to care for their terminally ill patients at home, as Kübler-Ross recommended. Hospice programs have proliferated in the decades since; there are now more than four thousand across the United States. They offer services exclusively for the dying, for patients who are beyond treatment and are seeking a painless transition from life. Kübler-Ross was heartened by expansion of hospice and palliative care, a specialization that focuses on pain relief and that did not exist when she began her research. But her point was never really about the expansion of *services;* it was about doctors expanding their capacity for empathy, so they'd learn to treat patients with compassion and not checklists.

In the 1990s, Kübler-Ross experienced a series of strokes. She couldn't walk or feed herself; she spent her last years sitting on the porch of her son's Arizona ranch, staring out at the endless sky. She had visitors from all over the world. One woman flew in from Japan just for the day so she could have tea with Kübler-Ross before she died. When she was admitted into the hospital, a group of Native

Americans in traditional garb showed up on Ken's lawn, built a tee-pee, and smoked a pipe. There was a constant parade of journalists, who all wanted to know the same thing: How was the world's expert on death responding to the loss of her own life? The answer: not well. She was crotchety, tired, and largely immobile, in a world of endless pain. She was "angrier than angry," she told CNN. The journalist described Kübler-Ross's response to dying as "very human." Her reaction, the journalist wrote, was "not fully what I expected from the woman who created the model for coping well with death and dying."

"People love my stages," Kübler-Ross told Kessler shortly after the article came out and not long before she died, at the age of seventy-eight. "They just didn't want me to be in one of them."

TWELVE

Guide to the Stars

Joan Quigley

MERV GRIFFIN, THE HOST OF *THE MERV GRIFFIN SHOW*, had a toothy smile and a healthy pad of gray hair. He was the contrarian uncle of 1970s talk shows. Unlike Johnny Carson, who opted for sunny celebrities, Griffin preferred less-obvious guests: authors like Norman Mailer, racy comedians like Richard Pryor and George Carlin. He wanted *The Merv Griffin Show* to be a place where guests talked about sex, race, and the Vietnam War, and he did not care if this made his producers panic.

In May 1972, Griffin invited Joan Quigley onto the show. Quigley must have seemed more conservative than a typical Griffin guest. She dressed like a card-carrying member of the Daughters of the American Revolution on her way to a luncheon. She was in her fifties, with thinly plucked eyebrows, her blonde hair secured in a bob.

He introduced Quigley as a California astrologer whom he had invited to make predictions about the future. Before the show, Quigley would recall, one of his producers had supplied her with Griffin's birthdate and place. Griffin had been born in San Mateo, California, on July 6, 1925. With that, Quigley could divine what lay ahead. She told Griffin that his marriage was about to implode. He laughed and shook his head. Impossible.

Two weeks later, Griffin's wife served him with divorce papers. Griffin, in turn, lost his tolerance for surprises and became a great fan of Quigley and astrology. He invited Quigley on the show several more times to predict political and world events. Off the air, she sent him letters that detailed when the electrical devices in his house were likely to malfunction and the days when he'd feel fuzzy or ill.

That summer, Nancy Reagan, then the first lady of California, who was also born on July 6, asked Griffin for Quigley's number. "He asked my permission to have her call me," Quigley recalls in her memoir. She was ecstatic, honored at very thought. She adored the Reagans.

Nancy called a few weeks later. She supplied Quigley with her exact birth time—an important data point for an astrologer. She explained that her husband was making a run for president and she was looking for any insight, any competitive edge the universe made possible. Quigley drew up Nancy's chart and told her that she "hadn't seen so superlative a stellium since Jackie's." Nancy didn't know what a stellium was—it's astrological jargon for a grouping of planets—but she was delighted to hear this. She and her husband needed all the help they could get.

⌒‿⌒

JOAN QUIGLEY WAS a Republican long before she became Nancy Reagan's astrologer. She was raised in a genteel San Francisco family, the closest California comes to old money. Her father owned a hotel and sent Joan and her sister, Ruth, to one of San Francisco's toniest private schools, the kind that breeds students for colleges on the East Coast. Joan went to Vassar and, upon graduation, apprenticed herself to an astrologer she'd met as a teenager through her mother. The astrologer went by her married name, Mrs. Jerome J. Pearson. When Joan was fifteen, she'd sat in on one of her mother's consultations with Mrs. Pearson and had been amazed by the certainty with which Pearson could see the future and by the clean, almost mathematical quality of her methods. There was no communing with far-off spirits, no chanting, no tinctures, no grotesque velvet table covers. There was a consistent logic to astrology, based on verifiable externalities—planets do, indeed, orbit around the sun. It was a bit like meteorology, except instead of predicting weather patterns, astrologers could predict anything.

Those predictions weren't always accurate, but accuracy has never been astrology's primary draw. Americans have long relied on astrology for a combination of advice and entertainment. Like Benjamin Franklin's *Poor Richard's Almanack,* it's the inherent absurdity of monthly horoscopes that make them so readable. Horoscopes are an invitation for wishful thinking. We read that the seventeenth bodes well for a promotion, that the weekend of the twenty-fifth might present an opportunity for travel, and it's an excuse to search for cheap flights or fantasize about your next job.

Magazine horoscopes are perceived as child's play by the more rigorous practitioners of astrology. "A person must be very credulous indeed to believe that the same thing is happening to one twelfth of the world's population during a given day or month," Quigley wrote. She turned down numerous offers to write a monthly column. That was beneath her. She became an astrologer in the early 1950s, before hippies and LSD and the proliferation of self-help; she was not a member of an esoteric community but rather did a job and served her clients. She shared a two-bedroom apartment in a doorman-attended building with her sister, Ruth, who worked as a financial analyst. "Joan's predictions came out correctly more often than mine did," Ruth said. "Though I had a high enough average to keep my clients happy." Joan was a member at the opera house and subscribed to the *Wall Street Journal.* In her memoir, she emphasizes that her work required the use of a computer, as if that proved something about its merits. Ruth emphasized that her sister used the same astronomical maps as NASA.

Quigley perceived herself as a scholar of American astrology, like J. G. Dalton, who published textbooks in the late 1800s that described the movements of the planets and their moons. The decades after the Civil War were a profitable time for spiritualists. More than six hundred thousand soldiers died in the war—2 percent of the country's population—and their widows and mothers hired mediums to help them communicate with their departed loved ones. There were dozens of different kinds of practitioners to choose from: rhythmical dancers, spirit photographers, graphologists, numerologists, and clairvoyants known as "table-tippers," who rapped the responses they received from beyond.

Many of these mediums were eventually accused of running scams, charging exorbitant fees for predictions that never materialized. In the early twentieth century, fortune-telling was illegalized in many major cities and mediums were forced underground. In New York, city detectives would go undercover to catch fortune-tellers in the act. They'd visit the offices of popular fortune-tellers, buy a forecast for five dollars, and then arrest the medium on the spot. In 1914, the New York police conducted a sting operation on an expensive New York astrologer named Evangeline Adams and accused her of fortune-telling, astrology, and palmistry. She'd been charged once before, in 1911.

Adams's trial was held on December 11, 1914. Her lawyer argued that astrologers weren't psychics or charlatans; they did not claim to see the future. They drew astrological charts for their clients based on their birth dates and advised them on which days were best suited for traveling or throwing a party. It was up to client to decide if they trusted the logic of the stars. "There is no claim here that the defendant was garbed in special garments or that there was any air of mysticism about the place; it was a simple apartment with library furniture," noted the judge. "She claims no faculty of foretelling by supernatural or magical means that which is the future, or of discovering what was hidden or obscure; but she does claim that nature is to be interpreted by the influences that surround it." Adams was acquitted: she was not a fortune-teller but an expert in her own odd but rigorous school of thinking. In interviews, Adams told reporters that she believed her case would mark the moment when astrology was treated, rightfully, as a science and not a superstition.

That prediction proved false. (As did many of Adams's predictions. She also foresaw that the "Dow Jones might climb to heaven" a few weeks before the 1929 crash.) But astrology became, in the view of the wider public, a harmless hobby, perfectly harmonious with Christian ideals. President Theodore Roosevelt is said to have kept his astrological chart pasted to the bottom of his chessboard, which he kept in his bedroom for easy reference. Presidents Calvin Coolidge, Franklin Roosevelt, and Richard Nixon were all fond of reading their horoscopes. And Joan Quigley, a wealthy Vassar girl from an established San Francisco family, saw nothing wrong with devoting her life to it.

The Reagans were from California, home to the American New Age. There were astrologers in their friend circle and they attended cocktail parties where it was a standard conversational practice to ask someone their "sign." In Ronald Reagan's 1965 memoir, *Where's the Rest of Me?*, he describes checking his horoscope every morning and refers to Carroll Righter, a popular Hollywood astrologer, as a dear friend.

As governor and a presidential candidate, Reagan wanted to appear like a genuine statesman, not like an actor who had lucked into a part. His flimsier hobbies and questionable friends from Hollywood were expunged from his profile. That included anything related to astrology. When he first won the governor seat, in 1968, the media questioned why he had scheduled to take the oath of office at exactly 12:10 a.m. on January 2, since inaugurations are typically daytime affairs. Several California newspapers, after consulting with astrologers, reported that Reagan appeared to be postponing the oath until the planets reached an ideal alignment. Reagan was annoyed by the rumors, changed his plans, and had an aide release a statement: "We do not intend to have stargazers in this Administration," it said.

QUIGLEY WAS UNEASY about Reagan's chances when he first ran for the presidency, in 1976. "He had a kind of adverse configuration of Saturn to his horoscope that always causes political leaders to suffer a defeat. Fortunately, that Saturn only comes once in 28 years," she wrote some years later. Still, she sent a calendar to his office that marked the dates when Reagan's chart was poorly configured for public speeches.

Reagan lost the nomination to Gerald Ford, and Quigley lost touch with Nancy Reagan for a few years. In 1980, after Reagan secured the Republican presidential nomination, Quigley reached out to Nancy to see if she might be interested in her services. Nancy asked her to draw up a calendar for the remainder of the campaign that indicated all of her husband's lucky and unlucky days. Quigley did so. One of the unluckiest days in that period was August 19. Quigley was so concerned that she underlined it in red pen.

On Saturday, August 16, George H. Bush, Reagan's running mate, flew off to Asia to meet with various government leaders and Reagan marked his departure by holding a press conference in which he discussed his plans to reestablish relations with Taiwan. By Tuesday, August 19, China's Communist Party had released a statement criticizing what they called Reagan's "two-China policy." "Everybody knows that relations between the U.S. and China were built on the U.S. recognition of only one China," it read. All the papers carried the story, and they made Reagan, already considered weak on foreign policy, seem dangerously naïve. At some point, Nancy must have combed through a stack of files and saw Quigley's forecast, with August 19 underlined in red. From then on, according to Quigley, Nancy consulted her before every campaign event.

Quigley recommended that Reagan debate President Carter on October 28, in Cleveland, at precisely 9:30 p.m. Reagan's chart was aligned for a victory, but more importantly, Carter's chart was aligned for failure. "Carter's Mercury (the planet of speech) in Virgo and his Pisces Uranus (planet of the sudden and unexpected) were opposite one another. Any configuration between Virgo and Pisces can make someone untidy or unable to see the big picture," Quigley wrote. She often went on the offensive, drawing the charts of world leaders and suggested scheduling diplomatic negotiations on days when Reagan's opponents were weakest. (She was careful never to reveal his or Nancy's time of birth, fearful that their enemies might employ astrologers of their own.)

One of the cornerstones of Carter's campaign was nuclear disarmament. But when he introduced the subject during the October 28 debate, he acted as if the matter had only recently crossed his mind. "I had a discussion with my daughter Amy the other day, before I came here, to ask her what the most important question was. She said she thought nuclear weaponry." His response had likely been plotted to make him appear relatable, but his delivery made him seem less familiar than incompetent, as if he consulted his eleven-year-old daughter on national security policy. Later in the debate, President Carter accused Reagan of opposing Medicaid, and Governor Reagan fired back with what's become one of his most famous comebacks. "There you go again," he said, his delivery mellow and commanding.

A week later, Reagan won the election in a landslide. Nancy called Quigley the morning after the election to tell her stories from the celebration the night before, about driving late at night through Los Angeles and people running out the sidewalks to cheer them on as they passed. "Congratulate Ronnie for me," Quigley said before hanging up. Quigley always referred to the president as "Ronnie," just as his wife did, like they were all old friends.

After the election, Quigley returned to her normal life— attending the opera with her sister and advising her regular clients. She didn't hear from Nancy for a few months. She was surprised to have never received "so much as a perfunctory thank you note." Despite her ingratitude, Quigley came to miss Nancy, the adrenaline of the campaign, and all the little lies she told friends to excuse herself whenever Nancy called. Quigley was bred to be close to power, and being an astrologer to an incoming president must have felt like she was fulfilling her fate. Her father had never entirely approved of her decision to become an astrologer. But Ruth says that changed when her sister started working for the Reagans. Their father loved the Reagans.

Nancy called in early April. A few weeks earlier, Reagan had been shot in the chest as he was exiting the Washington Hilton hotel, where he had given an address to a collection of trade unions. He had been rushed to the hospital and survived. "Could you have told about the assassination attempt?" Nancy asked Quigley. Yes, Quigley assured her, she could have. Quigley was delighted to resume her position in Nancy's inner circle but worried about sacrifices the work would require. She knew her involvement would need to be kept secret, as it was during the campaign; Nancy feared that if the press found out about her consultations with an astrologer it would tarnish the graceful image she had carefully calibrated. "I knew that if I decided to take the Reagans on, I would be giving up my time and effort like all those who take part in any administration, sacrificing the rewards they commanded in the private sector in order to serve their country. I was aware, however, that unlike them I would not have the prestige they had while serving." But she worried about Reagan's safety; his chart suggested that he was entering a risky period, and she felt it was her duty as an American to protect her president from harm. Ruth recalls that Joan charged the Reagans three thousand dollars a month, though she spent hours on their charts each week. "She could not afford to pay me even a fraction of what I was worth," Quigley wrote. "It was very self-sacrificing for her, but she was very patriotic," said Ruth. "She felt she could help Ronald Reagan achieve world peace."

"VIRTUALLY EVERY MAJOR move and decision the Reagans made during my time as White House Chief of Staff was cleared in advance with this woman in San Francisco who drew up horoscopes to make certain that the planets were in a favorable alignment for the enterprise," writes Don Regan, Reagan's chief of staff, in his memoir, *For the Record*. Regan kept a color-coded calendar on his desk, with "good" days highlighted in green and "bad" days highlighted in red. Reagan's schedulers had no choice but to work around the days this mystery woman had blacked out. Mrs. Reagan forbade the president from traveling on "red" days, of which there were many. Here's the calendar Quigley provided for the first few months of 1986:

> Jan 16–23 very bad
> Jan 20 nothing outside the WH—possible attempt
> Feb 20–26 be careful
> March 7–14 bad period
> March 10–14 no outside activity
> March 16 very bad
> March 21 no
> March 27 no
> March 12–19 no trips exposure
> March 19–25 no public exposure
> April 1 careful
> April 11 careful
> April 17 careful
> April 21–28 stay home

Regan came to feel that Quigley held disproportionate power over global politics, far more than many cabinet members vetted by Congress. "The president's schedule is the single most potent tool in the White House, because it determines what the most powerful man in the world is going to do and when he is going to do it," Regan wrote. The first lady spoke to Quigley on Saturday afternoons and grew furious when the White House staff made last-minute adjustments to the schedule without leaving time for Quigley's approval. "I wish you'd make up your mind," she once barked at Regan. "It's costing me a lot of money, calling up my Friend with all these changes."

"Friend." That was one of the White House's code words for the first lady's astrologer. The other code name was "Joan Frisco," which both Joan and Ruth thought too obvious, but it was Nancy's invention and it felt inappropriate to question her. Regan writes that he never learned Quigley's real name. No one at the White House spoke to Quigley, aside from Nancy. West Wing staffers were often left waiting for the latest astrological forecast to arrive. Mike Deaver, the deputy chief of staff and chief scheduler, learned to delicately punt a commitment until Quigley's forecast arrived. When a communications officer suggested, say, a trip to Michigan to mark the opening of a new factory, Deaver would say, "Let me play around with this," or "Let me see what can be done."

It's unclear if President Reagan was aware of Quigley or if he simply allowed his wife to monitor his schedule how she pleased. He was, however, promiscuously superstitious. He named his dog Lucky, always kept a talisman or three in his pocket, and felt there was a distinct possibility that ghosts inhabited the Lincoln bedroom. (He also casually acknowledged the possibility of extraterrestrial life. "I occasionally think how quickly our differences worldwide would vanish if we were facing an alien threat from outside this world," he said in a 1985 speech to the United Nations.)

Nancy and Quigley's calls could last a few minutes or a few hours, depending on the astrological and political prognosis. They could go weeks without speaking or talk several times a day. The schedule was unpredictable, but Quigley was always on call. She was discreet: No one in her San Francisco social circle, aside from her sister and parents, knew that Nancy Reagan was a client. She spilled nothing to her assistant, Nikki, who was told that the charts were for a client who did a lot of work abroad. She cut back on her television appearances, even though that was not an explicit part of her agreement with Nancy. Talk shows were risky: she could slip and say something that embarrassed Nancy or the president or, even worse, disclose a matter of national security.

Quigley worked from her living room as she determined what time the president should deliver his State of the Union address or what day he should invite a foreign leader to the White House. Quigley says that it was she who decided that President Reagan's flight to Geneva to meet with Mikhail Gorbachev should depart on November 16, 1985, at 8:35 in the morning.

She did more, in her own estimation, than sorting months into lucky and unlucky days. She read the chart of every foreign dignitary and offered Nancy her insights. "I suggested to Nancy that the way to begin the Geneva talks was by being friendly, that Ronnie's consummate charm could be used constructively to convince an open-minded, modern, highly intelligent Gorbachev to accept ideas heretofore unacceptable ideologically but now of practical value in the Soviet Union," Quigley wrote in her memoir. "Whenever I hear the 'tear down that wall' speech, I get such a thrill because Joan really set that in motion," Ruth said. In September 1986, Nancy called Quigley in a panic: Gorbachev had proposed a secret meeting in Reykjavik, and she wasn't sure if President Reagan should attend. "Ronnie and I are the only two people in the country who know this. You will be the third person." Quigley's mother had died the previous day, but she dried her tears and consulted her charts. She was, after all, a patriot. Quigley says she told the first lady that the president had to go to Reykjavik, but that the meeting should be made public. And that's precisely what happened.

In her memoir, Quigley credits herself with constructing Nancy's image. "I want everyone to love me," Nancy once told Quigley, but instead she was mocked in the press for being snobbish and cold. Quigley says she advised her to refrain from doing interviews in fashion magazines. Although she was an astrologer by profession,

Quigley had studied politics and art history at Vassar, and on the phone with Nancy, she often shared her thoughts on foreign policy and the Constitution, her theories on how, say, the Boland Amendment pertained to the Iran-Contra scandal. It's unclear what the first lady made of her astrologer's political analysis, if she appreciated Quigley's contributions or struggled not to laugh—if the first lady's belief in astrology, and in Quigley, was boundless or restricted to sorting "good" days from "bad" ones.

The first lady was, by all accounts, a charismatic and slippery person, so focused on her husband that she could instinctively devour someone if it meant protecting or bolstering him. "She was very protective of the President," Quigley wrote. "She was almost psychic in her awareness of his best interests and the motives of those surrounding him." She must have sensed that Quigley's motives were pure, that all Quigley cared about was protecting the president from harm. "I had the knowledge, the experience, the resourcefulness, and the willingness to take the infinite pains that were needed to guide Ronald Reagan safely from May 1981 until June 1 of his last year in office, when his own chart indicated that his life would no longer be in danger," Quigley wrote.

Millions of Americans read their horoscopes each month. "You can leave an awful lot of things out of a newspaper, but if you leave your astrology column out, you're in trouble," said Lou Schwartz, the president of the *Los Angeles Times* syndicate, in 1988. Newspapers frame these monthly horoscopes as entertainment, and their devoted readers assure their skeptical friends that they skim them with breakfast "for fun," too ashamed to admit to their instinct for magical thinking. People consult horoscopes for the same reason they consult advice columns—because everyone craves reassurance and because they address our ambitions and fantasies, the subjects that quietly consume us but that our daily lives often require us to ignore. They are a small indulgence, the kind Mildred Newman would have endorsed.

But unlike advice-givers, there's never been an astrologer who's ascended to household name. The practice has too witchy an association. If Nancy Reagan had been open about her relationship with Quigley, if she had admitted that she trusted an astrologer more than she did her husband's advisers and that Quigley's forecasts afforded her a greater sense of safety than an FBI report, the practice might have lost its taint and Quigley might have become America's first celebrity astrologer, remembered less for the accuracy of her predictions than for the way she made people feel.

QUIGLEY WAITED AND waited for a formal invitation to the White House. She was not invited to the party celebrating Reagan's election in 1980 or his reelection in 1984—even though she considered herself largely responsible for both victories. She was not invited to either inaugural ball. Although she and Nancy spoke on the phone constantly, they'd only met once in person, and quickly, at an election event in San Francisco in 1976.

In March 1983, Nancy Reagan hosted a state dinner for Queen Elizabeth II in San Francisco. She told Quigley to expect an invitation by mail. It never arrived. "There must have been some mistake," Nancy said a few days after the dinner. "I know I put your name on the list."

In April 1985, Quigley booked a trip to DC. She didn't tell any friends or family she'd be in town. Her trip had only one purpose: to take up Nancy on her open-ended invitation to tea in the White House residence. There was a state dinner scheduled then to honor the president of Algeria, and Nancy had promised a proper invitation this time. She didn't want Quigley, who was nearly sixty, to attend the function alone, so she arranged for a marine guard to escort her. "Everyone I know here is married," Nancy said over the phone.

Quigley was careful not to wear any of the cocktail dresses she'd worn on *The Merv Griffin Show*. She went with an inconspicuous pale blue gown. She was desperate to wear a new red dress, but she knew that red was Nancy's color and didn't want to upset her. Quigley hobnobbed with the editor of *Newsweek*, the actress Cheryl Ladd—who had recently starred in *Purple Hearts*, a Vietnam-based romantic drama—and various journalists and political types. Quigley introduced herself as a writer from California and evaded further questions. She stepped out of the way anytime she saw the flash of a camera—for Nancy's sake, she wanted no photographic evidence of her presence. "Nancy quite obviously did not want to make a point of my being there," she later wrote. She was seated at the same table as Vice President George H. W. Bush, whom she complimented for his debating skills. She ate seafood mousse and drank champagne and danced with her young marine escort. She had only a brief moment with the president in the receiving line. "Hello, Joan," he said, as if they'd met before. They shook hands and she said to him, "Mr. President, I feel that you have been chosen to bring peace."

The next day she finally had her long-awaited tea at the White House. "Tea with Nancy was much more interesting than the state dinner," Quigley wrote. Quigley reminded Nancy that she had eaten lunch at the White House before, as a child; she'd gone to grade school with Franklin Roosevelt's granddaughter, Ellie, who had invited Joan and her parents for a tour while they were sightseeing in DC. Nancy's White House was more spectacular than Quigley remembered; the first lady had renovated, mining the White House basement for decorations and discovering ivory and emerald sculptures from China, which she displayed prominently around the residence. There were hand-painted gold flecks on the walls of the bedroom and the sitting room was painted a thick, brooding burgundy.

They gossiped about the state dinner; Quigley complimented the flower arrangements and the food, which Nancy had taste-tested in advance. They laughed at George Schultz, the secretary of labor, who had forced the actress Cheryl Ladd to dance with him—"he loves to dance with all the pretty young glamour girls," Nancy said. They debated Bush's chances at the presidency; Quigley believed he was fated to win and Nancy believed he was too weak to lead. They talked about Nancy's marriage, her horoscope, about Ronnie's place in history. Quigley told her about the museums and galleries she'd visited in DC—it was important to her that Nancy see her as educated and cultured, not as some grungy outsider with a sixth sense. Nancy was curious about what was happening in DC, as she never got out herself: being first lady, she said, felt like serving a prison sentence sometimes. Nancy didn't ask her many questions. After the tour, Nancy hugged Quigley and kissed her cheek, and Quigley thought to herself, "This woman could chew someone up and swallow and spit up the bones and never feel a thing."

QUIGLEY EXPECTED A thank-you. Nancy had promised as much—that one day, after they were out of office, Nancy would tell the world just how much Quigley had done for the Reagans and the country. "She told Joan that after they were out of office she would say how great her contributions had been," Ruth said.

Shortly after Donald Regan published his memoir, in which he complained at length about the unchecked powers of an unnamed astrologer, someone within the administration leaked Quigley's name to the press. Nancy was frantic to discredit the story. Quigley was on vacation in Paris when it broke. It was Ruth who picked up Nancy's call.

"This must never come out!" Nancy said.

"Not while you're in office," Ruth replied. "But what about after you are out of office?" She, too, hoped that her sister would receive her proper due.

"Never," said Nancy.

Nancy reached Quigley, finally, at her Paris hotel, and they had a similar exchange. Nancy begged her not to talk to the media and Quigley refused. "I am determined to show who and what I am and represent reputable astrologers honorably. I will in no way injure you. But I will not refuse to be interviewed," Quigley recalled saying. The two women never spoke again. Quigley gave interviews to every major network, and each time, she described her work as being "very technical." "It's fabulous being able to work with Air Force One because you can say, you know, 'Do this at six minutes after six,' and they'll do it," she told Mike Wallace on *CBS Evening News*.

Although Nancy Reagan was humiliated by her affiliation with astrology, she was not the only first lady curious about mystical traditions. Eleanor Roosevelt consulted a palm reader, Jacqueline Kennedy experimented with rune stones, and Mamie Eisenhower had her tea leaves read. Florence Harding relied on a medium named Madame Marcia, who entered clairvoyant trances from which she could see the future. Mary Lincoln consulted medium after medium following the death of her son, Willie, whom she was desperate to see again. These women looked to these practices, in part, to lessen the power gap between them and their husbands. The occult and the pseudo-religious, across its many iterations—astrology, tarot, yoga, and so on—are among America's longest-running matriarchies. Their citizens and many of their leaders are women who have grown so tired of competing with men for social power that they opt to chase another kind of power instead: they concede the world to men while they focus on controlling the universe.

In 1989, Nancy Reagan published her own memoir, *My Turn*, in which she addressed Regan's allegations about her dependence on astrology. "Astrology was simply one of the ways I coped with the fear I felt after my husband almost died," she wrote. "My relationship with Joan began as a crutch, one of several ways I tried to alleviate my concern about Ronnie."

Quigley was so offended by Nancy Reagan's dismissive portrayal of her that in 1990 she wrote a memoir of her own, *What Does Joan*

Say? The title is, purportedly, what Reagan would ask Nancy before scheduling an important event. Joan had, in her own estimation, assisted with important trade negotiations, assured the success of crucial public addresses, and helped keep the president safe. ("Ronald Reagan is the first president elected in a zero year to survive his terms of office since William Henry Harrison died after a month in office on April 4, 1981," she wrote.) Quigley felt that she had earned more than her portrayal in *My Turn* and that astrology, as field, deserved better. "Astrology is so generally misunderstood, even among uninformed believers," she wrote. She was tired of being referred to as a "clairvoyant," of having her work maligned as some kind of sorcery. The Reagans' shame about astrology was, to her, a symptom of a much bigger problem. "My conclusions are based on this accurate scientific material in the same way your doctor supports his diagnosis by laboratory reports or an economist bases his predictions on statistics," she wrote. She wanted astrology to go mainstream. She suggested that astrologers take a qualifying exam.

Quigley, who died in 2014, said she foresaw Nancy's betrayal. "Struggle has been in my charts," she once told a reporter. She knew she could "expect no gratitude" from the Reagans, and yet, she said she did not foresee writing a memoir defending her place in history. Knowing in advance that the Reagans would hurt her made no difference in the end. It hurt all the same.

part four

Advice for All, by All

How did we learn it? That talent for insatiability.

—Margaret Atwood, *The Handmaid's Tale*

IN 1991, A MAN NAMED TIM KECK DECIDED TO LAUNCH a new magazine in Seattle, and his friend Dan Savage, then a manager at a video store, said this: "Make sure your paper has an advice column. Everybody claims to hate 'em, but everybody seems to read 'em." The first issue of Kreck's magazine, *The Stranger*, came out later that year and included Savage's advice column, "Savage Love."

Most people would agree: no one likes to be told what to do. And yet, as Savage pointed out, people *really* like advice columns. "Savage Love" has turned into a multimedia advice-giving franchise that includes a podcast and a column. Advice-giving is too diffuse to be treated as an industry, so there's no official body tracking new columns and podcasts as they launch, but about five years ago, I noticed that every website and magazine had started to offer advice—unlikely places like *n+1*, a cerebral Brooklyn journal;

Outside, a publication for adventure sports enthusiasts; and *The Nation*, the high-minded lefty rag, among others. They each published old-fashioned advice columns, with readers sending intimate, anonymous questions about life and love. Every week, it seems, there's a new podcast offering some kind of advice on love or work or "becoming an adult."

Advice-giving depends on an active, involved audience—the questions, after all, need to come from somewhere. David Grossvogel, a professor at Cornell who wrote a book about Ann Landers, found that fans of advice columns aren't there to receive advice but to practice giving it. "Everybody reads her column with one hand over the answers to see if they can come up with better advice," he said in an interview. "They all think they'd be terrific at it." Anyone can give advice, and many of us do so, daily. Technology has enabled people to share advice outside their families and social circles. Anyone with a laptop or a smartphone can make a YouTube video or start a blog, and anyone with a microphone and an internet connection can start a podcast. Why read an advice column or listen to a podcast when you can start your own?

Technology, social media in particular, has also allowed audiences to expect more intimacy and transparency from their favorite celebrities. Instead of watching their favorite actresses pose on the red carpet, they want to be taken behind the scenes, watch them select the dress and apply makeup, catch a glimpse of what they ate for breakfast that morning. It's natural, then, for a celebrity become an advice-giver, to explain how she selects a dress to flatter her body, how she applies makeup for a black-tie event, and her method for soft-boiling an egg. Many actresses, like Gwyneth Paltrow, Jessica Alba, Lena Dunham, and Blake Lively, have founded their own "lifestyle" brands, providing style, dieting, and career tips. Successful screenwriters placate fans by offering advice on writing; successful tech entrepreneurs offer advice on starting a company; socialites and other nebulously famous people offer advice on how to be more like them.

The internet has advice for everyone, for aspiring masseuses and aspiring firefighters, for women over sixty and for teenagers transitioning gender identities, for black professionals and for new immigrants from China. The advice tends to be provided by people who mirror their audiences, by famous masseuses and transgender teens. This is nothing new. In 1907, the *Jewish Daily Forward* created an advice column called "A Bintel Brief" (A Bundle of Letters) to answer questions from recent Eastern European immigrants struggling to adjust to American culture.

"Worthy editor," one "Bintel Brief" letter began, "I recently met a wonderful girl. She has a flaw however: a dimple in her chin. I'm told that people who have such a dimple quickly lose their spouses. I love her very much, but I'm afraid to marry her, lest I die because of that dimple."

The response: "The tragedy is not that the girl has a dimple, but that some people have a screw loose in their heads."

There are now hundreds of websites and blogs that, like "A Bintel Brief," offer advice for a tailored audience, for new mothers, or older mothers, or single mothers, or women struggling with infertility. Given this landscape, why would anyone still try to be a full-time, gets-it-all advice-giver?

And yet such people still exist. This section profiles five of them: Harville Hendrix, the so-called marriage whisperer, and his wife, Helen Hunt, who claim to know the secret to making every marriage work; Judith Martin, or Miss Manners, a self-designated expert on social rules; Martha Beck, a prominent life coach who says she can help anyone achieve their dreams; and Michael King, who answers questions on Quora, a popular social media site, on everything from relationships to stock tips to politics. They all write with an anachronistic omniscience, but they have made certain adjustments to update the generalized advice-giver to the internet era, when personal experience often supplants expertise. They tend, for instance, to disclose far more personal information than mid-century advice-givers and write candidly of their own turnarounds. They're also more professionalized than the advice columnists of yore. Unlike, say, Dorothy Dix, their advice is based on more than instinct and draws from copious research.

Ultimately, they provide the same services as mid-century advice columnists, striving to be helpful however they can. They are basically normal people—aside from their belief that everyone has something to learn from them.

THIRTEEN

Stand by Me

Harville Hendrix and Helen Hunt

I FIRST LEARNED ABOUT AMERICA'S MOST FAMOUS marriage evangelists, Harville Hendrix and his wife, Helen LaKelly Hunt, because a friend of mine told me about an instructional video she'd seen online that taught a reconciliation technique known as Imago dialogue. I had eleven weddings to go to that summer and was spending many evenings listening to friends talk about their premarital counseling plans, which ranged from rigorous to make-shift. Imago, I learned, is a formalized conversation that Hendrix and Hunt have devised to defuse conflict between couples. It in-volves repeating and verifying what the other person says. The lis-tener is supposed to keep asking, "Did I get that right?".

Imago dialogue might seem like a straightforward solution to conflict, but, I soon learned, Hendrix and Hunt conceive of it as part of a larger effort. They want to use Imago to prevent divorce—first in America and then, presumably, everywhere.

"We've each been divorced, and we think it's wrong," Hunt told me the first time we met, at a restaurant near their apartment on the Upper West Side. Hunt has a gentle smile, a high-frequency energy, and a Texan twang to her speech.

Hendrix joined in. "If you could end divorce," he said, "you can save American families and the American economy." Hendrix is eighty-two, with a full, gray beard.

Hunt and Hendrix speak proudly of their differences and believe it can be scientifically proven that opposites attract. Hendrix comes from poverty. His parents died before he turned six, and he was raised by his older sister on a small farm in southern Georgia. Hunt, sixty-nine, comes from money. She is a daughter of billionaire oil tycoon H. L. Hunt, one of the inspirations for the television series *Dallas*. Hendrix is studious, Hunt is expressive; he's the thinker, she's the doer; he's calm, while she always needs to be busy. Hendrix warned me that his wife would probably sit down with me for only twenty minutes at a time. Sure enough, exactly twenty minutes after she arrived, she excused herself. He stayed on for almost two hours.

Studying marriage with the person you're married to might be the surest way to never get a day off. Hunt and Hendrix have published eleven books since 1988, including their first, the best-seller *Getting the Love You Want*. Oprah Winfrey refers to Hendrix as the "marriage whisperer," and she had him on her show twelve times. Hendrix and Hunt never stop speaking in Imago dialogue. Hunt repeated my interview questions back to me: "You want to know why we think our work resonates with people. Did I get that right?" They told me they were trying to add more fun to their marriage and had started to watch Stephen Colbert and David Letterman. They talked about laughter the way other people talk about vitamins.

In 2008, Hendrix closed his private couples-therapy practice in Manhattan, and he and Hunt started two new projects. The first was the launch of a think tank, Relationships First, which aims to strengthen couples. (They were excited to have Alanis Morissette and her husband, the rapper Souleye, as board members.) The second was to launch their movement to promote coupledom and end divorce. They believe that the world would be a better place if there were more couples in it. In recent years, conservative lawmakers in more than a dozen states have introduced bills imposing various measures to make getting a divorce more difficult, such as longer waiting periods and mandated couples counseling. Hunt and Hendrix have taken a different approach. They're not trying to ban divorce but prevent it. They believe that if more couples learn Imago dialogue, they'll never want to break up.

The starting point of their movement is Dallas, a city they see as big enough to make a meaningful impact but small enough that they can track their progress. Dallas also has sentimental value: it's where Hendrix and Hunt met. Hendrix's hope is that the city's measures of well-being will climb as the movement catches on.

Most adherents of Imago therapy, the kinds of patients Hendrix saw in New York and wrote about in his books, are the sort who drive Audis and make last-minute plans to see Gilbert and Sullivan operettas. But Hendrix and Hunt want to bring Imago to people of all backgrounds. They believe there's no one they can't help: rich or poor, religious or nonreligious, young or old, gay or straight. "We've had a three-hundred-year focus on individuals, and that period and paradigm has run out of value," Hendrix told me. "There's an emergence into the collective happening right now, a critique of individualism, capitalism, and self-centered living." People, all people, want and need Imago.

A FEW MONTHS after meeting Hendrix and Hunt in Manhattan, I traveled down to Dallas, where they were hosting their fourth workshop, called Safe Conversations. The location was a windowless conference room in the Momentous Institute, a children's nonprofit in southwest Dallas.

Two hundred and twenty people were in the audience, about half of them Hispanic (there was live Spanish translation available) and the rest divided evenly between black and white. Most lived in the surrounding neighborhood, Oak Cliff, a largely working-class, Hispanic area. Volunteers in turquoise T-shirts roamed the room handing out snacks and passing the microphone to people, and twenty-two clinical volunteers in navy T-shirts patrolled the workshop for couples in distress.

Onstage, Hendrix was trying to get a young couple to engage in a dialogue sequence. The pair sat in armchairs facing each other, and Hendrix told the man, Michael, to pay his wife of three months, Tara, a compliment.

"What I appreciate most about you is that you're a good cook," Michael said.

"So what I'm hearing you saying is that you appreciate that I'm a good cook," Tara said. She seemed bored.

To prompt Michael, Hendrix began, "When I think about you as a good cook, I feel—"

"When I think about you as a good cook," Michael said, "I feel full, sleepy, and—sexy."

"Really?" asked Tara, a little annoyed. The woman sitting next to me groaned.

Hendrix jumped in: "When I think about you as a good cook, it reminds me of . . . Try to find something from your childhood."

"When I think about you as a good cook, I—" Michael stopped, then started over. "When the house smells good, it reminds me of home and when my mom cooked and I felt loved."

Tara repeated him, her eyes now glassy with affection. Unprompted, she spoke the next line in the sequence: "Is there anything more about that?" There wasn't. They hugged for sixty seconds as the rest of us watched. Hendrix told the crowd that the length of an average hug is three to nine seconds, but that a good hug, one that "pushes the boundaries of relationship," takes a whole minute.

Hendrix has a trove of mysteriously sourced facts like this. He is dauntless in that way that sometimes comes with old age. Most of his information, he says, comes from research conducted either by him or by fellow Imago counselors, of whom there are more than a thousand across the globe. He holds a PhD from the University of Chicago Divinity School and started to study relationships in the late 1970s, shortly after his own divorce. His ideas are inspired by physics as well as sources ranging from Freud to the New Testament. "There's a dyadic structure of nature," he explained. "Whenever a particle comes out of a void and into space, it comes with another particle."

For all the grand theories of love, the workshop emphasized actions. During a segment dedicated to "high-energy fun," Hendrix and Hunt jumped up and down synchronously, breathing heavily, until they burst into laughter. They say that regular belly laughs are key to a happy marriage, even if they're forced. Like Dale Carnegie, they believe that smiling can *make* you happy.

As the day went on, people around me were conducting exercises and being driven to tears, revelations, and reconciliations. I talked to Darrel and Kayla Young, who had been married for ten years. They had been to the previous Dallas workshops and hoped to attend more. They've become such adherents of Imago that they plan to launch a petition to require a premarital course and exam for anyone in Dallas who wants a marriage license. "You gotta take a test before you get your hunting license or your fishing license," Kayla said. "Marriage is harder than fishing."

Hendrix and Hunt cater mainly to people who are married, but all varieties of couples are encouraged to come to the workshops. One couple in Dallas was a pair of sisters who sprinted through every exercise and jumped up to give each other long hugs. Down the hall, where free day care was being offered, children of parents in the workshops were likewise learning Imago dialogue, and I stopped in to watch. "What I'm hearing you saying is my bike was in the driveway and you hurt your leg," one second grader told another kid. "Did I get that right?"

LIKE SO MANY institutions of American life, marriage gets drawn into the culture wars. Many politicians, especially conservatives, have promoted marriage as an antidote to social decline and welfare expansion or, as Senator Marco Rubio put it, as "the greatest tool to lift children and families from poverty." On the other side are those who argue that marriage is a benefit, not a generator, of wealth—an interpretation that is common among social scientists. "Having a good relationship is not about knowledge and it's not about skill. It's about having resources," said University of California, Los Angeles, psychologist Benjamin Karney, laying out the latter view. "You have to improve the community in which that marriage is and the lives of the people in the relationship."

What we can say for sure is this: the rate of marriage in the United States, while in slow decline, remains higher than that of Japan, Germany, or Sweden. For the past three decades, the rate of divorce has also been in decline. At the same time, poor Americans are getting married at much lower rates than wealthy Americans, and their rates of divorce are much higher. This is one reason that Hendrix and Hunt offered their Dallas workshops, which would normally run about five hundred dollars a head, for free, putting up their own money. They hope the lessons will help couples who could not normally afford them.

Hunt and Hendrix have spent most of their marriage and careers on the Upper West Side, and they contribute to the Democratic Congressional Campaign Committee. Hunt, who was inducted into the National Women's Hall of Fame for her philanthropic work, counts the feminist Gloria Steinem among her closest friends. When they enter the marriage debate, however, they hope to avoid partisanship. Economic statistics are not their main concern. Rather, they believe being in a couple is natural and being single is not. "As individuals, we each have emotional wounds that need healing," Hendrix and Hunt write in one of their workbooks, "and on some level, we know that it is only in the context of a committed relationship that this healing can occur."

One of their favorite examples is their own. Hendrix and Hunt first met in 1977. He was teaching psychology at Southern Methodist University, where she was completing a master's degree in counseling. They met at a party and discovered they shared an interest in Martin Buber and Dostoevsky. Each also had two children from a previous marriage. They fell in love, and they married five years later.

Their trouble started in the mid-1990s. It should have been a joyful time. *Getting the Love You Want* had become a runaway hit following an appearance by Hendrix, his first, on *Oprah*. Imago was just beginning to take off. But they were miserable. He would claim to be buried in work and lock the door to his office and watch *Star Trek* late into the night; she would draw up lists of all the things he was doing wrong, like wearing too many earth tones and cracking bad jokes at parties. They had become critical of one another, passive-aggressive, and finicky. They tore through marriage therapists; number five, they say, called them "the couple from hell." At a conference for Imago therapists in 1998, they confessed that they were heading toward divorce.

To save their marriage, they decided to devote one year to trying to fix it. The first policy was to eliminate all negativity from their interactions. Neither of them was allowed to say anything spiteful. Ever. They taped a calendar to the refrigerator and drew a smiley face when they made it through a day with no negativity and a frowny face when one of them slipped.

Once Hendrix and Hunt had eliminated all the negativity from their relationship, they didn't have much left to say. "We had a silent love," Hunt said, laughing. They filled the silence with compliments and all the belly laughs they could muster.

The Zero Negativity Challenge is now a tenet of their relationship philosophy and has been added to the twentieth-anniversary edition of *Getting the Love You Want*. At workshops, volunteers pass out blue silicone bracelets bearing the letters ZN (for Zero Negativity) and information on how to download a Safe Conversation app for their mobile devices. The app offers a digitized version of the calendar that once hung on Hendrix and Hunt's refrigerator, reminders to pay your partner a compliment, assistance with Imago dialogue, and a short-cut to the Couples Store, where you can buy their books.

Hunt and Hendrix held hands during one of our interviews. They kissed onstage during the Dallas workshop. They're very attentive to each other. "Do you need to take a minute?" Hendrix asked Hunt before the workshop. She did. She's careful to give him time alone to watch *Star Trek*. *Effortless* is not a word anyone would use to describe their manner. They show their love through well-practiced and calibrated interactions.

⌒‿⌒

SCHOLARS HAVE DEVOTED extensive study to individual therapy but surprisingly little to couples therapy. "A dirty little secret in the therapy field is that couples therapy may be the hardest form of therapy, and most therapists aren't good at it," wrote William Doherty, the director of the marriage and family therapy project at the University of Minnesota, in an article for the *Psychotherapy Networker*. Even the goal of most couples counseling remains unclear. Virginia Satir, a psychologist who practiced in the 1960s and '70s and is considered a pioneer of family therapy, has said that her goal with couples was "not to maintain the relationship nor to separate the pair but to help each other to take charge of himself."

Hunt and Hendrix think that traditional couples counseling is pointless, that it's essentially therapeutically sanctioned bickering. (They both make air quotes around the phrase "constructive criticism"—criticism, to their minds, is never constructive.) Unlike most conventional marriage therapy, Imago has a clear and simple definition of success: reconciliation. This appeals to many practitioners and clients alike. Sessions are civil and feel productive. Imago therapists say that for couples who truly want to stay together, Hendrix's methods are among the most effective out there.

But is keeping a couple together always a sound goal? Hunt and Hendrix believe so. According to their findings, we are all instinctually attracted to people who can help us heal from childhood traumas. They argue that it's impossible to fall out of love, that conflict is a sign that you're with the right person, and that fighting is essential to emotional and spiritual growth. (I asked them if that meant they should both still be with their first spouses; they said Imago was a powerful tool but did not enable time travel.) Mismatches, by this logic, are effectively ruled out. You're with the right person if you are happy, and you're with the right person if you're miserable and fighting.

This has made Hendrix and Hunt into absolutists. "You end the relationship when the person is brain-dead or brain-damaged," Hendrix says in one video, in response to a question of when to call it quits. "As long as they can talk and relate, there's hope for a relationship."

Even cases of spousal violence are resolvable, they insist. "It takes two to create this warped ballet," Hendrix and Hunt write in *Keeping the Love You Find.* "What is rarely acknowledged is that the battered wife knows only one way—the way she learned from her own mother—to get attention, and that is to provoke her distant, silent husband with relentless, though perhaps subtle, criticism, complaints, and rejection—until he explodes."

Later in that chapter, Hendrix and Hunt acknowledge that abuse by an unrepentant partner should spell the end of a relationship, but "when the addict or abuser is willing to acknowledge and work on the problems," then "the attempt to save the relationship should be made." Some weeks after the conference, I sent Hendrix and Hunt an email asking them to comment on these passages, but they did not respond.

In Dallas, I met Tammy and David, who had been married for thirty years and separated for six months. "I was being abused," Tammy told me while David was in the bathroom. "He threatened to kill me in front of my kids." She moved into a women's shelter, but a divorce group made her decide never to have one. She wanted to stay with David and had read Hendrix and Hunt's books. "Separation is painful enough," Tammy said. "I don't want to end up repeating the same patterns with someone new."

HUNT AND HENDRIX perceive themselves as revolutionaries on the precipice of a new social order. But in reality, their idealization of marriage is old-fashioned, and their counsel to stay together at any costs harkens back to Dorothy Dix, Dear Abby, and Ann Landers, who wrote in times when a woman might remain in a relationship because it was her only means of solvency. Hendrix speaks of a "three-hundred-year-focus on the individual," a paradigm he's keen to shatter, but our society has long bestowed married couples with special privileges, like tax breaks and the ability to share health-care plans and social security benefits.

Marriage also offers the legal and social license to declare certain matters none of anyone else's business. The first time the Supreme Court invoked a constitutional right to privacy was in 1965 in *Griswold v. Connecticut,* in which the court ruled that a married couple had the right to use birth control even in states where it was illegal. After I was married, I noticed that extended relatives stopped asking me how my relationship was "going"—they had questioned me relentlessly when I was living with my now husband. Privacy is crucial to romance: you can't be a pair until you stop telling other people things. Coupledom has an isolating quality, as anyone who's watched a friend disappear into a relationship can attest. But Hendrix and Hunt believe that couples, these typically interior animals, will be the force that changes the world.

There are now, of course, alternatives to marriage that didn't exist in Dear Abby's heyday. Marriage is a common prerequisite to purchasing a home or having a child, but it's not a mandatory one. Studies indicate that a growing number of single women over thirty are choosing to become single parents through adoption or artificial insemination. There is less stigma around divorce—humiliation is only one of many culturally approved ways of processing it. Fashionable celebrities, some divorced, others never married, are photographed in tabloids alongside their loving, supportive "co-parents."

Still, in most parts of America, these alternative family structures are tolerated but far from normal. There is still no domestic arrangement as idolized and celebrated as the traditional monogamous marriage. Spinsterhood has not lost its taint. Most young people still aspire to marry one day, even if they're waiting until they're older. (The average age of an American woman at her first marriage, according to the latest statistics, is 26.5; for men it's 28.7. In 1920, in the age of Dorothy Dix, it was twenty-one for women and twenty-four for men.) Stephanie Coontz, a professor at Evergreen State College and the author of *Marriage: A History*, says that the instinct to postpone marriage reflects a greater reverence for the institution.

All of this raises the question: Who, or what, are Hendrix and Hunt saving us *from*?

Hunt and Hendrix don't name a straw man. Their intellectual opponents are elusive but omnipresent: they decry a nationwide, top-to-bottom neglect of the marital bond. They were coordinating with Dallas-area schools to teach Imago in classrooms. "We want them learning English, arithmetic, biology, and relationship," Hunt says. Hendrix believes that modern American society overemphasizes the importance of sex in a healthy marriage. He does not specify the worst offenders; he has no prepared screed against *Cosmopolitan* magazine, Dr. Ruth, or *The Joy of Sex*. He fears, however, that happily married people are abandoning relationships because they've gleaned from television that they're having too little sex. Hendrix goes so far as to say that less sex is a *good* thing, that it's a sign of a more authentic, deeper connection. "In a safe marriage, you're making love all the time. You might want to explore it genitally, you might want to read poetry to each other," he says. Hendrix may believe in soul mates, but he is not a romantic. He thinks intense romantic feelings indicate something sinister. He has a loosely Freudian theory about romance, that sexual desires are a manifestation of the affection denied by one's parents. "Right now it's really clear that the more wounded you were in childhood the more intense your romantic love experience will be," he says. "If it's not a severe need deprivation then romantic love won't have same intensive energy. It'll be a gentler, sweeter, less chaotic experience when you fall in love." Hendrix believes that future generations raised by older, more attentive parents, will be more emotionally stable and their romantic desires won't be so sharp or overwhelming. They'll have no dark, unmentionable longings, just a clear-eyed need for commitment.

AS A METHOD of communication, Imago appears to be effective. In Dallas, as I saw the reactions among participants, the desire among couples to reconnect in love, it was hard not be moved. "I felt respected," a woman in a pale pink T-shirt told the audience, clutching the microphone with one hand and her stomach with the other. "I started crying because I don't think I've ever felt that way before." Many couples at the workshop told me of their wonder and gratitude toward Hendrix and Hunt for offering free counseling, as well as complimentary day care and lunch. Having a full day alone with a spouse was normally out of reach. Many left the workshop grinning.

But Imago is also an ideology, one that aims for simplicity and universality. To preserve the notion that Imago is right for every couple, Hendrix and Hunt are loath to make exceptions. "It is the case that every couple is different, as is every leaf on a tree," Hendrix and Hunt wrote me in an email, "but every couple is also similar in their relational needs."

When I got married, plenty of older friends offered the classic warning that marriage takes work, but no one took me aside and explained what the work looks like. Marriage affords a couple privacy, but perhaps not enough support. "With my mom friends, we talk about taking our kids to the dentist, to speech therapists, to tutors," said Beth Reeder Johnson, who coordinates the clinical volunteers for the Dallas workshops. "But no one talks about their plan for their marriage or their marriage philosophy." Because marriages are private, they can be difficult to emulate.

Imago, with its rigid and programmatic rules, is easy to emulate. It offers simple answers, and that is the appeal. It might not be an ideal model, but amid the eternal uncertainties of love and partnership, people are eager to have a model at all.

FOURTEEN

Politeness vs. Honesty, Part 2

Judith Martin

MISS MANNERS, OR JUDITH MARTIN, FINDS THE REST of us rather amusing. She receives fifty-some emails a day from people whining about their irritating neighbors or irritating in-laws, pleading for a bit of compassion from the last reasonable human on earth.

Martin is seventy-nine. ("My mother would be shocked if she knew that I give my age when people ask!") She has written an advice column on manners since January 2, 1978, when she published a short essay for the *Washington Post* about what to do if you wake up on New Year's Day with a blurry memory and a nagging suspicion that you owe someone an apology. "How Do I Apologize When I Don't Know What It Was I Did?" read the headline. "Miss Manners recognizes that even the most well-bred person may be subject to a fit of bad behavior at a holiday party," she wrote. She recommended forgoing an apology and sending a small gift to the possibly offended host. "This does not incriminate you, as an apology would, and on the fat chance that she thought you were cute, too, it can be seen simply as a gracious gesture." The letters came pouring in. People had *thoughts* about these things, about these minor, seemingly insignificant social infractions. People all across the country were spiraling because their niece hadn't written a thank-you note or their friend never replied to a wedding invitation. No one could agree on the appropriate amount of money to spend on a graduation gift, when an air kiss was a proper greeting, how to eat asparagus, or the appropriate age for a girl to have her ears pierced. It was incredible, Martin thought, how easily we drive each other crazy.

She turned people's proclivity for driving one another insane into a business. In addition to the column, which she's published three times a week for forty years and which is carried in more than two hundred papers, she's written thirteen books on manners, including *Miss Manners' Basic Training*, *Miss Manners' Guide to Domestic Tranquility*, *Miss Manners' Guide for the Turn-of-the Millennium*, and *Miss Manners' Guide to Excruciatingly Correct Behavior*. In recent years, she's published volumes on texting, aging, and wedding etiquette. A disproportionate number of the letters she receives concern weddings. "They get etiquette-conscious at that time, so they ask silly things: 'Who should do the third dance with whom?' Well, I don't care! Those are non-questions. But meanwhile, they are violating the most basic decencies of manners by trying to charge their guests!" She's found that many wedding hosts ask their guests to help cover the cost of the event and finds the practice despicable.

In her books and columns, Miss Manners refers to herself in the third person. For instance: "Not a day goes by that Miss Manners doesn't receive several questions about how to do something—throw a party, take a trip, buy household items, entertain in a restaurant—that the writer states being unable to afford." Her tone is huffy, erudite, and witty, the voice of a person who perversely delights in the minor misfortunes of others but is careful to emphasize that she hasn't the time to care. She reads like a blend of a Jane Austen heroine and Anna Wintour, a close observer with an unabashed obsession with appearances. She seems repressed and stiff, the kind of person to say *peeved* in place of *angry*. I pictured her in head-to-toe black, elegant and slick, with a stoic expression on her face.

But Judith Martin is not at all like this. She suggested we meet at the Cosmos Club, a members-only restaurant and bar in DC. (A private club! I thought. How Miss Manners of her!) She met me in the lobby. She wore a green-and-blue plaid dress and leather boots that reached her knees. She was dressed as if for a picnic, and she looked terrific. Her white hair was soft and loose, and when she smiled, her eyes shone with the sympathy of a mother in a Vicks commercial. She spoke with the unmistakable nasal inflections of a person raised by Yiddish speakers. She was tiny, the top of her head barely reaching my collarbone, and after she settled onto an uphol-stered bench in the so-called Gold Room—shaking her head, "Well, this room isn't very cozy, is it?"—she crossed her ankles, smiled, and said, "So, what do you want to know?"

I asked her if she felt that American manners had deteriorated since the 1970s. She's suggested as much in many of her books. (Her books include complaints like, "The assumption that people know and follow the simplest methods for annoyance control is wildly optimistic.") Manners don't work in polarities, Martin told me; they don't get "better" or "worse." Like language, they evolve. "The best change of all was that it was no longer accepted, so-cially, to make bigoted remarks. That was the huge and wonderful change, and we're now experiencing some backlash from that," she said. President Trump had been in office a few months when we met, and there'd been a reported uptick in hate speech. I told her about a freshly painted white swastika I'd seen on my way to work. She shook her head, like a matriarch who expected more of her children.

I had been thinking about Lord Chesterfield, about how panicked and angry Americans felt at his call for strategic self-censorship, at his instruction to exercise restraint. I asked Martin where she drew the line between candor and politeness, between our obligation to be honest and our obligation to be civil. She angled her eye toward me. "Well, they don't call me Miss Morals!"

———~·~———

JUDITH PERLMAN WAS born in 1938 in Washington, DC. Her father, Jacob Perlman, was a Russian immigrant who worked as an economist for the United Nations. Her mother, Helen, was an elementary school teacher, and when they lived overseas, she would find work at the English-speaking school where Judith and her brother, Matthew, were students. For a time, they moved every few years. By the time Martin reached high school, they'd lived in Colombia, Greece, Bolivia, and the Philippines. "That exposed me to the idea that the way people behave is not universal. There are differences. And that interested me," she said. She appears to have been born middle-aged; as a child, she enjoyed reading, visiting museums, and chatting with her parents. "When I was eight or ten, my father looked at me and said, 'You know, I could just picture you as an old lady with a stick and a high-collared blouse tyrannizing over generations of your descendants.' I was a little girl in pigtails at the time, and I thought, 'My daddy understands me.'"

Her parents were devout liberals. Her father was the only economist in his field who hired female researchers, and when the family settled back in DC, they sent Judith to the city's only integrated high school—Georgetown Day School, where her mother worked as a teacher. Her uncle Selig Perlman was a famous labor economist who wrote the seminal text *A Theory of the Labor Movement*. Her authoritative book *Miss Manners' Guide to Excruciatingly Correct Behavior* includes a chapter about etiquette for picketers. "Miss Manners would especially urge consideration for picketers on the part of the public, quite aside from the moral or social issues," she writes. "Proper dress for picketers is either outdoor apparel appropriate for the weather, or the working clothes of the striking profession. Miss Manners was once glad to see Washington striking musicians wearing white tie and was even willing to waive for the occasion the general rule about not wearing evening dress during the day."

American manners have long had a poor reputation abroad, associated with rowdy children and slovenly dress. Martin appreciates them anyway. "I think American manners are the best in the world," she said. "We would never say, as the British do, 'So-and-so is *in trade*. Isn't that awful?' We have the idea of treating everybody equally," she said. The goal of most American customs, she pointed out, is to collapse, not highlight, the divisions between classes. She considers that a worthy goal. Ask for her critique of contemporary American manners and she'll critique capitalism instead. "Our chief etiquette problem is greed. It's unabashed greed," she said. She had plenty of examples: "Money is tight, but I want to buy my husband a boat," went a letter she received recently. She finds that too many of the people seeking her guidance are really asking that she endorse their extortion scheme, angling to solicit money from friends and family so they can afford a luxury item (or a wedding). She finds the wedding industry, in general, to be "hideously vulgar."

After high school, Judith went to Wellesley College, where she studied English literature and hoped to become a drama critic. Her parents insisted she find a job after her freshman year, but Judith preferred to spend the summer relaxing with a book. She procrastinated the job search until she thought it too late for any responsible institution to hire her and then applied to be a "copy kid" at the *Washington Post*, the equivalent of a news assistant, a job that typically required a year hustling at the student paper and genuflecting before a well-connected family friend. To her surprise, she was offered the job. And to her even greater surprise, she loved it. She worked there all three summers of college, and when she graduated, in 1959, she accepted a job as a reporter for the women's section, the only section of the paper where women were regularly permitted bylines. As a reporter, she covered the DC party circuit. At a White House party near the end of Lyndon Johnson's presidency, Johnson invited Martin and several other women reporters up to the residence. "We stayed for two hours, eating popcorn from a silver bowl while he swore he had never wanted to be president," she said. She was dying to write about it—he'd seemed undone— but her editor found it inappropriate. "I have great respect for our government, but I don't necessarily respect the people in those positions," she said. "You would think politicians would learn to stop being such bigots."

She was one of a dozen female staffers who sued the *Washington Post* for gender discrimination in 1972. Their suit was one of a fleet of gender discrimination cases filed by female reporters in the 1970s that accused major publications like *Newsweek* of systematically denying them bylines and promotions. The *Post* women won their suit and Martin began to write features and drama criticism, as she always hoped.

She saw movies in the morning, went to the theater in the evening, and wrote her reviews during the day. She had gotten married soon after graduating from Wellesley, to a molecular biologist named Robert Martin, whom she'd met through a mutual friend. The couple had two children, Nicholas and Jacobina. The children attended Georgetown Day School, as Judith had, and were sent to an after-school program at the Washington National Opera to develop their appreciation for theater. They were both required to get jobs by seventh grade. "I misunderstood Take Your Child to Work Day. I thought it was Put Your Child to Work Day," she said.

Nicholas is now the director of operations at the Lyric Opera of Chicago; Jacobina is an instructor at Second City, the famed school for comedians. They have both cowritten Miss Manners books with their mother and ghostwrite the column on occasion. The Miss Manners voice is now a shared one, a kind of heirloom. "There are times when something comes up and we don't know which of the three of us wrote it," she said.

Miss Manners says that etiquette shouldn't be complicated, that it's simply a matter of treating people with respect. The minor details, the holding of forks and doors, are a side note; few people will notice social peccadillos if you commit to the Golden Rule. Martin is a proud descendant and a proud ancestor; she finds it shameful how many Americans treat their families as "optional appendages." She recognizes, however, that not everyone had the great privilege of her upbringing, or her children's upbringing. And that's why she invented Miss Manners.

SHE STARTED THE column to amuse herself and assumed no one would read it. She thought any discussion of etiquette would be deemed anachronistic, linked to the Gilded Age, a world of white gloves and coattails and formality—the very things the feminist movement had struggled to liberate women from. Martin, who identifies as a feminist, did not want to be falsely identified with the "sissies and smoothies," as she put it. But the subject interested her. She likened social rules to costume or set design—they established character, incited conflict, enriched the world of the story.

But people *were* interested. They were confounded and often infuriated by how their family, friends, and coworkers behaved, their insensitive questions and inattention to details. Many Americans felt that life had grown so informal that it was unclear what rules, if any, still applied. Did you have to write a thank-you note after a job interview or receiving a gift or going to a friend's place for dinner? (Yes.) Was it stuffy to ask your son's friend to address you formally, as Mr. Smith? (No.) Were you supposed to buy your boss a Christmas present? (No.) Her column was a refuge for those who believed that manners still mattered, that informality was not license to be rude, and that friends, relatives, and coworkers were still entitled to expect things from one another.

"How do you figure out what the social rules are?" I asked her.

"Well, I pronounce them!" she laughed.

She defined social rules small and large, making decrees on subjects ranging from flatware, to baby showers, to appropriate

boundaries between parents and adult children. She has studied etiquette manuals from France, Japan, and Great Britain, as well as ancient Egypt and ancient Greece, and American manuals from every
decade. She considers Ralph Waldo Emerson, Benjamin Franklin,
and George Washington to be among America's best writers on etiquette. Washington was obsessed with manners. When he was sixteen, he jotted down a list of 110 crucial social behaviors (#97: "Put
not another bit into your Mouth til the former be Swallowed."), and
as president, he was committed to crafting an image of a humble
and accessible leader; he took great care in how he dressed and
in determining the menu at White House events. Martin sees her
passion for etiquette as a matter of patriotism: if Washington had
the time to think about these things, then surely they're important to the country he hoped to create. She believes that American
manners should be more centralized, that customs have become so
fragmented that many Americans have mistakenly come to believe
that they live in a country *without* social rules. "A combination of
acrimony and ignorance has left us in a state of etiquette chaos in
which we are still flailing. The absence of a universally accepted
standard, along with the habit of suspiciously analyzing whatever
forms are proposed, means that no one is safe," she wrote.

Martin often lectures at universities. Law students are her favorite. They understand the importance of etiquette—without it,
the mildest conflicts would flood the courts. "There are two systems
for regulating society: law and etiquette," Martin said. "The law
handles momentous things—you know, danger to life, liberty, and
property—and etiquette handles the everyday little problems that
the law is too clumsy to handle. And I have a fascinating time at law
schools, because they understand it as an extra regulatory system."
She points out that democratic governments don't need to litigate
every minor conflict, that the civic system relies on social pressure to
moderate behavior. It is perfectly legal, for instance, to dress as we
please, shout obscenities at public figures, and occupy excessive space
on the subway. "As far as we know, however, the intention was not

to create a society that was perfectly free and perfectly unbearable. It was taken for granted that custom and social pressure, if not our vaunted sense of fairness, would be a powerful deterrent from keeping people from routinely exercising their freedom without regard to how ugly this might make life for their fellow citizens," she wrote.

But if etiquette is such an effective extralegal regulatory system, then why, I asked her, are so many people so rude? She laughed. "Human nature!" She has grouped humanity into two categories: those who behave "none of the time" and those who behave "some of the time." She reminds the frustrated people who write her that it's best to not read into the offensive behavior of others, that most people are trying the best they can.

ABOUT A MONTH after President Trump's inauguration, Martin published a story in *The Atlantic* under the headline "Miss Manners on Rudeness in the Age of Trump." The story bore Martin's byline and was written in the first person, though it sounded like Miss Manners, biting and formal. "Manners transgressions have always been harder to live down. A single instance of screaming doomed the 2004 presidential campaign of Democratic National Committee chairman Howard Dean. Gaffes that smacked of jeering, bullying, or defaming brought down many a political career," she wrote. "So why did so many citizens elect a president of the United States who unabashedly—even proudly—violated those expectations?" Her fear was that Americans voted for Trump *because* of those violations; they were intrigued by his neglect for basic civility. His voters, she thought, either couldn't tear their eyes from the Trump road show or admired his ability to behave as he pleased and suffer no consequences. They envied the impunity they'd granted him.

Martin understands rudeness as a kind of virus. "If rudeness begets more rudeness, which begets more rudeness, where will it all end?" she once wrote. She believes we are living in a period of peak rudeness, but she places only some of the blame on the current administration. The internet is also at fault. She thinks that the internet offers too much freedom, allowing people to hurl insults and threats at strangers as if their words have no meaning. Martin also resents what she calls the "busyness cult" that's overtaken modern society, in which it's considered a sign of puritanical piety to lack time for others. Unlike Lord Chesterfield, who was solely concerned with manners as a means to personal ends, Martin cares about social cohesion and—though she may claim otherwise—about morals, too.

For the most part, Martin admires the American insistence on informality, that people have more freedom to dress and speak as they please. But what she finds odd and somewhat disconcerting is that *everything* is informal. When she started writing the column, there were various registers of speech or dress—you wore a tie to work, jeans to a friend's dinner party, and sweatpants when lounging at home. Today, a woman might wear yoga pants all day. This doesn't offend Martin—it bores her. The emphasis on informality has had a certain flattening effect; everyone was once required to be socially multilingual, fluent in a variety of settings. Now, everything has been mashed together into a kind of behavioral Esperanto. She bemoans the disintegration of a distinctive professional etiquette. She dislikes when offices refer to themselves as "families"—unlike real families, those relationships are finite, purposeful, and unlikely to last into retirement. Miss Manners thinks the insistence on informality is a ploy to convince people to work longer hours because they're surrounded by "friends." She's enraged when doctors refer to their patients by their first names. "I once went to battle with the Mayo Clinic over this," she said. "They say it's friendlier. It really isn't friendly. Among friends, either both of us have our clothes on or both of us have our clothes off." She does not see how two people could ever be equals when only one of them is holding a scalpel and sees no reason to act otherwise.

A generation ago, she points out, white people were always addressed with an honorific, while black people never were. In 1963, a black teacher named Mary Hamilton was held in contempt of court when she refused to respond to a judge until he called her "Miss Hamilton." Martin would prefer that everyone receive "dignity and a title" rather than abolishing these signs of respect. Not long ago, she took her new iPhone to the Apple Genius Bar because she wanted Siri to address her as "Ms. Martin" rather than "Judith." She mocks people who don't want to be addressed formally because it makes them feel old—they *are* old, she reasons; why not relish the dignity that comes with it?

She collects examples about the efficacy of kindness. When we met, she had recently read that doctors in malpractice suits can save thousands of dollars in legal fees if they apologize to the patient and admit wrongdoing before trial. "It's like a criminal showing remorse in court. You can't really look into their hearts and see if they're really sorry, but showing remorse goes a long way toward mitigating the punishment," she said.

She recognizes that these are superficial behaviors, that demonstrating remorse is a performance and in no way undoes the crime. But, at the moment, she would welcome more surface-level civility. She thinks Americans have become too honest, too sincere. She's not the only one. On *Saturday Night Live,* the day after Trump's inauguration, the comedian Aziz Ansari begged President Trump's most virulent supporters to be politer. "The problem is there is a new group. A tiny slice of people who have gotten way too excited about Trump for the wrong reasons. As soon as Trump got elected, they were like, 'We don't have to pretend like we're not racist anymore! We can be racist again,'" Ansari said. "If you're one of these people, please go back to pretending, you gotta go back to pretending."

Martin, like Chesterfield, is a longtime advocate of pretending. She praises Americans' general aptitude for pulling off a "skillful performance of false cheer." Pretending, she argues, is what makes America great. The ruling class pretends to be humble; immigrants pretend to be versed in American customs, and when they misspeak they're forgiven by Americans who can remember when they, or their ancestors, had to pretend as well. "It's no accident that Americans have an aptitude for show business. Every immigrant family had someone who walked out on whatever was playing at home. These individuals had flipped through the particular scripts they had inherited and the scenarios they could foresee and decided they could do better," she wrote. Etiquette may be associated with pretentiousness, but Martin's point is that it enables the very kind social shape-shifting that Americans pride themselves on, that it makes it possible to strive for more.

FIFTEEN

How to Coach a Life Coach

Martha Beck

"LIFE COACH" IS A NEWLY OFFICIAL JOB TITLE FOR AN ancient practice: helping others make decisions. Coaches assist clients who are unsure if their job is the right job or if their relationship is the right relationship, who may be tempted to move across the country and start over. There's no degree required to be a life coach. I can call myself a life coach, you can call yourself a life coach. It's a nebulous but growing profession. Clients spend over a billion dollars on coaching each year, according to *Harvard Business Review*, with coaches charging, on average, five hundred dollars an hour.

"Ninety-nine percent of what you get from a life coach you can get from a thoughtful friend, but if you pay for it, you pay more attention to it," said Martha Beck, likely the world's most famous life coach. "I'm really doing them a favor when they hand me money." Beck dislikes the term *life coach*—"what a gnarly-sounding term," she said. She prefers "guide." She has also done more than perhaps anyone to legitimize life coaching.

The Martha Beck Institute offers a certification course for life coaches. The course costs $7,500, takes nine months, and is mostly held online. Since 2001, when she started the certificate program, Beck has trained more than three thousand life coaches—most of them women—who go on to employ their Martha Beck certificates to build careers as "corporate coaches," "healers," "MindBody coaches," "Intuitive readers," and "facilitators." The degree is as validating as it is flexible; it's a liberal arts course in empathy.

Beck coordinates her school for freelance empathizers from a ranch in central California, where I went to visit her recently. It's a sprawling and stunning property, on the peak of a hill, surrounded by vineyards. Beck saw this very ranch in a dream when she was a girl, with its bay windows and its two horse pens, and auspiciously enough, when the house went to market right around her fiftieth birthday, the listing price was precisely her life's savings. Beck is fifty-five but told me that a variety of medical tests determined her "biological age" to be thirty-six. This makes perfect sense upon meeting her. She's as spry as a meerkat. She has short auburn hair that accentuates her angular face, with cheekbones that resemble the knobs of a coat rack.

Beck is a self-described socialite who holds multiple degrees from Harvard, including a PhD in sociology. She identifies as a social scientist and brags about her score on the logic portion of the SAT. ("I got a perfect score on my logic SAT. That's how I think. Logic, logic, logic.") She also begins a surprising number of sentences with phrases like "All my shaman friends." An example: "All my shaman friends would say that's a healer's disease." A "healer's disease," Beck says, is a chronic condition commonly suffered by spiritualists that can only be kept at bay by constant attendance to others. There are signs, Beck says, that one is destined to become a healer—one of them being an incurable illness. "It means that you have to train as a medicine person, and you have to act as a medicine person. If you ever stop serving others, you get sick again." Beck has several chronic diseases, including interstitial cystitis in her bladder, but demonstrates no symptoms.

"The surgeon who diagnosed me said, and I quote, 'Pound for pound, you have the biggest bladder I've ever seen.' I thought, 'This is my gift from the heavens!' Because I can literally sit and coach a group for twelve hours and never need to pee."

Beck is glib for a person who believes in destiny. She told me about the animal spirit who frequented her dreams as a child—as her shaman friends would say, regular dreams about animal friends are a telltale sign that a child will grow up to be a healer. "I had dreams when I was little, little, little. Like, three or four. I would go to this river at night and I would dive in and down at the bottom of the river was an albino beaver. I would sit down with him and he would tell me things about math and physics," she said. "Yeah, I had my friend, my pure white beaver, which I can't really write about because of the pun problem. I just wish it had been an otter. I would talk about it all the time."

Beck disdains the trappings of modern society that have made life coaching so popular. She hates how hard everyone seems to work, how little time people have for pleasure, how everyone seems to live an atomized existence, motivated by money and cut off from the people they love. She has retreated to her ranch, where she lives with her partner, Karen, her adult son, Adam, and rotating coterie of friends and visitors. She is the best-selling author of a dozen advice books, including *Finding Your Own North Star*, but in 2016, she founded her own press, Cynosure, so she could self-publish. "I just wanted to divest myself from dependency on every major system," she said. She continues to write an advice column in *O, The Oprah Magazine*, as she's done for over a decade. She's been told by prison wardens that her column is among the items commonly found under the mattresses of female inmates. Other than her columnist duties, Beck makes no long-term commitments; she has no five-year plan. Every morning, she covers herself in birdseed and meditates under a tree for an hour or so. "The birds land on you and the chipmunks sit in your lap. It's very blissful." When she's finished, she brushes off the birdseed and determines how to best spend her time. She'll often pause in the middle of a conversation or meeting to ask herself, "Is this what I really want to be doing?" She calls these moments "integrity checks." She is intent to waste as little time as possible on obligations. When clients or aspiring coaches come to her because they want a job, a partner, children, a better title, more money—the standard checkboxes of personal achievement—she's glad to assist. Her obligation, after all, is to the client. But she can't help but coach them, or *guide* them, to want more.

BECK WAS TWENTY when she got married. Her husband, John, was a fellow Harvard student and a fellow Mormon. They attended the same Utah high school, where he was a senior when she was a sophomore, and though they hardly knew each other then, something about him intrigued her, and she applied to Harvard to be close to him. They had their first child, a daughter, when Beck was twenty-three and finishing her master's degree. "You grow up Mormon, you get socialized to think that that is right on time," she said. She became pregnant again less than two years later. At a routine sonogram almost six months into her pregnancy, the doctor realized that the child, a boy, would be born with Down syndrome. "I had a two-week window to have a god-awful type of abortion. I mean, I'm very pro-choice, but at that stage of pregnancy, it's horrible. They just kill the fetus slowly and you give birth to a dead baby. I couldn't do it. I just couldn't do it." Adam was born in May 1988. "It broke my social contract with everyone at Harvard. With my advisers, with my professors, I was now sort of a pariah for having made the wrong choice." Her thesis adviser encouraged her to put up Adam for adoption. "I remember him telling me that and thinking, as he told me, 'What is the value of human existence? Is it to sit in an office like this one and write articles that no one will ever read for pleasure? How is this better than what Adam's life will be?'" She was so insulted that she left Harvard. She and John returned to

Utah and Beck commuted by plane to Cambridge to fulfill her final course requirements.

In Utah, the Becks were offered jobs at Brigham Young University, where Martha's father, Hugh Nibley, was a noted scholar of Mormon and biblical texts. They had a third child, a daughter, and cowrote a psychology book about addictions, *Breaking the Cycle of Compulsive Behavior*, which includes instructions on how to overcome homosexual feelings.

In 1993, the Church of Jesus Christ of Latter-Day Saints excommunicated or disciplined six notable Mormon scholars. In solidarity, the Becks disavowed Mormonism, and soon after, both John and Martha came out as gay and then divorced. The separation was amicable; they're still in close touch. Her separation from Mormonism was more explosive. She wrote a book, *Leaving the Saints: How I Lost the Mormons and Found My Faith*, in which she discusses an epidemic of sexual assault within the church's highest echelons and accuses her father of sexual abuse. (Her father, now deceased, and her seven siblings have all denied these charges.)

After leaving her position at BYU, Beck moved to Phoenix and taught a career development course at Arizona State University. Her students kept lingering after class and, eventually, offered to pay Beck for private counseling. "I'd been very happy to pay therapists," she said. "I figured it was sort of comparable. The therapist I'd gone to for a while charged eighty dollars an hour, so I charged fifty dollars an hour." Her students referred more students, and she found herself running a small career-consulting business. Her clients were a young, driven bunch, struggling to choose between offers and industries, but there tended to be existential matters looming over their job fears. Her fiftieth client, for instance, was a woman who had to choose between two different jobs on different sides of the country. "I couldn't feel any joy or enthusiasm connected to either of these positions or to her work in general or to anyone or anything," Beck said. "And finally as just sort of a throwaway, she said, 'You know, either way I have to sell my horse.' And I said, 'Tell me about your horse.' And her energy completely changed, and it soon became clear that the horse was the most important relationship in her life. And I was like, 'Why the hell would you give away a being you love for either of these jobs? Who gives a crap if you're making ten thousand dollars less a year? You've got something you love. If you can't take the horse, don't take it at all.'" The line between career coaching and life coaching was thin, and Beck was inclined to cross it. "I do a lot of research on entrepreneurialism. I know how to help people find a job if that's what they want. I know how to help them build a business if that's what they want. But I am prone to ask them, 'Okay, what if you had a really, really, really successful business and you'd achieved the pinnacle of everything you want. Let's go there, imagine that.' They're like, 'Oh, yeah. I'd have a boat and I'd have a mansion or have whatever.' 'Okay, feel that, really get it. There, you're done. You just felt it. All you're going to get is a feeling, you know? And you can start now. You can start feeling that any time you want.'"

It struck Beck, in her role as a career counselor, that offering improvised career advice was not a stable career plan. She felt she needed a theory to legitimize her coaching methods and set to work on *Finding Your Own North Star*, her first self-help book. She carried residual animosity toward academia and Mormonism, but her coaching methodologies were influenced by both. "I have cautious respect for shamanic traditions and cautious respect for academia and cautious respect for religion. It's all good. There's a baby in every bathwater. As soon as you start ruling anybody out you're being a dogmatist, which is what I don't like." The thesis of the book is that the purpose of life is joy; the presence of joy means a decision is right, the absence of joy means a decision is wrong. She writes that the body is joy's best odometer; when you feel a pit in your stomach or tension in your shoulders, you are feeling something other than joy and should delicately but swiftly excise yourself from the situation.

The necessity of joy and the so-called body check remain the basic tenets of the Martha Beck life coaching method. "I made up the methodology. I've never even looked into other life coaching methodologies, which is probably a bad thing," she said. Beck and her acolytes bristle at the word *advice*—only you, your body, can know what brings it joy. But she has a fairly definitive dos-and-don'ts list for joyful living. Do meditate. Do use agential verbs, as in "I *choose* to pull an all-nighter." Don't use passive words, as in "I *have* to pull an all-nighter." Do what you love. Don't succumb to other people's expectations. She believes the body is your friend and the brain is not, that language is the root cause of most psychic pain. "We're the only species that can create a belief in reality because of the use of abstract language," she said. She likes to point to Adam, her son, as evidence: he has limited capacity for language but is among the most mellow and content people she knows.

A coaching session works like this: The coach asks the client to describe the greatest source of pain in his or her life. The client talks, the coach asks follow-up questions, and as soon as the coach forms an opinion, she discloses it to her client. The technique is supposed to distinguish the life coach from a quiet, diffident therapist. "The first thing I teach coaches to say is, 'Here's what I think is going on with you. Your job is to please, please tell me where I'm wrong and tell me precisely.' Asking for this confirmation, number one, it builds trust. Number two, it puts you in a position of servant rather than overseer. It creates humility and an open mind." She tried it on me.

"There are times when you look at what's happening in journalism and go, 'Wow, I wonder where I'm going to be in ten years.' I would guess you spend a fair amount of time wondering that. Tell me where I'm wrong," she said.

I told her she was right.

Beck admits that coaching is a luxury activity. "A coach is to a therapist as a personal trainer is to a physician. You go to a therapist if you are mentally ill and you want to get well. If you are well but want to have higher levels of satisfaction than normal, then you go to a trainer or coach. One of the first things I also teach [coaches is], 'Here are the signs of someone being mentally ill. Send them to a therapist.'" Many of Beck's clients are celebrities, Fortune 500 CEOs, Silicon Valley millionaires, though she was hesitant to name names. "A lot of the people at the very top are the most miserable people. It's bloodcurdling, actually," she said. "I know a lot of celebrities. I don't like very many of them." Maria Shriver, the former first lady of California, called several times during my visit, and Beck was constantly texting Elizabeth Gilbert, the author of *Eat, Pray, Love.* Neither are clients, exactly. Beck says she informally coaches many of her dear friends. It's habit by now.

She says that many of her coaching clients arrive at their first session with the same fantasy. "The guys always want to buy a bar on the beach and they're going to work in the bar and they're going to lie on the beach and they're going to fish," she said. "The women want to wake up in a room that is almost all windows, and it looks out over a beach and everything is white in the room, and they dress in white, floaty peasant outfits. It's kind of like *Under the Tuscan Sun,* without color." The dream is a life of effortlessness and simplicity, and Beck's point is that such a life can be found through mental practice—they don't have to buy a beach house. Her ideas recall Dale Carnegie, William James, and other evangelists of positive thinking. She believes that our minds shape our reality.

Beck doesn't have much time for private coaching anymore. She spends her time writing, training new coaches, and training master coaches, who train the coaches. She's building an army of life coaches, and it's all part of her plan to change the world.

⟨~×~⟩

"MAYBE YOU CAN get the air conditioner out of the shot?" said Rowan Mangan, one of eight women on Beck's staff. Rowan lives in one of the houses on Beck's ranch, but she was in Australia at the moment, visiting family, and was trying to produce Beck's video shoot by Skype. Her face was smiley and pixilated.

Beck, her eyebrows squinted and her focus pure, tilted her laptop for a tighter angle. She was making a short video for Architects of Change, part of Maria Shriver's website. She's been making more videos lately. "One thing I found about writing these days is that people are primarily visual, and if you can get visual images, the concepts go down a lot more easily," she said. She tilted the laptop again, noticed a case of Tic Tacs in the shot and moved them aside, and brushed off the blanket she'd refashioned as a tablecloth. "Video is such a pain in the neck."

"I ate some almond flour bread that I had put away carefully wrapped. It was off. And it was so off that I thought, 'I think I better do this film very fast in case I start puking my lungs out in three minutes,'" Beck said.

"That's really weird," Rowan said. "I'm really feeling ill, and maybe I'm feeling your—"

"That's it! I've sympathetically transferred food poisoning to you in Australia. It happens all the time." It can be hard to know when Beck is marveling at the oneness of the universe and when she is kidding.

Beck sat at a small table. On top of the table there were three things: a platter containing a short pyramid of sugar cubes, a pie plate of indigo-dyed water, and a clear pitcher with the same purple liquid. The cheap setup resembled a booth at a third-grade science fair, which was odd considering that Beck grossed $3.5 million in 2016.

"Is there anything I can do from this continent?" Rowan asked.

"Encourage me and soak up my food poisoning."

"I am, and it's bad."

"I'm so sorry. Better you than me is what I'm thinking."

Beck pressed record. She took a deep breath, found a wide smile, and began. "Some of you guys know that I have a PhD in sociology. And some of you know that I'm also a woo-woo person who has always believed that sometime in my lifetime I would experience a global transformation of human consciousness." She motioned at the sugar pyramid, which she explained was supposed to symbolize our current society, with its hierarchies and inequities, while the pool in the pie plate symbolized the enlightened society Beck sought to build. She poured the contents of the pitcher onto the pyramid, and as the base dissolved, Beck narrated, "The people who dissolve first, who give up the old way of being first, are the ones who have the least to lose. So they're on the bottom. They just absorb the people around them because they are made of inclusion and love." The sugar pyramid collapsed and resembled the indigo pool in the pie plate, and Beck explained, "That is how civilizations become clear and equal and sweet and inclusive." After the demolition, she read a quote from an essay Toni Morrison had written for *The Nation*: "There is no time for despair, no place for self-pity, no need for silence, no room for fear. We speak, we write, we do language. That is how civilizations heal." Beck had mentioned to me earlier that she was planning to turn the Morrison quote into a meme. "We have a corporate mission of creating memes," she said. "If you can create a meme, memes drive culture, and culture drives behavior. Like *Star Wars*. Suddenly everybody could talk about their spirituality without feeling like they had to get religious. Everyone knows, 'The Force be with you.'"

"I hope this helps, and I'll see you on the internet. Love you, ciao," Beck said, and signed off.

"Holy shit," said Rowan, who'd been following along through Skype. "That was brilliant."

"I pay you to say that," said Beck.

Like all of Beck's staff, Rowan is a certified master coach. Master coaches are the black belts of the Martha Beck coaching universe. They receive specialized training, which also takes place online, but from Beck's telling the course sounds more like a baptism than a licensing program. Masters, Beck says, learn to disassociate from their egos, perform miracles, and channel the unknown. "About halfway through the training, they all start experiencing miracles; not just little synchronicities, but really odd things that shouldn't have happened," Beck said. "Hearing really clear instructions—not really spoken, but language in their brains saying, 'This is what you need to do. There's been an accident at this address. You need to go there.'" Beck told me that her pony, Tinker Bell, is psychic, that she can time travel and communicate with herself in the past and future, and that she can make it rain in California.

These are unbelievable claims, but realism is not what Beck's followers are after. They're looking for an excuse to dream. Her followers tend to be people who are successful but miserable—the "worried well," as Beck calls them. Her goal is to free them, the women in particular, from the tyranny of expectations that hover over their lives. She encourages her followers to experiment a bit, to window-shop for meaning in places they may consider strange or out-there, because who knows where something can lead?

"Who knows?" is the underlying question of Martha Beck's philosophy. Who knows if time travel is real or if the pony is really psychic—as long as an idea brings joy, who cares if it's wacky or even true? Beck is a promiscuous thinker whose references range from Brian Greene, to Carl Jung, to Confucius. (She studied Chinese as an undergraduate.) She spends much of each day surfing the internet, eyes alert to possibilities. "I read a lot of blogs and things to see what people are saying, what the zeitgeist is," she said. "The internet is one huge, beautiful sociological study fest, you know?" The internet, of course, is also a magnificent time suck, a planet of endless rabbit holes. But Beck is as gloriously open-minded as a freshman in a late-night bull session. Every book, every philosopher has the sheen of a new discovery. In her *O* columns and in her books, Beck comes across as a reformed socialite still delighting in having untethered herself from a life she didn't want. She refers to herself as a "hot mess" or a "human train wreck" and complains about being a prisoner of her own perfectionistic mind. In other words, she appears to have a lot in common with her primary audiences: impressive but unhappy women in the heart of middle age. "You write self-help books," Beck told me, "because you struggle to get through the day." In her Twitter bio, she identifies as having "ADD plus high anxiety."

My first night with Beck, she told me, "I had many times in my life where I could have either chased despair or been weird. I chose weird." Beck says that a third of the people who sign up for life-coach training don't know what they want from it. They are looking for something different. Something weird. This is where Beck comes in, with her shaman friends and her psychic ponies. Her coaching is designed to give women permission to be weird, because who knows? Beck believes that weirdness, or being open to weirdness, is the key to a more meaningful existence. Dorothy Dix advised women on how to disguise their weirdness; she believed that there was always a way, even without a husband, for a woman to contribute to society. Dear Abby and Ann Landers were dogged in their insistence that there were only a select number of ways to live. Beck continues in the tradition of Mildred Newman, training her followers to ignore the judgments of others and their own self-doubt. But Newman was concerned only with the health and satisfaction of her patients and readers, whereas Beck thinks that all this self-care leads to something awesome, in the most literal sense of the word, that it generates miracles and time travel and a new world order. She senses, perhaps, that this is what her readers need to hear. Newman's followers, especially the celebrity set, were focused on and delighted by their own achievements, but Beck's followers are more self-conscious and coy. Their self-care needs to be justified.

Some of the life-coaching trainees know precisely why they're there: they want an easy way to make a living from home. Beck would rather talk about a revolution of human consciousness than career-coaching methodologies, but she would also hate to disappoint the people who have signed up for her class; she hates disappointing anyone. "That's the hardest part of my integrity plan, is not doing what everyone wants all the time," she told me. For those who have no interest in the "woo-woo" element of the Beck method, who want to help clients build careers they enjoy, she urges that they make their services as specific as possible. "If you say, 'I'm a life coach; I'll make your life better,' you're going to be far less interesting from a Google sense than someone who says, 'I use dog training to change your life.'"

Beck is working on a second novel and hopes to build out her press and convert one of the homes on her property into an artist residency. Every day, she jumps on a video conference with her staff and they decide what they want to make—a video, a meme, a new online course. "I believe some people are fully enlightened, but I don't think I'll ever be," Beck said. "I'll always be going out on the hero's quest."

SIXTEEN

The King of Quora

Michael King

Why do so many startups fail?
Why are all the hosts on CouchSurfing male?
Are we going to be tweeting for the rest of our lives?
Why do Silicon Valley billionaires choose
average-looking wives?

What makes a startup ecosystem thrive?
What do people plan to do once they're over 35?
Is an income of $160K enough to survive?
What kind of car does Mark Zuckerberg drive?

Are the real estate prices in Palo Alto crazy?
Do welfare programs make poor people lazy?
What are some of the biggest lies ever told?
How do I explain Bitcoin to a 6-year-old?

Why is Powdered Alcohol not successful so far?
How does UberX handle vomiting in the car?

Is being worth $10 million considered 'rich'?
What can be causing my upper lip to twitch?
Why has crowdfunding not worked for me?
Is it worth pre-ordering a Tesla Model 3?

How is Clinkle different from Venmo and Square?
Can karma, sometimes, be unfair?
Why are successful entrepreneurs stereotypically jerks?
Which Silicon Valley company has the best intern perks?
What looks easy until you actually try it?
How did your excretions change under a full Soylent diet?

What are alternatives to online dating?
Is living in small apartments debilitating?
Why don't more entrepreneurs focus on solving world hunger?
What do you regret not doing when you were younger?

—Jason O. Gilbert, "A Poem About Silicon
Valley, Assembled from Quora Questions
About Silicon Valley," Splinter

Quora is a website for people with questions. Some users post fairly specific questions: "What are the rules regarding eating cheese tortellini while pregnant?" "Is staring at the moon dangerous?" But, generally, the questions lean broad, even philosophical: "When did you realize you were officially an adult?" "How is life in Libya currently?" "What is the one thing that teachers wish they could tell their students but don't?" The company says there are one hundred million users across the world, all of them burning with questions they don't know where else to take. It was founded on the same premise on which John Dunton founded the *Athenian Mercury*—"concealing the Querist and answering his question." The people posing the questions on Quora tend to remain anonymous, while those answering them have some kind of public-facing identity that may or may not be consistent with who they are offline. All social media sites have personalities: Facebook is the arrogant jock who never does the reading but talks at length anyway; Twitter is the brainy, type A student who started preparing for the SATs in eighth grade; Instagram is the cool girl who's somehow impossible to dislike; Reddit is the taunted nerd preparing for world domination. Quora is the sensitive one who sings in the choir and journals compulsively. It's where the internet goes to be earnest.

Anyone can answer a question on Quora. Every now and again someone famous will reply: you can request Sheryl Sandberg or Hillary Clinton to tell you how to rally your confidence before a big presentation and they just might answer. Vinod Khosla and Keith Rabois, famous venture capitalists, may respond to your question about pitching investors, or Jimmy Wales, one of the founders of Wikipedia, may answer your questions about how to launch a website. But most of the replies are written by people whose celebrity begins and ends on Quora. They are users who have answered hundreds, if not thousands, of questions and have developed an expertise in particular areas, like "dogs," "planetary science," "the World," or "creation." If they're particularly prolific, they may be given the honorific of "Top Writer," which comes with swag, like fleeces and messenger bags, and invitations to events in New York and Mountain View, California. Quora is not a place for people who need their advice-givers vetted by their favorite paper or their favorite celebrity. Rather, it's for readers who instinctively trust people more than they do institutions. With the Athenian Society, John Dunton played up his intellectual pedigree, but on Quora, that kind of pretentiousness might be a liability. It's a world where intimacy is the most prized currency.

Most Top Writers have two or maybe three areas of expertise. But Mike King is a Top Writer in fifty subjects, including "Mental Health," "Psychiatry," "Ex-Boyfriends and Ex-Girlfriends," "Empathy," "Life Advice," and "Long Beach, California." He has written more than eleven thousand posts, and while Quora does not officially rank users across categories, a company representative told me that King was likely the most prolific contributor the site has ever had. While most Quora authors list only a couple credentials on their page, King lists twenty-seven. He describes himself as a retired psychologist who holds a PhD and who has worked as a counselor for teen runaways and as an epidemiologist at the Centers for Disease Control and Prevention. He also describes himself as an "Infantry paratrooper (no hero)" and a "Semi-retired dirt kicker and feeder of stray cats Still In The Game" (capitalization his). Every author has a fixed bio page, but every time you answer a question you're prompted to write a one-line bio, like "Teenager, fried chicken lover, and self proclaimed egotist" or "Stay-at-home, hands on mom, trying to raise productive little humans." Most people keep their bios consistent; King carefully tailors his credentials to the question. He'll identify as having "twenty years investing experience" when offering a stock tip, or as a "follower of the 2016 election campaign" when replying to a question about Donald Trump. He responds, on average, to about ten questions each day, even on weekends. Occasionally, he goes on an empathy bender. On March 21, 2017, for instance, he replied to thirty questions, including:

> "Every time I sleep, I wake up with shortness of breath and a tight throat and chest feeling. Are these symptoms of anxiety or something more serious?"
>
> "What are the cons and pros of my employer knowing that I am diagnosed with a mental illness?"
>
> "My mother says she feels lost, and her head feels empty as if she doesn't know what she's supposed to do on a daily basis, what does this mean?"
>
> "I'm 25 never been in a relationship and never held a job for more than 4+ months. I'm about to graduate university but I feel worthless. What can I do?"
>
> "Should I let my girlfriend go to senior ball with her friend?"

"My moms brother had a kid but didn't marry the person. Then
she remarried and has a step son now can I date that person?"
"I get along with teachers, but not my peers. Is there something
wrong with me?"

The remaining twenty-three questions concerned suicidal thoughts,
narcissistic personality disorder, bipolar disorder, getting back together with an ex, and Donald Trump. King has advised people
to leave their partners, stay with their partners, go to therapy with
their partners, and he has sent dozens of people the number for a
suicide hotline. I showed King's profile to a friend who works as a
children's social worker, who regularly loses sleep over her clients.
After flipping through his responses, she concluded that his advice
was measured and warm and that he had volunteered himself to
roughly three times her caseload. Since joining Quora three years
ago, King's posts have been viewed 9.1 million times. He has also
posted about a dozen questions, most of them about cats or Quora
itself: "What do you do if you know a person is lying on Quora?" "I
brought my new cat home from the shelter and she keeps sneezing.
What's happening?"

There's no money to be made on Quora. It "pays in exposure,"
as the tech millionaires like to tell the rest of us. Popularity on
Quora does not necessarily transfer to popularity elsewhere: King,
for instance, has only a couple hundred followers on Twitter.
Quora, unlike Twitter, Facebook, or Instagram, offers few opportunities for self-aggrandizement; there's no place to brag or fish for
compliments or "likes," no chance at a corporate sponsorship. The
only tangible validation the site offers is "upvotes," which is when
a reader thinks a response deserves to be placed near the top of
the page, where the most people will see it. But it's not *you* being
voted on; it's the pertinence of your answer and the quality of your
advice. "We're not really focused on people promoting themselves,"
Adam D'Angelo, Quora's thirty-three-year-old founder, said in an
interview. "On Quora, you're not answering questions because you

want to get points or because you have nothing else to do. You're answering questions because you want to build your reputation or you genuinely, intrinsically enjoy helping people."

King has a plainspoken, almost folksy writing style. "I'm sorry you're feeling bad," he told the restless twenty-five-year-old who was about to graduate from college; he passed along a hotline for a nearby clinic. In his profile photo, King appears somewhat thunderstruck, his eyes peeled open and his lips pursed. He has gray hair and a matching handlebar mustache, and he wears oversized wire-rim glasses. He's photographed in what appears to be a cramped closet—above his shoulder are shelves overstuffed with shoeboxes and half a dozen hanging shirts. Who, I wondered, was this man in a closet who had quietly and without fanfare devoted himself to the complicated problems of strangers? And were Quora users right to trust him?

KING AND I corresponded by Facebook for a while and he agreed to talk by phone. I assumed, based on his areas of expertise, that he lived in Long Beach. But he lived in Nevada, ten miles southeast of Vegas, with his cat, who had recovered from the sneeze she'd brought home from the shelter. King named her Chelsea Handler in homage to the raunchy comedian. "She's very feisty!" he told me. "I've had her for six weeks and she's been quite a challenge, going through some illnesses with her and some strange psychological things, but she's pulled through it!" His voice was eager and high-pitched, like that of a child who's spotted an ice cream truck.

King wakes up every morning at 3 a.m., makes himself a mug of hot cocoa, lets out Chelsea Handler, starts his computer, and signs in to Quora. He answers questions for three hours and then heads back to bed for a few more hours of rest. After his midmorning sleep, he runs errands, makes breakfast, and plays with Chelsea Handler. When it's nice out, he'll ride his motorcycle to town. By the afternoon, he's back in front of the computer. He remains there, answering questions, breaking for the bathroom or when he needs a nap or snack, until he heads to sleep at eight. "It's been a full-time job for me," King said. "It started to be an addiction." After you post a question on Quora, a drop-down menu appears on screen that prompts you to request a reply from a specific Quora user. King receives about twenty-five requests a day. "I answered twenty-eight last night and twenty-six the night before," he said the first time we spoke. "I have a hard time saying no." It takes him two hours, on average, to craft a response. "People are insistent on quality. Everything you do, they want it to be researched and they want it to be well-written," he said.

In the mid-1960s, King trained as a paratrooper in Fort Benning, Georgia. During an exercise, he landed on a fence post that punctured his left leg. "I'm all connected up with rods and stuff," he said. He was in a wheelchair for a while but now walks independently and is more mobile than he appears. "I have a limp and people automatically open the door for me, and suddenly I'm an infant and it's like, here, 'Let me pick you up and carry you around the store.'" He can drive, ride a motorcycle. He even taught himself to ride a bike with one leg.

But some days, it can feel like he's drowning in pain. He's seventy and has arthritis in his knees, elbows, and hands. There are days he can't type, when all he can do is lie down and rest. On those days, he said, he can get short-tempered and lash out at someone for their insistence on existing. When that happens, he's happy he retired, as much as he loved working as a counselor. "It was never a hard job for me; it always came naturally to me. I got good strokes from it," he said. On Quora, he can control his schedule. "I can quit any time, take a break, take a nap," he said. "I'm at a stage in my life when I recognize my limitations." He said he gets "good strokes" from Quora, too.

After his accident, King accepted a job as an epidemiologist with the Centers for Disease Control and Prevention. He traveled across the states, studying the spread of syphilis. By night, he earned a PhD in psychology. He wrote his dissertation on addiction and codependency. It was called *What's the Fantasy Behind That Smile?*, and it was published in 1983. He left the CDC and began counseling families dealing with substance abuse. "Families are neglected when it comes to treatment," King said. He speaks from personal experience. His mother was an addict and abandoned him and his sister for much of their childhood. King saw a therapist weekly for fifteen years. But he doesn't like talking about that, or writing about himself at all on Quora. "I don't need catharsis anymore. I've had enough of catharsis! I don't need insight anymore."

King is in the minority on this front. Quora, like any forum on the internet, inspires a lot of confessional, diaristic writing. Most of the people who answer questions tend to write from their own experience, about their own breakups or battles with depression. There's one Top Writer named Athena Walker who identifies as a psychotic. People tend to ask her whether they're psychotic, if their spouse, boss, or parent is psychotic, and what it's like inside her brain. "Can a psychopath feel pity for himself?" a Quora user asked her recently. No, Walker wrote. "I have no empathy for anyone. That includes myself."

King dislikes confessional writing; he finds it gratuitous. "People want to hear the gore, about body parts and blood, and I don't write for that kind of audience," he said. His approach is more clinical. He'll often encourage people to seek professional treatment or attend an Al-Anon meeting, a support group for the families of addicts. "I try to steer them in the right direction, to see a therapist, to get a book, to do something different," he said.

King has four children of his own, two daughters and two sons. They all live in Southern California and he doesn't see them much. The boys are married; the girls are not and live with their mother on a ranch overlooking a lake. I asked King if, as a father of four, he often finds himself giving advice in real life—offline. "Nope, not really," he said. His last relationship ended seventeen years ago. His girlfriend was a special-education teacher and quilter, and every year when school got out, they used to load up their truck, a black 1966 GMC, and spend the summer trekking across California and Nevada, sleeping in a tent or in air-conditioned motel rooms if it got too hot. About five years into their relationship, his girlfriend started spending more time at the casinos. She liked blackjack, slots, craps, she didn't discriminate, and when she lost twenty thousand dollars in less than three weeks, King told her she needed help. She didn't want help, she wanted out of the Vegas exurbs, and she moved to Arizona, near Phoenix. King hasn't seen her since. "I've been in three relationships," King said, each of which lasted seven years. "Seven years seems to be my cutoff. Isn't that funny?" he chuckled. I asked him if he'd been alone since his last relationship ended. He told me he'd had a housekeeper for a while but had recently let her go. "It didn't work out. She was pretty narcissistic and was trying to run my life and the way I worked."

On Quora, King specializes in dating and relationships. He also receives questions about parenting, Muslim culture, interpretations of the Bible, and pregnancy scares. "Should I move on from my marriage?" "Should Muslims be allowed to practice Shariah law in western countries?" "Can I name my son or daughter after a superhero?" "Is a pregnancy test still reliable if you didn't urinate on it for 5 seconds?" To the last question, King replied: "Read the instructions. It's highly unlikely a company would market a product that would self destruct in just 5 seconds. There should be a complete set of instructions that came with the kit. Thanks for the request." His responses tend to be brief but heartfelt: "I feel for you and what you have gone through. I can only imagine the pain and how lonely you must feel," he wrote to a man who wanted to know if it was time to move on from his marriage. His wife had left him a year earlier. "Your wife must have been terribly disturbed to leave you and your son and not get in touch. I really am sorry and I think you should move on." His motto, King told me, is "try to leave people with the impression that they're not stupid, even if they are."

King will answer any question that enters his inbox, no matter what it pertains to. The one exception is medical questions. There are women, he said, who will message him describing the consistency and color of their urine, or an unpleasant burning sensation during sex. He'll message these women privately and recommend a visit to the emergency room. "They say, 'I can't talk to my doctor about this.' But they'll talk to Quora! To strangers!"

IN 1987, JEFFREY Zaslow, a journalist at the *Wall Street Journal*, got an assignment from his editor. Ann Landers was stepping down at the *Chicago Sun-Times* and the paper was hosting a contest to find her replacement. Zaslow's editor wanted him to enter the competition and write a breezy, first-person piece about his experience. Zaslow agreed, but he failed to mention that this was more than a story to him: replacing Ann Landers was his dream job.

As part of his reporting, Zaslow sat in as the judges whittled down the 12,000 applicants to 108 semifinalists, and later he learned that he was among the chosen. His application kept getting bumped along as he chronicled the experience in the *Journal*. He won the competition, quit the *Journal,* and took over the column in June of that year. They named it "All That Zazz."

Zaslow was taken aback at first by the severity of problems in the letters addressed to him. People wrote to him because they were depressed and had lost the will to live. "People who can't afford a therapist, don't know one social agency from another, and, in essence, have nowhere else to go. They're lonely, unhappy, or disenfranchised," Zaslow wrote in his memoir, *Tell Me All About It.* They didn't seem to realize who he was: a reporter who'd won an essay competition.

Similarly, many of the people who seek King's support on Quora don't appear to have any other option. They complain that therapy is too expensive or too difficult to reach by public transit; they struggle, for one reason or another, to make it to an Al-Anon meeting. Social media is known as a place where powerless people go to feel powerful, where people who are bullied at school become trolls, where you can tell an actress you hate her face or tell a politician you hate his guts, and they might even see it. The internet that King inhabits, on the other hand, is a place where people are free to admit just how powerless they are. Quora is filled with desperate pleas for help, like "Who do I go to if I have nobody and no money to help me get through depression?" or "Is there any online psychiatrist service (for free)?" The internet is often treated as a consequence-free space, where nothing one writes matters. But the stakes of King's life on Quora are far higher than they are in Nevada. There are people relying on him. He knows that a certain percentage of the questions, especially the dramatic ones, were written by teenagers messing around. But he treats each request like it's a lifeline.

King had recently looked up the other Top Writers in one of his Quora categories, though he couldn't remember which one. "I had 353 answers and the next highest was 30 answers. I'm getting very few views compared to what they're getting," he said. But in most other ways, King is a fairly typical citizen of Quora—emotionally generous, eager to help. There's one user who lives in Bangladesh, holds a MBA, and "loves to help people"; he's written thoughtful responses on questions ranging from "How do you defeat depression in your own life?" to "How does it feel when you miss your mother?" Dozens, sometimes hundreds of people weigh in on questions like "How do you tell people that you want be alone?" "What are the five most important things for a man to learn in life?" or "How do I forgive myself for staying in an unhealthy relationship?" There was this question: "I binge ate 2000 calories today. What should I do?" More than a hundred people explained that two thousand calories a day was a normal and healthy diet.

Even after the question was exposed as a hoax, written by some known Quora troll, people kept replying, using the opportunity to issue generalized warnings about eating disorders. Everyone seemed to want the last word, to be the Quora user who knew best. Quora is not a competitive space except when it comes to kindness.

A large percentage of the questions appear to come from teenagers, who have happened upon the most eager collection of mentors in the world, a virtual village of doting godparents. The difference, of course, is that Quora users are strangers. A widely known rule of the internet is that few things come as advertised. It's up to you—the reader—to decide whether to trust the Quora user who "loves to help people" or who claims to be a millionaire or psychopath or therapist.

There are no binds to the advice one solicits online. No one checks up to make sure you broke up with the terrible boyfriend or apologized to your mother; no one can be offended if you choose a different path. No one's watching. It's free advice in every sense of the word—an unlimited shopping spree in the superstore of wisdom. King told me that the most satisfying moments of his time on Quora are when someone follows up, weeks or months after he's answered their question. "Someone will write and say how well they're doing. It's always nice to hear that they changed their life." But mostly, King helps people he won't hear from ever again. He has no way of knowing if the people he meets on Quora follow his advice, if they're well, or alive, or even real.

D'Angelo, Quora's founder, has said that the majority of Quora's users don't post questions or answer them. They're there to observe. "When we first started, we thought that Quora was going to be a place where people come when they have a question and where they come when they want to write answers. It turned out that the most popular thing among the users was not asking questions or writing answers, but just reading answers that were already there," D'Angelo said in an interview with *Recode.* Zaslow found that the best part of being an advice columnist was the stories. "Few other jobs allow such access to real life in America," he wrote in his memoir. Quora has opened that particular perk to everyone. King and a few others do the work so the rest of the internet can be voyeurs.

KING WARNED ME that I might be surprised by the way he acts offline. He's much goofier in person, he said, more sarcastic, even "edgy." (Quora is quick to suspend users for inappropriate comments and King is careful not to offend anyone. "They want people to be courteous to each other," he said.) I told him that I struggled to imagine this, how a person who spent his retirement showering anonymous strangers with empathy, who wrote "I'm sorry" that many times a day, could ever be edgy. He didn't offer any examples, or at least none I found convincing. He'd told me that his idea of a fun afternoon was people-watching at the local dollar store and buying a gag gift to bring home.

King evaded questions about his father's family, his time in the military, and his schooling. "Don't want identifying information out there. Been burned twice," he wrote me in a Facebook message. He sent me a few woozy, late-night messages, mostly about Chelsea Handler (the cat), each of them written as if he'd never mentioned her before. "Ran away . . . pooped in my bed. Now she's depressed. I stayed up all night loving her last night and today she is under the bed. Anyway. Vet doesnt know. I will keep loving her anyway. Her name is Chelsea Handler."

I thought about paying King a visit but decided not to. I also thought about calling his children and ex-girlfriend and decided against that as well. What if they told me he was a terrible father? What if I found King creepy or cruel? There were millions of people on Quora who depended on him. They had questions like, "What's the point of life?" "What does it feel like to be an unattractive woman?" and "How do husbands remain faithful to their wives?" And without King, and a few others like him, there would be nothing but a silent majority cruising for answers.

Conclusion

WHENEVER I TELL SOMEONE THAT I'M WRITING A BOOK about American advice-givers, they inevitably ask if I'm writing about someone I'd never heard of. "I love Carolyn Hax," they say. Or, "Do you listen to Delilah?"

"I'll check them out," I reply, and sometimes I mean it. I leave these conversations feeling guilty and lazy—I should know these people!—and wondering why I ever took on such a boundless topic. This book could easily have twenty more chapters, or fifty. I have obviously not included chapters on Carolyn Hax or Delilah. (But I do know who they are!) I also haven't said much, if anything, about Dr. Ruth, Dr. Drew, Beatrix Fairfax, Muriel Nissen, Ask Polly, Dan Savage, or Gwyneth Paltrow, among many others.

Paltrow, who stopped acting some years ago to focus on her website, GOOP, is a modern-day Miss Lonelyhearts, dispensing advice she's in no place to give. She has no background in health care but peddles nebulous medical treatments that carry the promise of beauty and "wellness." She has, for instance, recommended that

GOOP readers insert jade stones into their vaginas to "detox" their reproductive systems. In response, a gynecologist wrote a blog post imploring women not to buy and use these stones, which could put them at risk of toxic shock syndrome. Paltrow said these concerns were totally unfounded, and the stones remain on sale at GOOP's website for sixty-six dollars apiece.

This is the stereotypical narrative of an advice-giver: a guru makes her fortune preying upon gullible Americans with money to spare. There are indeed many unqualified people with potent megaphones providing disturbing instructions on how to live. Facebook has attempted to distinguish "real" journalists from "fake" journalists to prevent made-up stories from going viral. But advice-giving, unlike journalism, is a practice and not a profession. Advice can come from everywhere—a gym teacher, a woman you overhear on the subway, your uncle Bert. It cannot be regulated or measured objectively; good advice to one person is terrible advice to another.

It's not dangerous to enjoy an advice column, but it is dangerous to automatically believe whatever someone says. None of the people I've profiled should be categorized as wholesale gurus or as utter quacks. I've tried to present advice-givers as an empathic, ambitious, complicated class of people, and I hope other writers examine the figures I've left out.

There used to be a handful of advice-givers that all Americans listened to. But today, the country is more divided with everyone retreating to their like-minded corners of the internet where they can find advice that suits them. But even the contemporary advice-givers in this book hope to reach a mass audience. Like Samuel Wells, the nineteenth-century etiquette writer, they want to inspire the "spontaneous recognition of human solidarity." Advice-givers tend to be populists and they use the same set of tactics to draw a plurality of people to their side. It was John Dunton's idea to offer his readers the cover of anonymity. Advice, more than any other genre, requires a high level of audience participation, and by "concealing the Querist," Dunton discovered a way to trick readers into delivering copy. Benjamin Franklin, Dear Abby, and Ann Landers realized that sarcasm was one of the more effective ways to get people to take you seriously. William Alcott recognized that diets can be a spiritual practice. Dorothy Dix and Mike King after her understood the power of the phrase "I'm sorry," while Dale Carnegie saw the appeal of endless encouragement. Sylvia Porter recognized that Americans prefer financial wizzes who talk like their local bartender. Mildred Newman argued that there was nothing superficial about self-gratification. Dr. Spock determined that the best-received advice isn't prescriptive but rather empowers readers to make their own choices. Elisabeth Kübler-Ross had an open relationship with scientific convention, toggling between academic research and conversations with ghosts and fairies—a tradition that Martha Beck has continued. Joan Quigley's relationship with Nancy Reagan illuminates the particular comforts of astrology. Hendrix and Hunt reveal snippets from their own relationship as evidence that their theory works.

The works of these advice-givers highlight the emotional landscape at different moments in history. In fact, their advice—and the debates they sparked among fans and enemies—offers us a history of American culture wars. In the 1770s, Chesterfield's letters offended many readers who considered stifling one's true feelings a sign of cowardice, not to mention an affront to the American way. In the 1960s, Dear Abby and Ann Landers scrunched all their advice into witty, quotable one-liners, attempting to make light of the fact that America seemed to be going to hell. Kübler-Ross made it socially permissible to talk about death at a time when the bereaved were told to mourn in silence. In 2016, after the inauguration of President Trump, Judith Martin begged readers to embrace higher levels of self-censorship.

Advice-giving is a job that requires, above all, a willingness to be proven wrong. Advice-givers are people employed to shape social rules though they are aware that these rules will soon be outdated. The most successful advice-givers admit when they've changed their minds: Dr. Spock recognized that his views on gender roles were old-fashioned and Ann Landers publicly reckoned with the fact that divorce was sometimes unavoidable. We need advice-givers in America because we need people who are curious (or fame-hungry) enough to determine the current guardrails of civilization. It's a job that usually falls to politicians or some other kind of expert, but advice-givers, with their collaborative ethos, ever-changing opinions, and precarious claims to authority, are reminders that these social codes are not set in stone, that they're supposed to evolve with time. "Manners is the basic bargain of civilization. I will try not to annoy you to the point of violence or retaliation if you will do the same for me," Miss Manners said in a 2006 interview on *The Colbert Report*. Advice-givers have a reputation for social conservatism, but the very existence of the profession, a class of people tasked with defining and redefining cultural norms, should ideally prevent norms from becoming entrenched and ensure that these social bargains are renegotiated every generation. Advice-givers recognize that we're not meant to date, raise our children, and mourn in the same exact ways our parents did. They don't give stump speeches about preserving American values; they understand that the most supreme American value of all is an openness to change.

The advice offered in the *Athenian Mercury* has little in common with what one finds on Quora or hears from life coaches like Martha Beck. The *Athenian Mercury* was designed to create a social playbook, rules of engagement that applied to every last Londoner, while today's advice tends to be more individuated, giving people the tools they need to self-actualize—to "find themselves," as we say. The advice-givers have changed; they've shifted from distant authority figures to complicated individuals who are still sorting out the answers themselves. But the people seeking their advice are still, centuries later, struggling to find love, unsure what love even *is*, lonely, uncertain, and burning with questions so intimate and humiliating that they can only be shared with a stranger.

Acknowledgments

THIS BOOK WOULD NOT HAVE BEEN POSSIBLE WITHOUT the tremendous editors of Nation Books, Katy O'Donnell and Alessandra Bastagli. Thank you both for your patience, thoughtfulness, and various improvements to the manuscript. Thanks as well to all their dedicated colleagues at Hachette, especially Melissa Veronesi, my copy editor, Erin Granville, and my publicist Kristina Fazzarlo. I'm also grateful to my agent, Nathaniel Jacks, who was a great source of support at every stage of the book-writing process.

Portions of the book first appeared on the *New Yorker*'s website, where they were edited by the brilliant Sasha Weiss. Much of the chapter on Harville Hendrix and Helen Hunt first appeared in *Pacific Standard* magazine, where it was deftly edited by T. A. Frank and Maria Streshinsky and doggedly fact-checked by Paul Bisceglio.

Speaking of advice, Kathryn Schultz, Elizabeth Little, and Alia Malek offered generous quantities of it as I was first setting out. Michele Choy managed to perform essential research while also working two other jobs and preparing for graduate school. Rob Weiner and the Chinati Foundation gave me a room of my own when I most needed one.

In my research, I consulted primary sources as much as possible, but I also relied on the scholarship and reporting of many great historians and journalists. I am particularly grateful for the work of Lili Loofbourow, Walter Isaacson, Adam D. Shprintzen, Jan Pottker, Bob Speziale, Thomas Maier, Steven Watts, Tracy Lucht, Barbara Ehrenreich, Deirdre English, and Peter N. Stearns. I urge everyone reading this to seek out their work.

Thanks to Mom, Dad, Cary, Tracy, Lindsay, Sandra, and Fiona and the many friends who plied me with encouragement and snacks as I hunkered down.

This book is dedicated to Ben, my husband. Thank you for pushing me to write this book in the first place and bearing with me as I did, for your inspiring kindness, your curious and magnificent mind, and for being my partner in every sense.

Notes

Preface

2 **hundreds of thousands of people signed one for the first time:** Robert Ian Dowbiggin, *A Merciful End: The Euthanasia Movement in Modern America* (New York: Oxford University Press, 2004), 121.

3 **eleven billion dollars a year on self-help books:** Melanie Lindner, "What People Are Still Willing to Pay For," *Forbes*, January 15, 2009.

3 **"Here's Sound Advice: Write a Book, Become Rich":** Dan Ackman and Jeff Bauer, "Here's Sound Advice: Write Book, Become Rich," *Forbes*, May 13, 2003.

4 **"look for newer and fresher paths":** Nathanael West, *Miss Lonelyhearts and The Day of the Locusts* (New York: New Directions, 1950), 4.

4 **"Her sureness was based on the power to limit experience arbitrarily":** Ibid., 11.

4 **four of Trump's companies had filed for bankruptcy:** Michelle Lee, "Fact Check: Has Trump Declared Bankruptcy Four or Six Times?" *Washington Post*, September 26, 2016, www.washingtonpost .com/politics/2016/live-updates/general-election/real-time-fact -checking-and-analysis-of-the-first-presidential-debate/fact-check -has-trump-declared-bankruptcy-four-or-six-times/.

5 **If you were looking for straightforward advice, Sugar was not the person to turn to:** Much of this paragraph is taken from my article "The Advice Columnist We Deserve," *The New Yorker,* October 9, 2012.

5 **"sweet arrogant beautiful crazy talented tortured rising star glowbug":** Cheryl Strayed [Sugar], "Dear Sugar #48: "Write Like a Motherfucker," The Rumpus, August 19, 2010, therumpus .net/2010/08/dear-sugar-the-rumpus-advice-column-48-write-like -a-motherfucker/.

6 **"WTF, WTF, WTF?":** Cheryl Strayed [Sugar], "Dear Sugar #39: "The Baby Bird,"The Rumpus, June 3, 2010, therumpus.net/2010/06 /dear-sugar-the-rumpus-advice-column-39-the-baby-bird/.

6 **"I don't have a definite question for you":** Cheryl Strayed [Sugar], "Dear Sugar #78: The Obliterated Place,"The Rumpus, July 1, 2011, therumpus.net/2011/07/dear-sugar-the-rumpus-advice-column -78-the-obliterated-place/.

6 **"strange stirring, a sense of dissatisfaction":** Betty Friedan, *The Feminine Mystique,* 50th anniversary ed. (New York: W. W. Norton, 2013), 11.

6 **"How painful":** Cheryl Strayed [Sugar], "Dear Sugar #76: The Woman Hanging on the End of the Line," The Rumpus, June 16, 2011, therumpus.net/2011/06/dear-sugar-the-rumpus-advice -column-76-the-woman-hanging-on-the-end-of-a-line/.

6 **"suffering is what happens when truly horrible things happen to us":** Cheryl Strayed [Sugar], "Dear Sugar #44: How You Get Unstuck," The Rumpus, July 15, 2010, therumpus.net/2010/07 /dear-sugar-the-rumpus-advice-column-44-how-you-get-unstuck/.

PART ONE: OLD, WISE MEN

12 **diet heavy in barley:** Plato, *The Republic,* trans. G. H. Wells (London: George Bell and Sons, 1887), 13.

Chapter 1: *In Praise of the Maggot,* John Dunton

16 **"table, where the victuals were ill-sorted and worse dressed":** Quoted in John Boyer Nichols, introduction to John Dunton, *The Life and Errors of John Dunton, Citizen of London* (London: J. Nichols, Son & Bently, 1818), v.

16 **"For I had a thousand little things to say":** Ibid., 23.

16 **"I have been a Rambler ever since I was 14 years Old"**: Quoted in Gilbert D. McEwan, *The Oracle of the Coffee House: John Dunton's "Athenian Mercury"* (Kingsport, TN: Kingsport Press, 1972), 15.

17 **"I began to love books to the same excess that I hated them before"**: Dunton, *Life and Errors*, 43.

17 **one of his top sellers**: Ibid., ix.

17 **"conscious reader of public tastes and trends"**: J. Paul Hunter, *Before Novels: The Cultural Contexts of Eighteenth-Century English Fiction* (New York: W. W. Norton, 1934), 318.

17 **"Were I to begin the Trade of Bookselling once again"**: Ibid., 72.

17 **would "not exchange [it] for Fifty Guineas"**: Dunton, *Life and Errors*, 188.

17 **"concealing the Querist and answering his question"**: Dunton, *Life and Errors*, 188.

18 **"unwilling to lay out a shilling or a crown on a Journal of Travels"**: Quoted in McEwan, *The Oracle of the Coffee House*, 15–16.

18 **"lovers of Novelty"**: Hunter, *Before Novels*, 105.

19 **"The Design is briefly, to satisfy all ingenious and curious Enquirers"**: Quoted in McEwan, *The Oracle of the Coffee House*, 23.

19 **"Whether all souls are alike?"**: *The Athenian Oracle, Being an Entire Collection of All the Valuable Questions and Answers in the Old Athenian Mercuries* (1704; repr. Memphis, TN: General Books, 2012), 5.

20 ***These* were supposed to be the men answering the questions**: "'The Athenian Mercury': The World's First Advice Column," Professor Carmichael's Cabinet of Curiosities (blog), n.d., http://carmichaels cabinetofcuriosities.blogspot.com/2013/02/the-athenian-mercury -worlds-first.html.

20 **There was one reader who'd had a dream about a comet**: *The Athenian Oracle*, 12.

20 **"Pull 'em by the Nose"**: *The Athenian Oracle*, 18.

20 **consummating a marriage was stressful for everyone**: Quoted in Lili Loofbourow, "Dear Athenian Mercury: Questions and Answers from the First Advice Column in English," The Awl, March 28, 2011, www.theawl.com/2011/03/dear-athenian-mercury-questions -and-answers-from-the-first-advice-column-in-english/.

20 **"Whether I had not best immediately marry her"**: *The Athenian Oracle*, 245.

21 **There was a man who saw no point or pleasure in kissing**: Quoted in Lili Loofbourow, "Dear Athenian Mercury: The Non-Reproductive

Sex Issue," The Awl, April, 21, 2011, www.theawl.com/2011/04
/dear-athenian-mercury-the-non-reproductive-sex-issue/.

21 **over their six years, they published nearly six thousand:** McEwan,
The Oracle of the Coffee House, 3.

21 **"Send no more Obscene Questions":** Quoted in Loofbourow,
"Dear Athenian Mercury: Questions and Answers from the First
Advice Column in English."

21 **"Some *Questions* . . . we think not proper to take any notice of":**
Quoted in Joanna Picciotto, *Labors of Innocence in Early Modern England* (Cambridge, MA: Harvard University Press, 2010), 311.

21 **in love with a woman promised to another, much older man:** *The
Athenian Oracle,* 85.

21 **wanted to know if he was allowed to take a third:** Ibid., 93.

21 **why women preferred soldiers to intellectuals:** Ibid., 183.

22 **"Roguing here won't do because it has too large a Signification":**
Ibid., 210.

22 **The *London Mercury*, one of the parody rags, reprinted all the
questions:** McEwan, *The Oracle of the Coffee House,* 36.

22 **"When shall I be marry'd?":** Quoted in Lili Loofbourow, "The
Mouse That Crawled Up Inside a Man, and Other Urban Leg-
ends of the 17th Century," The Awl, June 3, 2011, www.theawl
.com/2011/06/the-mouse-that-crawled-up-inside-a-man-and
-other-urban-legends-of-the-17th-century/.

22 **a woman who wanted to know if she should tell her fiancé she was
a virgin:** Alison Adburgham, *Women in Print: Writing Women and
Women's Magazines from the Restoration to the Accession of Victoria*
(London: Faber and Faber, 2012), 23.

23 **"Oh, who could stand the stress of so much Light!":** *The Athenian
Oracle,* 97.

23 **"Such a friendship is not only innocent but commendable":** *The
Athenian Oracle,* 26.

24 **"According to Aristotle, this may proceed from the double Motion
of the Matter of Hairs":** *The Athenian Mercury,* vol. 20, June 14, 1697.
Courtesy of Brian Cowan.

24 **"first wife in a new edition":** Dunton, *Life and Errors,* 529.

24 **"a most Voluminous writer":** Ibid., v.

24 **"My first great care under the relation of Apprenticeship":** Ibid., 50.

25 **"Long before I had any articulate use of my tongue":** Ibid., 23.

25 **"There is nothing here without which English literature has suffered"**: Cecil A. Moore, "John Dunton, Pietist and Impostor," *Studies in Philology* 22, no. 4 (October 1925): 467–499. Courtesy of Lili Loofbourow.

Chapter 2: *Politeness vs. Honesty, Part 1*, Lord Chesterfield

27 **"plain almost to ugliness"**: Philip Stanhope, *The Letters of the Earl of Chesterfield to His Son*, vol. 1 (1744; repr. New York: G. P. Putnam's Sons, 1901), xliv.

27 **one for "gallantry" and the other for "attachment"**: Philip Stanhope, *Lord Chesterfield's Letters* (1744; repr. Oxford: Oxford University Press, 1992), xvi.

28 **when she gave birth to his brother:** James Manning and Archer Ryland, *Reports of Cases Argued and Determined in the Court of King's Bench, During Michaelmas Term, Eighth Geo. IV.* [1827–30] (London: S. Sweet, 1831), 106.

28 **"Admit me to your fireside"**: Stanhope, *The Letters of the Earl of Chesterfield*, vol. 2, 264.

28 **James Dodsley, a top English publisher:** Jenny Davidson, *Hypocrisy and the Politics of Politeness: Manners and Morals from Locke to Austen* (Cambridge: Cambridge University Press, 2004), 56.

29 **"looked like a stunted giant"**: William Henry Craig, *Life of Lord Chesterfield* (London: John Lane the Bodley Head, 1907), 79.

29 **"more conversible entertaining table-wit of any man of his time"**: Ibid., 80.

29 **"not above thirty could understand reason"**: Stanhope, *The Letters of the Earl of Chesterfield*, vol. 2, 328.

30 **"no mark of age or passion, envy, hate or discontent"**: Charles Dickens, *Barnaby Rudge and Hard Times* (Boston: Ticknor and Fields, 1867), 184.

30 **"Lord Chesterfield rarely or never acted on impulse"**: Craig, *Life of Lord Chesterfield*, 57.

31 **"I have been pushing on my work through difficulties"**: James Boswell, *The Life of Samuel Johnson*, vol. 1 (1791; repr. London: George Routledge and Sons, 1865), 145.

31 **"as perfect as the imperfections of human nature will allow"**: Stanhope, *The Letters of the Earl of Chesterfield*, vol. 1, 385.

32 "I am told you speak very quick and not distinctly": Ibid., 221.

32 "I have lately had extraordinary good accounts of you": Ibid., 359.

32 "Dress yourself fine where others are fine": Ibid., 306.

32 "Lord Chesterfield had two admirable qualities": Craig, *Life of Lord Chesterfield*, 97.

33 "Nothing is more engaging than a cheerful and easy conformity": Stanhope, *The Letters of the Earl of Chesterfield*, vol. 2, 204.

33 "Be serious with the serious": Ibid., 232.

33 "Perhaps you will say that it is impossible to please everybody": Ibid., 279.

33 "You cannot, and I'm sure you do not think yourself superior by nature": Ibid., 277.

33 "there are no persons so insignificant and inconsiderable": Ibid., vol. 1, 240.

33 "Every woman who is not absolutely ugly thinks herself handsome": Ibid., 262.

33 pretentious words like *namely:* Philip Stanhope, *The Letters of Philip Dormer Stanhope, Earl of Chesterfield*, vol. 4 (London: R. Bentley, 1845), 122.

34 "Talk often": Stanhope, *The Letters of the Earl of Chesterfield*, vol. 1, 281.

34 "I do not regret the time that I passed in pleasures": Ibid., 203.

34 "They teach the morals of a whore": Quoted in Boswell, *The Life of Samuel Johnson*, 202.

35 "I have no quarrel with the graces": Mercy Otis Warren, "A Letter from an American Lady to Her Son," *Boston Magazine*, June 1784.

35 "purity of sentiment": G. J. Barker-Benfield, *Abigail and John Adams: The Americanization of Sensibility* (Chicago: University of Chicago Press, 2010), 57–58.

36 "man of quality who never recovered from the ridicule": Stanhope, *The Letters of the Earl of Chesterfield*, vol. 2, 92.

36 many American parents reminded their own teenage children: Lorri Glover, *Southern Sons: Becoming Men in the New Nation* (Baltimore, MD: Johns Hopkins University Press, 2007), 87.

37 "Probity, virtue, honor": Quoted in Michael Kimmel, *Manhood in America: A Cultural History* (Oxford: Oxford University Press, 2011), 11–13.

38 "congruence between avowal and actual feeling": Lionel Trilling,

Sincerity and Authenticity (Cambridge, MA: Harvard University Press, 1972), 2.

38 **"I would much rather have the assent of your reason":** Stanhope, *The Letters of the Earl of Chesterfield*, vol. 1, 189.

39 **Americans were "frequently more sincere" than the French:** Alexis de Tocqueville, *Democracy in America, Book 2*, trans. Arthur Goldhammer (New York: Library of America, 2004), 713.

39 **"For most people, 'be yourself' is actually terrible advice":** Adam Grant, "Unless You're Oprah, Be Yourself Is Terrible Advice," *New York Times*, June 5, 2016.

40 **"Americans of all ages, all conditions, all minds constantly unite":** Tocqueville, *Democracy in America, Book 2*, 595.

40 **"His Serene Highness," "His Magistracy," and "His Elective Magisty":** Judith Martin, *Star-Spangled Manners: In Which Miss Manners Defends American Etiquette (For a Change)* (New York: W. W. Norton, 2003), 65.

40 **"truly American and republican school of politeness":** Samuel Wells, *How to Behave: A Pocket Manual of Republican Etiquette* (1857; repr. Amazon Digital Services, 2011).

41 **"Take, rather than give, the tone of the company you are in":** Stanhope, *The Letters of the Earl of Chesterfield*, vol. 1, 281.

Chapter 3: *Funny Business*, Benjamin Franklin

43 **"Diligence is the mother of good luck . . .":** Benjamin Franklin, *Poor Richard's Almanack* (1732; repr. Seedbox Press, 2011), Kindle edition, "On Money and Business."

44 **"A Penny saved is Twopence clear":** Ibid.

44 **"Where there's marriage without love, there will be love without marriage":** Ibid., "On Love, Marriage, and Family."

44 **"No Piece can properly be called good":** Benjamin Franklin, "On Literary Style," *Pennsylvania Gazette*, August 2, 1733.

44 **ten thousand copies:** James Srodes, *Benjamin Franklin: The Essential Founding Father* (Washington, DC: Regnery History, 2003), 66.

44 **more than the Bible:** Walter Isaacson, *Benjamin Franklin: An American Life* (New York: Simon and Schuster, 2004), 95.

44 **"I consider'd it as a proper vehicle for conveying instruction":** Benjamin Franklin, *The Autobiography of Benjamin Franklin* (1818; repr. Carlisle, MA: Applewood Books, 2008), 144.

45 **"I shall endeavor to enliven Morality with Wit, and to temper Wit with Morality":** Quoted in Isaacson, *Benjamin Franklin,* 28.

45 **"a hankering for the sea":** Franklin, *Autobiography,* 15.

46 **"those who were traveling thither were little better than dunces":** "Silence Dogood, No. 4," *New-England Courant,* May 14, 1722, The Papers of Benjamin Franklin, American Philosophical Society and Yale University / Packard Humanities Institute, franklinpapers.org.

46 **"A Man compounded of Law and Gospel, is able to cheat a whole Country":** "Silence Dogood, No. 5," *New-England Courant,* July 23, 1722, The Papers of Benjamin Franklin, American Philosophical Society and Yale University / Packard Humanities Institute, franklinpapers.org.

46 **"aversion to arbitrary power":** Franklin, *Autobiography,* 26.

47 **"make an Example of him for his Immodesty":** "Martha Careful and Caelia Shortface," *American Weekly Mercury,* January 28, 1729, The Papers of Benjamin Franklin, American Philosophical Society and Yale University / Packard Humanities Institute, franklinpapers.org.

47 **"Generality of People, now a days, are unwilling either to commend or dispraise":** "Silence Dogood, No. 1," *New-England Courant,* April 2, 1722, The Papers of Benjamin Franklin, American Philosophical Society and Yale University / Packard Humanities Institute, franklinpapers.org.

48 **"The Casuist" told him to "return not evil for evil, but repay evil with good":** Isaacson, *Benjamin Franklin,* 69.

48 **"Temperance, Eat not to dullness . . . ":** Franklin, *Autobiography,* 126–127.

49 **"I made a little book, in which I allotted a page for each of the virtues":** Ibid., 128.

49 **"If I have been a useful citizen, the public owes the advantage of it to that book":** Isaacson, *Benjamin Franklin,* 26.

51 **"Work expands so as to fill the time available":** C. Northcote Parkinson, *Parkinson's Law and Other Studies in Administration* (Boston: Houghton Mifflin, 1957), 2.

51 **The committee, he wrote, "takes root and grows":** Ibid., 33.

51 **"The more elaborate and expensive pieces of office machinery are seldom power symbols":** Michael Korda, *Power!: How to Get It, How to Use It* (New York: Ballantine Books, 1975), 220.

51 **there was a noted rush on blue suits and blue office furnishings:**

Michael Korda. *Another Life: A Memoir of Other People* (New York: Random House, 2000), 333.

52 **"Marriage . . . is the most natural State of Man":** Benjamin Franklin, "Reasons to Choose an Older Mistress," in *A Benjamin Franklin Reader,* ed. Walter Isaacson (New York: Simon and Schuster, 2005), 5.

53 **"Pennsylvania is heaven for farmers":** Srodes, *Benjamin Franklin,* 49.

53 **"Some thought [the almanac] had its share of influence":** Franklin, *Autobiography,* 145.

53 **"nobody has yet found a reliable way to teach kids to be grittier":** Paul Tough, "How Kids Learn Resilience," *The Atlantic,* June 2016.

54 **those in attendance "heard it, and approved the doctrine, and immediately practiced the contrary":** Benjamin Franklin, "The Way to Wealth," in *A Benjamin Franklin Reader,* ed. Isaacson, 182.

54 **"an atrocious debasement of human nature . . .":** Benjamin Franklin, "Address to Pennsylvania Society for Promoting the Abolition of Slavery and the Relief of Free Negros Unlawfully Held in Bondage," in *The Complete Works of Benjamin Franklin,* ed. John Bigelow (New York: G. P. Putnam's Sons, 1888), 167.

Chapter 4: *American Guru,* William Alcott

55 **"dietetic charlatanry":** Adam D. Shprintzen, *The Vegetarian Crusade: The Rise of an American Reform Movement, 1817–1921* (Chapel Hill: University of North Carolina Press, 2013), 25.

56 **"Flesh-eating is the key-stone to a wide-spread arch of superfluous wants . . .":** *Vegetarian Advocate* (London), July 1, 1850, ivu.org /congress/1850/convention.html.

57 **"everybody . . . understand that we are something more than grass eaters":** "Address of Dr. W. A. Allcott [sic]," *American Vegetarian and Health Journal* 1, no. 10 (October 1851): 167–169.

57 **the intent was not to outlaw the procedure:** Alesha Doan, *Opposition and Intimidation: The Abortion Wars and Strategies of Political Harassment* (Ann Arbor: University of Michigan Press, 2009), 46.

58 **"The schools were essentially private ventures, money-making in spirit and object":** Abraham Flexner, "Medical Education in America," *Atlantic Monthly,* June 1910.

58 **"renewed my declaration of independence with regard to those earthly props":** William Alcott, *Forty Years in the Wilderness of Pills*

and Powders; or, The Cogitations and Confessions of an Aged Physician (Boston: J. P. Jewett, 1859), 75.

59   "The strange belief that 'dirt is healthy'": William Alcott, *The Young Mother; or, Management of Children in Regard to Health* (Boston: George W. Light, 1838), 90.

59   "A physician of some eminence, now residing in Philadelphia": William Alcott, *The Vegetable Diet* (Boston: Marsh, Capen and Lyon, 1838), 167.

59   "Prof R. D. Mussey, of Hanover, New Hampshire": Ibid., 153.

60   "quite insoluble and unwholesome": William Alcott, *The Laws of Health; or, Sequel to the House I Live In* (Boston: Jewett, 1859), 149.

60   "If the infirmities of age come upon us, it is because we have disobeyed": Ibid., 10.

60   "There is no slavery in this world like the slavery of a man to his appetite": "Dr. Alcott's Sentiments and Remarks," *American Vegetarian and Health Journal* 1, no. 1 (November 1850): 25.

61   "crammed with animal abominations": Quoted in Shprintzen, *The Vegetarian Crusade,* 71.

61   "the vegetarian movement saw the diet as a catalyst for a total reform ideology": Ibid., 2.

61   "spontaneous recognition of human solidarity": Samuel R. Wells, *How to Behave: The Classic Pocket Manual of Good Manners* (1867; repr. Simon and Schuster, 2012), e-book, introduction.

61   "creating healthy, vital bodies best prepared to advance socially and economically": Shprintzen, *The Vegetarian Crusade,* 2.

62   powdered brewer's yeast, powdered skim milk, yogurt, wheat germ, and blackstrap molasses: Gaylord Hauser, *Look Younger, Live Longer* (New York: Farrar, Strauss and Company, 1950), 22.

63   Everything was healthy. Nothing was healthy. No one seemed to know: Steve Fishman, "The Diet Martyr," *New York,* March 15, 2004.

64   "doughbirds": Nina Teicholz, "How Americans Used to Eat," *The Atlantic,* June 2014.

64   "breakfast would have been no breakfast": Charles Dickens, *The Works of Charles Dickens,* vol. 15 (New York: Houghton Mifflin, 1877), 244.

65   "The immediate cause of his decease": "Death of Sylvester Graham," *American Vegetarian and Health Journal* 1, no. 10 (October 1851): 187–188.

66   an unkind piece about Graham: Shprintzen, *The Vegetarian Crusade,* 73.

PART TWO: AS A FRIEND

68 **"enraged woman":** Timothy Stone Pinneo, *The Hemans Reader for Female Schools* (New York: Clark, Austin, and Smith, 1847), 190.

68 **"natural and almost laudable to break down under all conceivable varieties of strain":** Mary Putnam Jacobi, "Modern Female Invalidism," *Boston Medical and Surgical Journal* 133, no. 7 (1895).

69 **"endure effort, exposure, and hardship":** Sylvanus Stall, *What a Young Man Ought to Know* (Philadelphia: Vir Publishing Company, 1904), 190.

69 **"By the time an emotion has fairly got us in its grip":** Woods Hutchinson, "Does the Mind Rule the Body?" *Saturday Evening Post* 181, no. 30 (January 23, 1909).

Chapter 5: *Sob Sister,* Dorothy Dix

Some of the material in this chapter was previously published in my article "The Advice Columnist We Deserve," *The New Yorker,* October 9, 2012.

69 **empathy is, in fact, a well-disguised sin:** Paul Bloom, *Against Empathy: The Case for Rational Compassion* (New York: Ecco, 2016).

72 **"most potent single agency" of "shaping the habits of thought":** Robert S. Lynd and Helen Merrell Lynd, *Middletown: A Study in Modern Culture* (Orlando, FL: Harcourt and Brace, 1929), 116.

72 **"half-portion sort of person":** Quoted in Harnett T. Kane with Ella Bentley Arthur, *Dear Dorothy Dix: The Story of a Compassionate Woman* (Garden City, NY: Doubleday, 1952), 29.

72 **"As I look back upon my life I see it as a battlefield":** Dorothy Dix [Elizabeth Gilmer], *Dorothy Dix—Her Book: Every-day Help for Every-day People* (New York: Funk and Wagnalls, 1926), xix.

73 **"There is no joy or sorrow that can tear at the human heart that I do not know":** Dorothy Dix [Elizabeth Gilmer], "Dorothy Dix Learns of Human Nature Through Talks with Girls and Women," *Indianapolis Star,* June 17, 1923.

73 **"Teachers were the Miss Annas and the Miss Marys":** Kane, *Dear Dorothy Dix,* 30.

74 **"The marriage was not my idea":** Ibid., 41.

74 **"matches with skin on them":** Ibid., 46.

75 **"Why God, child, you can write!":** Ibid., 50.

75 "She's the kind they speak of around editorial rooms as 'a damn good newspaperman'": Ibid., 57.

75 credited with coining the phrase "The way to a man's heart is through his stomach": Giuliana Lonigro, "Women's History Month Profile: Sara Payson Willis ('Fanny Fern')," New York Women in Communications, March 2, 2011, www.nywici.org/features/blogs /aloud/womens-history-month-profile-sara-payson-willis-fanny -fern.

75 "everything in the world had been written about women and for women, except the truth": Quoted in Kane, *Dear Dorothy Dix,* 59.

76 "told how women ought never to leave the sacred precincts of home . . .": Quoted in ibid., 61.

77 He resented it when people in New Orleans referred to him as "Mr. Dix": Ibid., 74.

77 "My husband is a brute . . .": Quoted in "Dorothy Dix: Advice Columnist," n.d., 1920-30.com: The 1920s in History, www.1920-30 .com/society/dorothy-dix.html.

78 She gave them ambitious titles: Dix, *Dorothy Dix—Her Book.*

78 "Make up your mind to be happy": Quoted in Kane, *Dear Dorothy Dix,* 273.

78 "I stood yesterday. I can stand today.": Quoted in ibid., 13.

78 In the preindustrial era, men and women had shared economic and domestic responsibilities: Joseph M. Hawes, *The Family in America: An Encyclopedia,* vol. 2 (Santa Barbara, CA: ABC-CLIO, 2001).

78 At the turn of the century, there was a boom of boys groups: Michael Kimmel, *Manhood in America: A Cultural History* (Oxford: Oxford University Press, 2011), 122.

79 an estimated seventeen thousand women died each year from botched abortions: Dorothy E. McBride, *Abortion in the United States: A Reference Handbook* (Santa Barbara, CA: ABC-CLIO, 2008), 10.

79 "try to find out what talents and aptitudes nature bestowed upon you": Dix, *Dorothy Dix—Her Book,* 67.

79 "The Ordinary Woman is the real heroine of life": Ibid., 25–26.

79 "degrade marriage into a kind of vaudeville show": Dorothy Dix [Elizabeth Gilmer], "Dorothy Dix Talks: About Advice to Women," *New Orleans Picayune,* February 13, 1898.

80 being a bachelorette in perpetuity was not something to mourn: Marilyn Coleman, Lawrence H. Ganong, and Kelly Warzinik, *Fam-*

ily Life in 20th-Century America (Westport, CT: Greenwood Publishing Group, 2007).

80 **"the husband who remains a gallant lover after three or four years of married life is about as rare as hens' teeth":** Dorothy Dix [Elizabeth Gilmer], *How to Win and Hold a Husband* (New York: Arno Press, 1974), 106.

80 **"Let him come home and find no dinner because the cook has struck for wages":** Dorothy Dix [Elizabeth Gilmer], "Dorothy Dix Talks: Sit Down Strike Warranted Here," *Evening Standard,* May 18, 1943.

80 **"If we take wages for housework as a political perspective":** Silvia Federici, *Wages Against Housework* (London: Falling Wall Press / The Power of Women Collective, 1975), 2.

81 **"must be believed in to hold society together":** Lynd and Lynd, *Middletown,* 115.

81 **"Men prefer mediocrity in women":** Quoted in "Dorothy Dix: Advice Columnist."

81 **"the right to be as ugly as nature made them":** Dorothy Dix [Elizabeth Gilmer], "Dorothy Dix Talks: The Homely Woman to the Front," *New Orleans Picayune,* July 3, 1898.

82 **"Flight from him, not with him, is your only salvation":** Quoted in Kane, *Dear Dorothy Dix,* 287.

83 **women deserved some slack, especially from one another:** Ibid., 8.

84 **"It took me a dozen years to realize the enormous responsibility people thrust upon me":** Ibid., 149.

Chapter 6: *Happy Thoughts,* Dale Carnegie

86 **"you'll see the certificate I got from the Dale Carnegie course":** *Becoming Warren Buffett,* dir. Peter W. Kunhardt, Kunhardt Films, January 2017.

86 **"a person's name is to that person the sweetest and most important sound":** Dale Carnegie, *How to Win Friends and Influence People* (1936; repr. New Delhi: General Press, 2016), Kindle edition, Chapter 3.

88 **"The work I loathed was churning the cream into butter":** Quoted in Steven Watts, *Self-Help Messiah: Dale Carnegie and Success in Modern America* (New York: Other Press, 2013), Kindle edition, Chapter 1.

89 **"I was so crushed, so beaten, so despondent, that I literally thought of suicide":** Ibid., Chapter 2.

90 **"It is far nobler work than selling meat":** Ibid., Chapter 3.

91 **a book about "the art of getting along with people":** Carnegie, *How to Win Friends and Influence People* (2016), Kindle edition, "How This Book Was Written—And How It Came to Be."

91 **unemployment in America was at 16.9 percent:** Bureau of Labor Statistics, "1934–36," *100 Years of U.S. Consumer Spending,* May 2006, www.bls.gov/opub/uscs/1934-36.pdf.

91 **don't "criticize, condemn, or complain":** Dale Carnegie, *How to Win Friends and Influence People* (New York: Simon and Schuster, 1937), 41.

91 **rules for getting people to like you:** Ibid., 146.

91 **rules for "winning people to your way of thinking":** Ibid., 242.

91 **"lavish praise" or "honest and sincere appreciation":** Ibid., 55.

92 **"Why don't we use praise instead of condemnation?":** Ibid., 265.

92 **"Dale Carnegie sells people what most of them desperately need":** Margaret Case Harriman, "He Sells Hope," *Saturday Evening Post,* August 14, 1937.

92 **"Skeptical? Well, I like skeptical people.":** Carnegie, *How to Win Friends and Influence People* (1937), 287.

93 **"all-saving power of healthy-minded attitudes":** William James, *Varieties of Religious Experience* (Mineola, NY: Dover Publications, 2013), 94–95.

93 **"one of the most distinguished psychologists and philosophers America has ever produced":** Carnegie, *How to Win Friends and Influence People* (1937), 269.

93 **"You don't feel like smiling?"** Ibid., 101.

93 **"act as though that particular trait was already one of his outstanding characteristics":** Ibid., 271.

94 **summarized the latest psychological research on positive thinking:** Emily Esfahani Smith, "The Benefits of Optimism Are Real," *The Atlantic,* March 1, 2013.

94 **"drain you of the energy you need to take action in pursuit of your goals":** Gabrielle Oettingen, "The Problem with Positive Thinking," *New York Times,* October 24, 2014.

94 **"Be a good listener. Encourage others to talk about themselves":** Carnegie, *How to Win Friends and Influence People* (1937), 125.

94 "let them realize in some subtle way that you recognize their importance": Carnegie, *How to Win Friends and Influence People* (1937), 135.

94 advises women to develop their confidence and guard themselves from men who take credit for their ideas: Sheryl Sandberg and Adam Grant, "Speaking While Female," *New York Times,* January 12, 2015.

95 40 percent of American workers will be freelancers: *Intuit 2020 Report,* Intuit, October 2010, https://http-download.intuit.com/http .intuit/CMO/intuit/futureofsmallbusiness/intuit_2020_report.pdf.

95 "Fifty years ago, when you went to business school": Alana Semuels, "How the Relationship Between Employers and Workers Changed," *Los Angeles Times,* April 7, 2013.

Chapter 7: *Everything Changes,* Dear Abby and Ann Landers

Some of the material in this chapter was previously published in my article "The Advice Columnist We Deserve," *The New Yorker,* October 9, 2012.

97 "they'd rather die": Jan Pottker and Bob Speziale, *Dear Ann, Dear Abby: The Unauthorized Biography of Ann Landers and Abigail Van Buren* (New York: Dodd, Mead, 1987), 21.

98 "Ann revealed certain Freudian flaws of character by going through with the operation": Paul O'Neil, "Twin Lovelorn Advisors Torn Asunder by Success," *Life,* April 7, 1958.

98 "like the kid who beats a dog until somebody looks, and then starts petting it": Ibid.

99 almost 10 percent of children grew up in a household without either parent: Stephanie Coontz, *The Way We Never Were: American Families and the Nostalgia Trap* (New York: Basic Books, 1992), 15.

99 reactions to this historical anomaly: Ibid., 25.

100 "She couldn't stand it": Pottker and Speziale, *Dear Ann, Dear Abby,* 95.

101 "Good morning, Ann Landers!" the man on the line said: Ibid., 105.

102 "I provided the sharp answers": Ibid., 116.

102 "she'd have thirteen assistants at a time": Sue Rochman, "Dear Ann Landers," *CR,* Fall 2010.

102 "She painted the walls of her office bubblegum pink and settled in": Jeffrey Zaslow, *Tell Me All About It* (New York: William Morrow, 1990), 33.

102 "Eppie should have given me credit, but she didn't": Pottker and Speziale, *Dear Ann, Dear Abby,* 138.

103 **"She was mad because her column wasn't in some paper in Aardvark, Arkansas":** Carol Felsenthal, "Dear Ann," *Chicago,* February 1, 2003.

103 **"Three strikes and a man is out, no matter how good his pitches":** Abigail Van Buren [Pauline Phillips], "Dear Abby: Her Ex Great to Date, Not to Mate," *Chicago Tribune,* August 26, 1989.

103 **"Snoring is the sweetest music this side of heaven. Ask any widow":** Abigail Van Buren [Pauline Phillips], *The Best of Dear Abby* (New York: Pocket Books, 1981), 41.

103 **Dear Abby's reply: "Probably.":** Quoted in "Lovelorn Columnist Takes Work Seriously Despite Humor; Column Is a Friend to Many," *Daily Chronicle* (Centralia, WA), November 5, 1957.

103 **"One cannot help what he feels":** Van Buren [Phillips], *Best of Dear Abby,* 195.

104 **"You've got a geranium in your cranium":** Ann Landers [Esther Lederer], "Ann Landers," *Dixon (IL) Evening Telegraph,* April 15, 1971.

104 **by the 1990s, only 34 percent of her letters did:** David Gudelunas, *Confidential to America: Newspaper Advice Columns and Sexual Education* (New Brunswick, NJ: Transaction Publishers, 2008), 123.

104 **"What is the difference between a mule, a jackass and a donkey?":** Van Buren [Phillips], *Best of Dear Abby,* 130.

105 **"Is there anything in insecticides that could excite a man?":** Abigail Van Buren [Pauline Phillips], "Dear Abby: Bug Bombs Ignite Husband's Ardor," *Chicago Tribune,* September 2, 1989.

105 **"I think it unwise for a married woman to hold down a full-time job outside her home":** Abigail Van Buren [Pauline Phillips], *Dear Abby on Marriage* (New York: Crest Books, 1963), 47.

105 **"content only with a husband who projects masculinity and authority":** Ibid., 38.

105 **"Marriage isn't a 50-50 proposition":** Ibid., 119.

105 **"there are no two people in the world who cannot live together in reasonable harmony if they really try":** Ibid., 122, 124.

105 **"In my book, marriage is forever":** Ann Landers [Esther Lederer], "Ann Landers: Your Problems," *Maryville (MO) Daily Forum,* July 14, 1960.

105 **divorce was an emergency measure, never the logical conclusion of a romantic disentanglement:** Stephanie Coontz, *Marriage, a History: How Love Conquered Marriage* (New York: Penguin Books, 2005), 225.

106 **for this column she was "Mrs. Jules Lederer":** Ann Landers [Mrs. Jules Lederer], "Ann Landers Wed 30 Years," *Journal Gazette* (Mattoon, IL), July 2, 1969.

106 **"Do not agree to engage in any practice you consider frightening, abnormal, or weird":** Abigail Van Buren [Pauline Phillips], "Dear Abby: Danger Lurks in Masochistic Tendency," *Los Angeles Times*, August 16, 1982.

107 **"dismiss it or rationalize it":** Felsenthal, "Dear Ann."

107 **"starving children born of parents who did not want them and could not feed them":** Abigail Van Buren [Pauline Phillips], "Dear Abby: Why Not Let God Plan Your Family?" *San Francisco Chronicle*, August 25, 1969.

107 **"I always say stick to your own kind":** Felsenthal, "Dear Ann."

107 **"whether you like it or not, this is the direction in which the world is moving":** Ann Landers [Esther Lederer], "Ann Landers: Interracial Marriages Have Built-In Hazards," *Ottawa Journal*, March 22, 1973.

107 **"unique opportunity to spotlight ignorance, fear, and stupidity":** Quoted in Pottker and Speziale, *Dear Ann, Dear Abby*, 189.

107 **"She had a Rolodex to kill for":** Pamela Paul, "Dear Reader, Get a Life," *Psychology Today*, July 1, 2003.

108 **"If you love her, accept her as she is and let her know it":** Abigail Van Buren [Pauline Phillips], "Dear Abby," *Honolulu Star-Bulletin*, September 10, 1975.

108 **it was perfectly appropriate for a gay couple to celebrate their commitment:** Abigail Van Buren [Pauline Phillips], "Dear Abby: Two Men Doth Not a Marriage Make," *Marshall (TX) News Messenger*, August 16, 1971.

108 **"If more men tried it, there would be fewer men in this country":** Ann Landers [Esther Lederer], "Ann Landers: He Spanks His Wife," *Oneata (NY) Star*, November 12, 1962.

108 **"These recent figures are enough to make an American hide his head in shame":** Ann Landers [Esther Lederer], "Ann Landers: No Need to Live with Guns," *Statesman Journal* (Salem, OR), March 3, 1982.

109 **"A nice idea, a weekend place, but not particularly useful":** Margo Howard, *Eppie: The Story of Ann Landers* (New York: Pinnacle Books, 1982), 121.

109 **"memorial to one of the world's best marriages that didn't make it to the finish line":** Ibid., 243.

109 "she never acknowledged the degree to which her life was her own": Ibid., 258.

110 "they and their friends taught me that maybe I was a little out of step": Pottker and Speziale, *Dear Ann, Dear Abby,* 179.

110 "I don't think that damages my credibility": Ibid., 181.

110 Popo did an interview with *Ladies' Home Journal:* Howard, *Eppie,* 266–268.

Chapter 8: *Indulgence Is a Virtue,* Mildred Newman

111 a "giant mistake": Ernest Jones, *Free Associations: Memories of a Psychoanalyst* (Piscataway, NJ: Transaction Publishers, 1990), 181.

112 Bjur would fund psychoanalytic research: Stephen Farber and Marc Green, *Hollywood on the Couch: A Candid Look at the Overheated Love Affair Between Psychiatrists and Moviemakers* (New York: William Morrow, 1993), 220.

114 a reverence that recalls druggy teenagers at their first music festival: Farber and Green, *Hollywood on the Couch,* 280–281.

114 *Interview* magazine published a conversation between Schumacher and Smith: Liz Smith and Joel Schumacher, "Joel Schumacher, Showbiz Whiz by Liz (Smith Of Course)," *Interview,* September 1977.

115 "they all kidded that they were her favorite": Neal Newman, interview with the author, January 5, 2017.

115 "It's not a doctor-patient relationship": Judy Kessler, "Mildred and Bernie Cash In as Their Own Best Friends," *People,* October 28, 1974.

115 "was either talking about Mildred and Bernie, as she called them, or she was with Mildred": *Everything Is Copy,* dir. Jacob Bernstein and Nick Hooker, HBO Documentary Films, 2015.

115 Rachel leans on her therapist, Vera Maxwell, who is Newman by a different name: Nora Ephron, *Heartburn* (New York: Vintage, 1983), 30–31.

116 "Vera looked at me and her eyes filled with tears": Ibid., 161.

116 "My mother didn't take away from the person that they were running their own life": Newman, interview.

116 "She inspired people, opened them up to a more fulfilled life":

Derek Rose, "Newman, Celeb Therapist," *New York Daily News,* November 8, 2001.

117 **There was a young boy who had a kreplach phobia:** Mildred Newman and Bernard Berkowitz, *How to Be Awake and Alive* (New York: Random House, 1975), 17–18.

117 **"each person can get what they needed from it":** Newman, interview.

117 **"the harm we do ourselves is a lot more dangerous to the environment":** Mildred Newman and Bernard Berkowitz with Jean Owen, *How to Be Your Own Best Friend* (New York: Ballantine Books, 1971), 26.

118 **"Doing what makes you feel good about yourself is really the opposite of self-indulgence":** Ibid., 35.

118 **"When we use our will power to achieve goals that do not spring out of us . . .":** Ibid., 44.

118 **"Don't judge yourself at all; accept yourself and move on from there":** Ibid., 83.

118 **"I owe the second half of my life to the years I spent in Newman's office":** Faber and Green, *Hollywood on the Couch,* 284–285.

119 **"Creative people have got to spend a certain amount of time in self obsession":** Ibid., 189.

119 **nearly half said that they'd gladly seek professional help if it weren't so expensive:** Amelia Gulliver, Kathleen M. Griffiths, and Helen Christensen, "Perceived Barriers and Facilitators to Mental Health Help-Seeking in Young People: A Systematic Review," *BMC Psychiatry* 10 (2010): 113, doi.org/10.1186/1471-244X-10-113.

121 **"This notion of oneself as a kind of continuing career . . .":** Joan Didion, "Letter from 'Manhattan,'" *New York Review of Books,* August 16, 1979.

122 **"It does mean being self-centered enough to care for yourself and to take care of yourself":** Newman and Berkowitz, *How to Be Your Own Best Friend,* 35.

PART THREE: EXPERTS AMONG US

124 **"The experts are terrible":** Sopan Deb, "Trump: The Experts Are Terrible," CBSNews.com, April 4, 2016, www.cbsnews.com/news/trump-the-experts-are-terrible/.

124 **"The complexity of modern life has steadily whittled away"**: Richard Hofstadter, *Anti-Intellectualism in American Life* (1963; repr. New York: Knopf Doubleday, 2012), 34.

Chapter 9: *Honorary Pants,* Sylvia Porter

127 **"The sun rose and set on my brother John"**: Jean L. Baer, *The Self-Chosen: "Our Crowd" Is Dead, Long Live Our Crowd* (Ramsey, NJ: Arbor Books, 1984), 259; Tracy Lucht, *Sylvia Porter: America's Original Personal Finance Columnist* (Syracuse, NY: Syracuse University Press, 2013), 17.

127 **"Of course, the Wall Street crowd knew what it was doing and sold the bonds when prices were high"**: Tracy Lucht, *Sylvia Porter,* 32.

128 **They'd "jot down whatever they were told"**: Ibid., 31.

129 **"The real significance of the Dominion of Canada's . . ."**: S. F. Porter, "Canada's Bond Offer 'Feeler' in U.S. Market," *New York Post,* August 6, 1935; Lucht, *Sylvia Porter,* 29.

129 **"battles with men on a basis of accomplishment, rather than personality"**: S. F. Porter, "Women in Finance . . . Louise Watson, Partner in Investment Firm, Finds Market Thrilling and Gives a Bit of Advice on Trading Risks," *New York Post,* June 6, 1936.

130 **"There are certain things we—women—can do to make the adjustment easier"**: S. F. Porter, "To the Women: Some Hints for Developing War Trends and Policies to Adopt," *New York Post,* December 12, 1941.

130 **"The first World War brought women into finance"**: S. F. Porter, "To the Women: You Can Get Jobs in the Financial Fields; Banks to Employ Thousands," *New York Post,* July 6, 1942.

130 **"I believe very definitely that the time has come for us to make capital of the fact that S. F. Porter is a woman"**: Lucht, *Sylvia Porter,* 11.

130 **"A financial editor can be beautiful!"**: Cliff Millen, "A Financial Editor Can Be Beautiful," *Des Moines Tribune,* October 18, 1949; Lucht, *Sylvia Porter,* 53.

131 **"Wall Street's Joan of Arc"**: Quoted in Lucht, *Sylvia Porter,* 53.

131 **"glamor girl of finance"**: Lucht, *Sylvia Porter,* 53.

131 **"Frumpy, one might guess about a woman writer on economics"**: Ibid., 54.

131 **"Sylvia is one of the boys. We hereby award her honorary pants":** Ibid., 1.

131 **Her "slip was showing":** Ibid., 65; Ferman Wilson, "The Lady Squawks?" *Miami Herald,* April 5, 1948.

132 **"As we belittle and neglect this class, we belittle and neglect America itself":** Sylvia Porter, "A Tax Plan for the Rich," *New York Post,* February 11, 1947; Lucht, *Sylvia Porter,* 81.

133 **"anytime but Christmas":** Sylvia Porter, *Sylvia Porter's Money Book: How to Earn It, Spend It, Save It, Invest It, Borrow It—and Use It to Better Your Life* (New York: Doubleday, 1975), 147.

133 **"men to whom your husband would wish you to turn for advice and financial counsel":** Sylvia Porter, "What Every Woman Should Know About Her Husband," *Good Housekeeping,* April 9, 1944.

133 **"There's no reason for being in a man's job":** Lucht, *Sylvia Porter,* 69.

134 **"Why can't economists talk straight like Sylvia?":** Christopher Anderson, "Sylvia Porter's Advice for Pinched Americans," *People,* October 29, 1979.

134 **Porter was put on the cover of *Time* magazine:** *Time,* November 28, 1960.

135 **the average married woman spent twenty-five years of her life at a job:** Porter, *Sylvia Porter's Money Book,* 465, 470.

135 **"don't you think you have a responsibility not to bring the whole structure down?":** William Galeota, "Miss Porter's School: A Columnist's Advice Wields Wide Influence from Coast to Coast," *Wall Street Journal,* March 24, 1972.

136 **"The higher the aspirations, the more chance that people will be disappointed":** Porter, *Sylvia Porter's Money Book,* 7.

136 **he turned to scripture and discovered the simplicity of a debt-free life:** Helen Olen, *Pound Foolish: Exposing the Dark Side of the Personal Finance Industry* (New York: Random House, 2012), Kindle edition, Chapter 4.

137 **her net worth is over twenty million dollars:** Susan Dominus, "Suze Orman Is Having a Moment," *New York Times Magazine,* May 14, 2009.

137 **"half of America reads Sylvia Porter, the other half writes it":** Lucht, *Sylvia Porter,* 15.

138 **"I took an early morning golf lesson":** Porter, *Sylvia Porter's Money Book,* 141.

Chapter 10: *Doctor's Orders,* Benjamin Spock

139 **"You know more than you think you do":** Benjamin Spock, *The Common Sense Book of Baby and Child Care* (New York: Duell, Sloan and Pearce, 1957), 3.

139 **"natural loving care that kindly parents give their children is a hundred times more valuable":** Ibid.

140 **"Pregnant mothers should avoid thinking of ugly people":** Quoted in Joanna Bourke, *Fear: A Cultural History* (Emery, CA: Shoemaker and Hoard, 2005), 84.

140 **"A baby should cry vigorously several times each day":** Quoted in Therese O'Neil, "'Don't Think of Ugly People': How Parenting Advice Has Changed," *The Atlantic,* April 19, 2013.

140 **advised mothers to never hug or kiss their sons:** Michael Kimmel, *Manhood in America: A Cultural History* (Oxford: Oxford University Press, 2011), 147.

140 **It's unclear how many young mothers actually followed this advice:** Margaret Talbot, "The Lives They Lived: Benjamin Spock, MD; A Spock-Marked Generation," *New York Times Magazine,* January 3, 1999.

141 **"He was grave but just":** Benjamin Spock and Mary Morgan, *Spock on Spock: A Memoir of Growing Up with the Century* (New York: Random House, 1985), 14.

142 **"Oh, you piddling creatures," she'd say:** Thomas Maier, *Dr. Spock: An American Life* (New York: Harcourt Brace, 1998), 4.

142 **"Instinct and maternal love are too often assumed to be a sufficient guide for a mother":** Quoted in Barbara Ehrenreich and Deirdre English, *For Her Own Good: Two Centuries of the Experts' Advice to Women* (New York: Anchor Books, 2005), 220.

142 **"Children should be kissed, if at all, upon the cheek or the forehead. But the less of this the better":** Dr. L. Emmett Holt, *The Care and Feeding of Children: A Catechism for the Use of Mothers and Children's Nurses* (New York: Appleton & Company, 1905), 131.

143 **"It conditioned him from the time of childhood to be fascinated with babies":** Maier, *Dr. Spock,* 9.

143 **"you should live at home to try to recover your ideals":** Quoted in ibid., 33.

144 **"The parents had no way to refrigerate milk except by putting the**

bottles out on the windowsill in the winter": Spock and Morgan, *Spock on Spock*, 100.

144 "I didn't know enough to take a fierce stance against it": Maier, *Dr. Spock*, 86.

144 "I conceived the idea that someone going into pediatrics should have psychological training": Spock and Morgan, *Spock on Spock*, 101.

145 "Don't be a booby," Spock would say: Ibid., 123.

145 "The more devoted she was in watching over and disciplining him": Quoted in Maier, *Dr. Spock*, 117.

145 "they had no experience at turning this into positive, practical advice for parents": Spock and Morgan, *Spock on Spock*, 130.

146 "We are only going to charge a quarter and can sell ten thousand copies a year easily": Ibid., 132.

146 "The main purpose of any schedule is to do right by the baby": Spock, *The Common Sense Book of Baby and Child Care*, 54.

146 "It sounds as if you're talking to me as if you think I'm a sensible person": Carol Lawson, "At 88, an Undiminished Dr. Spock," *New York Times*, March 5, 1992.

146 "I was scared that the book would be misunderstood": Ibid.

147 "He was a scary person, really scary": Maier, *Dr. Spock*, 251.

147 "I do care about what the neighbors think": Spock and Morgan, *Spock on Spock*, 124.

147 "it means she's very much a woman herself and has respect for the male sex as somewhat different": Benjamin Spock, *Problems of Parents* (New York: Bodley Head, 1963), 194.

147 every boy needed a male role model: Ibid., 187–189.

147 "vigorous self-confidence": Marvin S. Swartz, "Decent and Indecent," *Harvard Crimson*, March 23, 1970.

147 "parents and schools not encourage girls to be competitive with males if that is going to make them dissatisfied with raising children": Quoted in Lynn Z. Bloom, *Doctor Spock: Biography of a Radical Conservative* (New York: Bobbs-Merrill, 1972), 220.

148 "babies and young children have needs and rights too": Benjamin Spock, "Working Mothers: Some Possible Solutions for Child Care," *Redbook*, September 1970.

148 "major oppressor of women": Quoted in Ann Hulbert, *Raising America: Experts, Parents, and a Century of Advice About Children* (New York: Knopf Doubleday, 2011), 269.

148 **"We figured a lot of mothers would vote for Jack if they saw him with Spock":** Maier, *Dr. Spock*, 218.

149 **"I would try to take the worst wrinkles out of my suit":** Spock and Morgan, *Spock on Spock*, 194.

149 **spoke with "an earnest simplicity throughout":** Daniel Lang, "A Reporter at Large: The Trial of Dr. Spock," *The New Yorker*, September 7, 1968.

149 **it only cost twenty-five dollars to post bail:** Spock and Morgan, *Spock on Spock*, 188.

149 **"to have them killed in such numbers for a cause that is ignoble":** Lang, "The Trial of Dr. Spock."

150 **"They not only don't want to change the world, they don't even want to make money—that's how retired they are":** Ibid.

150 **"I want to be around lively people":** Spock and Morgan, *Spock on Spock*, 253.

150 **she'd reply that "they were both sixteen":** Mary Morgan, "My Life with Dr. Spock," *San Bernardino County Sun*, October 14, 1984.

151 **"paying the price of two generations that followed the Dr. Spock baby plan":** "Peale Raps Spock Advice," *Times* (Shreveport, LA), February 19, 1968.

151 **"Who do you suppose is to blame":** Richard D. Lyons, "Dr. Spock, Denying 'Permissiveness,' Says Agnew's Gibes Are 'a Compliment,'" *New York Times*, September 27, 1970.

151 **"as long as the parents are not afraid to be firm about those matters that do seem important":** Spock, *The Common Sense Book of Baby and Child Care*, 48.

152 **"nowadays there seems to be more chance of a conscientious parent's getting into trouble with permissiveness":** Benjamin Spock, *The Common Sense Book of Baby and Child Care*, 2nd ed. (New York: Pocket Books, 1958), 2.

152 **"a guilty feeling of 'Maybe I don't know enough,'":** Spock and Morgan, *Spock on Spock*, 133–134.

152 **"It is indicative of my sexism that it took me three years":** Ibid., 248.

153 **"Both parents have an equal right to a career if they want one":** Benjamin Spock, *Baby and Child Care*, 4th ed. (New York: Pocket Books, 1977), 37.

153 **the book sold more than forty million copies:** Kate Stone Lombardi, "Common Sense in Tow, Dr. Spock Returns to Sarah Lawrence," *New York Times*, May 22, 1994.

Chapter 11: *Death's Best Friend*, Elisabeth Kübler-Ross

155 "they pushed me to where they wanted me to go, not where I wanted to go": Elizabeth Kübler-Ross, *On Death and Dying: What the Dying Have to Teach Doctors, Nurses, Clergy and Their Own Families* (1969; repr. New York: Simon and Schuster, 2014), 67–68.

155 "They have not told me what they found during the operation": Ibid., 206.

156 "No two people are going to go through the stages exactly alike": David Kessler, interview with the author, April 28, 2017.

156 "It is simply an account of a new and challenging opportunity to refocus on the patient as a human being": Ibid., xvii.

157 "You do not register these events with your earthly consciousness, but rather with a new awareness": Elizabeth Kübler-Ross, *On Life After Death* (1991; repr. New York: Crown, 2008), 4–5.

157 "Many people say: 'Of course Doctor Ross has seen too many dying patients.'": Ibid., 2.

157 she was liberated by the possibilities of nonscientific inquiry: Elizabeth Kübler-Ross, *The Wheel of Life: A Memoir of Living and Dying* (New York: Touchstone, 1997), 128.

157 "I was destined to work with dying patients": Ibid., 16.

158 "You will never have to worry about this one": Ibid., 24.

158 "I want to find out the purpose of life": Ibid., 22.

158 "The best thing we gave those people was love and hope": Ibid., 62.

159 "what a sick child really needed was a parent to hold his hand and talk openly and honestly about life": Ibid., 109.

159 "Knowledge helps, but knowledge alone is not going to help anybody": Ibid., 119.

160 "Patients weren't shy about expressing their dissatisfaction with their medical care": Ibid., 145.

160 "I observed the desperate need of the hospital staff to deny the existence of terminally ill patients": Kübler-Ross, *On Death and Dying*, 237.

160 a doctor's right not to inform their patients of an incurable disease: Lawrence R. Samuel, *Death, American Style: A Cultural History of Dying in America* (Lanham, MD: Rowman and Littlefield, 2013), xv.

161 "death, which dominates European's thoughts, has been put in its proper place in America": Quoted in Peter N. Stearns, *American*

Cool: Constructing a Twentieth-Century Emotional Style (New York: New York University Press, 1994), 157.

161 **"difficult to function well in the company of an outwardly mourning person"**: Quoted in ibid., 164.

161 **"There are lonely people to visit, blind folks to read and write for"**: Abigail Van Buren [Pauline Phillips], "Dear Abby: Loneliness Worse Than Cancer," *Greensville (SC) News*, April 3, 1968.

161 **"Medicine has its limits, a fact not taught in medical school"**: Kübler-Ross, *The Wheel of Life*, 91.

161 **"the fear of death is a universal fear even when we think we have mastered it"**: Kübler-Ross, *On Death and Dying*, 2–3.

164 **"What you learn from dying patients, you can pass on to your children and to your neighbors"**: Kübler-Ross, *On Life After Death*, 14–15.

164 **"For me, death is a graduation"**: "Quotes," Elisabeth Kübler-Ross Foundation, www.ekrfoundation.org/quotes/.

164 **"Even the most accepting, the most realistic patients left the possibility open for some cure"**: Kübler-Ross, *On Death and Dying*, 134.

165 **"Our grief is as individual as our lives"**: Elisabeth Kübler-Ross and David Kessler, *On Grief and Grieving* (2005; repr. New York: Scribner, 2014), 7.

165 **"highly subjective data gathering"**: John S. Stephenson, *Death, Grief, and Mourning* (New York: Simon and Schuster, 1985), 90.

165 exercises **"geared towards helping people overcome the tears and anger in their lives"**: Kübler-Ross, *The Wheel of Life*, 187.

165 **"Sometimes it pays not to think with your head as much as with your instinct"**: Ibid., 197.

166 **"It's a fairy, isn't it?"**: Ibid.

166 **"At this time in my life, I was open to anything and everything"**: Ibid.

167 **forcing himself on grieving widows at her retreats**: Ron Rosenbaum, *The Secret Parts of Fortune: Three Decades of Intense Investigations and Edgy Enthusiasms* (New York: Random House, 2000), 445.

167 **"For years, I have been stalked by a bad reputation"**: Kübler-Ross, *The Wheel of Life*, 15.

167 **"all your life on earth was nothing but a school that you had to go through"**: Kübler-Ross, *On Life After Death*, 3, 11.

168 **government spending on nursing home care had more than**

doubled: Peter D. Fox and Steven B. Clauser, "Trends in Nursing Home Expenditures," *Health Care Financing Review* 2, no. 2 (Fall 1980): 65–70.

168 **"Medicare puts entirely too much emphasis upon institutionalization of patients":** US Congress, Senate, Special Committee on Aging, *Death with Dignity: An Inquiry into Related Public Issues,* Part 1, 92nd Congress, 2nd session, August 7, 1972, 3, www.aging.senate.gov/imo/media/doc/publications/871972.pdf.

169 **"They are reminders of our own mortality":** Ibid., 12.

169 **Hospice programs have proliferated:** "Hospice Care," National Center for Health Statistics, Centers for Disease Control and Prevention, July 6, 2016, www.cdc.gov/nchs/fastats/hospice-care.htm.

170 **response to dying as "very human":** Rhonda Roland, "'Death and Dying' Pioneer May Have Personal Lessons to Offer," CNN .com, March 26, 1999, www.cnn.com/SPECIALS/views/y/1999/03/rowland.kublerross.mar26/.

Chapter 12: *Guide to the Stars,* Joan Quigley

172 **"He asked my permission to have her call me":** Joan Quigley, *What Does Joan Say? My Seven Years as White House Astrologer to Nancy and Ronald Reagan* (Seacaucus, NJ: Birch Lane Press, 1990), 43.

172 **"hadn't seen so superlative a stellium since Jackie's":** Ibid.

173 **"astrologers could predict anything":** Cynthia Gorney, "The Reagan Chart Watch: Astrologer Joan Quigley, Eye on the Cosmos," *Washington Post,* May 11, 1988.

173 **"A person must be very credulous indeed":** Quigley, *What Does Joan Say?,* 13.

173 **I had a high enough average to keep my clients happy:** Ruth Quigley, interview with the author, April 17, 2017.

174 **2 percent of the country's population:** "Civil War Facts," The Civil War, PBS, www.pbs.org/kenburns/civil-war/war/civil-war-facts/.

174 **"she does claim that nature is to be interpreted by the influences that surround it":** Theodore Connoly, Henry L. Vilas, and William Henry, *The New York Criminal Reports,* vol. 32 (Albany, NY: W. C. Little, 1915), 339, 341.

175 **the moment when astrology was treated, rightfully, as a science:** Karen Christino, *Foreseeing the Future: Evangeline Adams and Astrology in America* (Amherst, MA: One Reed Publications, 2002), 89.

175   **"Dow Jones might climb to heaven"**: Lloyd Wendt, *"The Wall Street Journal": The Story of Dow Jones and the Nation's Business Newspaper* (Skokie, IL: Rand McNally, 1982), 197.

175   **refers to Carroll Righter, a popular Hollywood astrologer, as a dear friend**: Ronald Reagan with Richard G. Hubler, *Where's the Rest of Me? Ronald Reagan's Own Story* (1965; repr. New York: Karz-Segil Publishers, 1981), 249.

175   **"We do not intend to have stargazers in this Administration"**: Paul Houston, "Reagan Denies Astrology Influenced His Decisions," *Los Angeles Times*, May 4, 1988.

176   **"Fortunately, that Saturn only comes once in 28 years"**: Quigley, *What Does Joan Say?*, 46.

176   **they made Reagan, already considered weak on foreign policy, seem dangerously naïve**: "Bush Denies that Reagan Backs Two-China Policy," *Los Angeles Times*, August 19, 1980.

177   **"Any configuration between Virgo and Pisces can make someone untidy"**: Ibid., 64.

177   **"She said she thought nuclear weaponry"**: "1980 Presidential Debates," The Debates '96, All Politics, CNN/Time, www.cnn.com /ALLPOLITICS/1996/debates/history/1980/index.shtml.

177   **"There you go again"**: "Ronald Reagan: There You Go Again," YouTube video, 0:48, posted by sshillings, January 4, 2008, www .youtube.com/watch?v=Wi9y5-Vo61w.

177   **"Congratulate Ronnie for me"**: Quigley, *What Does Joan Say?*, 65.

177   **never received "so much as a perfunctory thank you note"**: Ibid., 27.

178   **"Could you have told about the assassination attempt?"**: Ibid., 24.

178   **"unlike them I would not have the prestige they had while serving"**: Ibid., 27.

178   **"She could not afford to pay me even a fraction of what I was worth"**: Ibid., 26.

178   **"She felt she could help Ronald Reagan achieve world peace"**: Quigley, interview.

179   **"Virtually every major move and decision the Reagans made"**: Donald T. Regan, *For the Record: From Wall Street to Washington* (New York: Hartcourt Brace Jovanovich, 1988), 3.

179   **"good" days highlighted in green and "bad" days highlighted in red**: Ibid., 4.

179   **the calendar Quigley provided for the first few months of 1986**: Ibid., 367.

179 "The president's schedule is the single most potent tool in the White House": Ibid., 74.

180 "It's costing me a lot of money, calling up my Friend with all these changes": Ibid.

180 "Let me see what can be done": Ibid., 290.

180 "I occasionally think how quickly our differences worldwide would vanish": "President Ronald Reagan Mentions Alien Threat at Fallston UN & National Strategy Forum," YouTube video, 2:21, posted by AT68TA, May 26, 2012, www.youtube.com/watch ?v=iQxzWpy7PKg.

181 "convince an open-minded, modern, highly intelligent Gorbachev to accept ideas": Quigley, *What Does Joan Say?*, 144.

181 "I get such a thrill because Joan really set that in motion": Quigley, interview.

181 "Ronnie and I are the only two people in the country who know this. You will be the third person": Quigley, *What Does Joan Say?*, 147.

181 "I want everyone to love me," Nancy once told Quigley: Ibid., 28.

182 "She was almost psychic in her awareness of his best interests and the motives of those surrounding him": Ibid., 30.

182 "his own chart indicated that his life would no longer be in danger": Ibid., 25–26.

182 "if you leave your astrology column out, you're in trouble": "Reagans / Astrology / Regan Book," *CBS Evening News*, May 9, 1988, Vanderbilt Television News Archive, tvnews.vanderbilt.edu /broadcasts/321602?.

183 "I know I put your name on the list": Quigley, *What Does Joan Say?*, 98.

183 "Everyone I know here is married": Ibid., 100.

184 "Nancy quite obviously did not want to make a point of my being there": Ibid., 105.

184 "Mr. President, I feel that you have been chosen to bring peace": Ibid., 106.

184 "Tea with Nancy was much more interesting than the state dinner": Ibid., 109.

185 "he loves to dance with all the pretty young glamour girls": Ibid., 111.

185 "This woman could chew someone up and swallow and spit up the bones and never feel a thing": Ibid., 117.

185 "after they were out of office she would say how great her contributions had been": Quigley, interview.

185 "This must never come out!" Nancy said: Quigley, *What Does Joan Say?*, 21.

186 "I will not refuse to be interviewed": Ibid., 22.

186 "It's fabulous being able to work with Air Force One": "Nancy Reagan / Book / Astrology," *CBS Evening News*, October 16, 1989, Vanderbilt Television News Archive, https://tvnews.vanderbilt.edu/broadcasts/324169?.

186 "My relationship with Joan began as a crutch": Nancy Reagan, *My Turn* (1989; repr. New York: Random House, 2011), 44.

187 "Ronald Reagan is the first president elected in a zero year to survive his terms of office since William Henry Harrison": Quigley, *What Does Joan Say?*, 25.

187 having her work maligned as some kind of sorcery: Ibid., 13.

187 "My conclusions are based on this accurate scientific material": Ibid.

187 "Struggle has been in my charts": Cynthia Gorney, "The Reagan Chart Watch: Astrologer Joan Quigley, Eye on the Cosmos," *Washington Post*, May 11, 1988.

187 she did not foresee writing a memoir defending her place in history: Quigley, *What Does Joan Say?*, 27.

PART FOUR: ADVICE FOR ALL, BY ALL

189 "Everybody claims to hate 'em, but everybody seems to read 'em": Dan Savage, *Savage Love: Straight Answers from America's Most Popular Sex Columnist* (New York: Penguin, 1998), 1–2.

190 "They all think they'd be terrific at it": Jeffrey Zaslow, *Tell Me All About It: A Personal Look at the Advice Business from the Man Who Replaced Ann Landers* (New York: William Morrow, 1990), 19.

191 "The tragedy is not that the girl has a dimple, but that some people have a screw loose in their heads": Zaslow, *Tell Me All About It*, 40.

Chapter 13: *Stand by Me*, Harville Hendrix and Helen Hunt

Much of the material in this chapter was previously published in my article "Harville Hendrix Wants to Save America, One Marriage at a Time," *Pacific Standard*, March 10, 2015.

198 **"the greatest tool to lift children and families from poverty":** Marco Rubio, "Reclaiming the Land of Opportunity: Conservative Reforms for Combating Poverty" (speech), Washington, DC, January 8, 2014, www.rubio.senate.gov/public/index.cfm/mobile/press -releases?ID=958d06fe-16a3-4e8e-b178-664fc10745bf.

198 **"You have to improve the community in which that marriage is":** Benjamin Karney, interview with the author, May 19, 2014.

198 **the rate of marriage in the United States, while in slow decline, remains higher:** "SF3.1: Marriage and Divorce Rates," OECD Family Database, Organisation for Economic Co-operation and Development, August 25, 2016, www.oecd.org/els/family/SF_3_1_Marriage _and_divorce_rates.pdf.

198 **For the past three decades, the rate of divorce has also been in decline:** Claire Cain Miller, "The Divorce Surge Is Over, but the Myth Lives On," The Upshot, *New York Times,* December 2, 2014, www .nytimes.com/2014/12/02/upshot/the-divorce-surge-is-over-but -the-myth-lives-on.html.

198 **"it is only in the context of a committed relationship that this healing can occur":** Harville Hendrix and Helen Hunt, *The Personal Companion: A Workbook for Singles* (New York: Simon and Schuster, 1995), 3.

200 **"couples therapy may be the hardest form of therapy, and most therapists aren't good at it":** William Doherty, "Bad Couples Therapy: Betting Past the Myth of Therapist Neutrality," *Psychotherapy Networker,* November/December 2002.

200 **her goal with couples was "not to maintain the relationship nor to separate the pair but to help each other to take charge of himself":** Mark B. Scholl, A. Scott McGowan, and James T. Hansen, *Humanistic Perspectives on Contemporary Counseling Issues* (New York: Routledge, 2013), 124.

201 **"As long as they can talk and relate, there's hope for a relationship":** This video is no longer available. Quoted in Jessica Weisberg, "The Man Who Wants to Save Your Marriage," *Pacific Standard,* March 16, 2015.

201 **"the battered wife knows only one way—the way she learned from her own mother—to get attention":** Harville Hendrix, *Keeping the Love You Find* (New York: Simon and Schuster, 1993), 125.

201 **"the attempt to save the relationship should be made":** Ibid., 132.

202 **a growing number of single women over thirty are choosing to**

become single parents: Isabel V. Sawhill, "Celebrating Single Mothers by Choice," Social Mobility Memos, Brookings Institution, May 8, 2015, www.brookings.edu/blog/social-mobility-memos/2015/05/08/celebrating-single-mothers-by-choice/.

203 **The average age of an American woman at her first marriage:** "Table MS-2. Estimated Median Age at First Marriage, by Sex: 1890 to Present," US Bureau of the Census, September 15, 2004, www.census.gov/population/socdemo/hh-fam/tabMS-2.pdf; D'Vera Cohn, Jeffrey S. Passel, Wendy Wang, and Gretchen Livingston, "Barely Half of U.S. Adults Are Married—A Record Low," Pew Research Center, December 14, 2011, www.pewsocialtrends.org/2011/12/14/barely-half-of-u-s-adults-are-married-a-record-low.

205 **"no one talks about their plan for their marriage or their marriage philosophy":** Beth Reeder Johnson, interview with the author, April 11, 2014.

Chapter 14: *Politeness vs. Honesty, Part 2*, Judith Martin

207 **"My mother would be shocked if she knew that I give my age when people ask!":** Judith Martin, interview with the author, March 16, 2017.

208 **"it can be seen simply as a gracious gesture":** Judith Martin, "How Do I Apologize When I Don't Know What It Was I Did?" *Washington Post*, January 2, 1978.

208 **"they are violating the most basic decencies of manners by trying to charge their guests!":** Martin, interview.

208 **"that the writer states being unable to afford":** Judith Martin, *Miss Manners' Guide to Excruciatingly Correct Behavior* (New York: W. W. Norton, 2011), 29.

209 **"The assumption that people know and follow the simplest methods for annoyance control is wildly optimistic":** Judith Martin, *Star-Spangled Manners: In Which Miss Manners Defends American Etiquette* (New York: W. W. Norton, 2003), 306.

210 **"I thought, 'My daddy understands me'":** "Live from Kanbar Hall—Miss Manners," YouTube video, 1:04:41, posted by 3200 Stories, October 22, 2013, www.youtube.com/watch?v=Bz5qyspU5Tc&t=166s.

210 **"Miss Manners would especially urge consideration for picketers**

on the part of the public": Martin, *Miss Manners' Guide to Excruciatingly Correct Behavior,* 143.

211   "We have the idea of treating everybody equally": "Live from Kanbar Hall."

212   "I thought it was Put Your Child to Work Day": Ibid.

213   Americans treat their families as "optional appendages": Martin, *Star-Spangled Manners,* 164.

214   "Put not another bit into your Mouth til the former be Swallowed": "Colonial Manners: Based on the Exercise of a Schoolboy," History, Colonial Williamsburg (website), www.history.org/almanack/life /manners/rules2.cfm.

214   "The absence of a universally accepted standard": Martin, *Star-Spangled Manners,* 192.

215   "without regard to how ugly this might make life for their fellow citizens": Ibid., 26.

215   those who behave "none of the time" and those who behave "some of the time": Martin, *Miss Manners' Guide to Excruciatingly Correct Behavior,* 33.

215   "a president of the United States who unabashedly—even proudly— violated those expectations": Judith Martin, "Miss Manners on Rudeness in the Age of Trump," *The Atlantic,* February 16, 2017.

215   "If rudeness begets more rudeness, which begets more rudeness, where will it all end?": Martin, *Miss Manners' Guide to Excruciatingly Correct Behavior,* 22.

216   "Among friends, either both of us have our clothes on or both of us have our clothes off": "Live from Kanbar Hall."

217   "If you're one of these people, please go back to pretending, you gotta go back to pretending": Aziz Ansari, *Saturday Night Live,* Season 42, Episode 12, NBC, January 21, 2017.

217   "skillful performance of false cheer": Martin, *Miss Manners' Guide to Excruciatingly Correct Behavior,* 291.

218   "It's no accident that Americans have an aptitude for show business": Martin, *Star-Spangled Manners,* 84.

Chapter 15: *How to Coach a Life Coach*, Martha Beck

219   "with coaches charging, on average, five hundred dollars an hour": Diane Coutu and Carol Kauffman, "What Can Coaches Do for You?" *Harvard Business Review,* January 2009.

219 **"I'm really doing them a favor when they hand me money"**: Martha Beck, interview with the author, March 5, 2017.

227 **"Beck grossed $3.5 million in 2016"**: Taffy Brodesser-Akner, "Even the World's Top Life Coaches Need a Life Coach. Meet Martha Beck," *Bloomberg Businessweek,* May 18, 2016.

228 **"That is how civilizations heal"**: Toni Morrison, "No Place for Self-Pity, No Room for Fear," *The Nation,* March 23, 2015.

Chapter 16: *The King of Quora,* Michael King

236 **"Teenager, fried chicken lover, and self proclaimed egotist"**: "What is the largest pizza chain in the world, and how did it became so big?" Quora, n.d., www.quora.com/What-is-the-largest-pizza-chain-in-the-world-and-how-did-it-became-so-big.

236 **"Stay-at-home, hands on mom, trying to raise productive little humans"**: "Do first children resemble their father more than their mother?" Quora, n.d., www.quora.com/Do-first-children-resemble-their-father-more-than-their-mother.

236 **"twenty years investing experience"**: "How can a 20 year old start trading stocks?" Quora, n.d., www.quora.com/How-can-a-20-year-old-start-trading-stocks#!n=12.

236 **"follower of the 2016 election campaign"**: "Why does the right wing in the US view the Democratic party as radical left?" Quora, n.d., www.quora.com/Why-does-the-right-wing-in-the-US-view-the-Democratic-party-as-radical-left.

236 **"Are these symptoms of anxiety or something more serious?"**: "Every time I sleep, I wake up . . . ," Quora, n.d., www.quora.com/Every-time-I-sleep-I-wake-up-with-shortness-of-breath-and-a-tight-throat-and-chest-feeling-Are-these-symptoms-of-anxiety-or-something-more-serious.

236 **"What are the cons and pros of my employer knowing that I am diagnosed with a mental illness?"**: "What are the cons and pros . . . ," Quora, n.d., www.quora.com/What-are-the-cons-and-pros-of-my-employer-knowing-that-I-am-diagnosed-with-a-mental-illness#!n=18.

236 **"My mother says she feels lost . . . "**: "My mother says she feels lost . . . ," Quora, n.d., www.quora.com/My-mother-says-she-feels-lost-and-her-head-feels-empty-as-if-she-doesnt-know-what-shes-supposed-to-do-on-a-daily-basis-what-does-this-mean.

236 **"I'm 25 never been in a relationship . . . "**: "I'm 25 never been in a relationship . . . ," Quora, n.d., www.quora.com/Im-25-never-been-in-a-relationship-and-never-held-a-job-for-more-than-4+-months-Im-about-to-graduate-university-but-I-feel-worthless-What-can-I-do.

237 **"I get along with teachers, but not my peers. Is there something wrong with me?"**: "I get along with teachers . . . ," Quora, n.d., www.quora.com/I-get-along-with-teachers-but-not-my-peers-Is-there-something-wrong-with-me.

237 **"What do you do if you know a person is lying on Quora?"**: "What do you do if you know a person is lying on Quora?" Quora, n.d., www.quora.com/What-do-you-do-if-you-know-a-person-is-lying-on-Quora.

237 **"I brought my new cat home from the shelter and she keeps sneezing"**: I brought my new cat home from the shelter . . . ," Quora, n.d., www.quora.com/I-brought-my-new-cat-home-from-the-shelter-and-she-keeps-sneezing-Whats-happening.

237 **"you're not answering questions because you want to get points or because you have nothing else to do"**: Alyson Shontell, "A Query With Quora: An Interview with Cofounder Adam D'Angelo," *Business Insider*, April 22, 2012.

238 **he passed along a hotline for a nearby clinic**: "I'm 25 never been in a relationship . . . ," Quora, n.d., www.quora.com/Im-25-never-been-in-a-relationship-and-never-held-a-job-for-more-than-4+-months-Im-about-to-graduate-university-but-I-feel-worthless-What-can-I-do.

240 **"I have no empathy for anyone. That includes myself"**: "Can a psychopath feel pity for himself?," Quora, www.quora.com/Can-a-psychopath-feel-pity-for-himself.

241 **"Read the instructions"**: "Is a pregnancy test still reliable if you didn't urinate on it for 5 seconds?" Quora, n.d., www.quora.com/Is-a-pregnancy-test-still-reliable-if-you-didnt-urinate-on-it-for-5-seconds.

241 **"Your wife must have been terribly disturbed to leave you"**: "Should I move on from my marriage?" Quora, n.d., www.quora.com/Should-I-move-on-from-my-marriage.

242 **"They're lonely, unhappy, or disenfranchised"**: Jeffrey Zaslow, *Tell Me All About It: A Personal Look at the Advice Business from the Man Who Replaced Ann Landers* (New York: William Morrow, 1990), 38–39.

243 **"I binge ate 2000 calories today":** "I binge ate 2000 calories to-
     day . . . ," Quora, n.d., www.quora.com/I-binge-ate-2000-calories
     -today-I-usually-only-eat-up-to-900-calories-a-day-or-less-I-am
     -thinking-of-fasting-tomorrow-I-have-tried-to-purge-but-it-didnt
     -work-I-hate-myself-for-doing-this-I-am-going-to-exercise-for-1
     -1-2-hours-What-should-I-do.
244 **"When we first started, we thought that Quora was going to be a
     place where people come when they have a question":** Kurt Wag-
     ner.,"A Q&A with the Q&A Boss—Quora's Adam D'Angelo Takes
     Our Questions," *Recode,* August 28, 2014.
244 **"Few other jobs allow such access to real life in America":** Zaslow,
     Tell Me All About It, 36.

Index

CASSANDRA GIRALDO

Jessica Weisberg is an award-winning writer and producer. Her writing has appeared in the *New Yorker,* the *New York Times, Harper's,* and the *Atavist,* among other publications, and has been nominated for a National Magazine Award. She was a producer on the podcast *Serial* and ran the features unit at *Vice News Tonight* on HBO, for which she was nominated for an Emmy. She works at Gimlet Media and lives in Brooklyn.

The Nation Institute

NATION BOOKS

Founded in 2000, **Nation Books** has become a leading voice in American independent publishing. The imprint's mission is to tell stories that inform and empower just as they inspire or entertain readers. We publish award-winning and bestselling journalists, thought leaders, whistleblowers, and truthtellers, and we are also committed to seeking out a new generation of emerging writers, particularly voices from underrepresented communities and writers from diverse backgrounds. As a publisher with a focused list, we work closely with all our authors to ensure that their books have broad and lasting impact. With each of our books we aim to constructively affect and amplify cultural and political discourse and to engender positive social change.

Nation Books is a project of The Nation Institute, a nonprofit media center established to extend the reach of democratic ideals and strengthen the independent press. The Nation Institute is home to a dynamic range of programs: the award-winning Investigative Fund, which supports groundbreaking investigative journalism; the widely read and syndicated website TomDispatch; journalism fellowships that support and cultivate over twenty-five emerging and high-profile reporters each year; and the Victor S. Navasky Internship Program.

For more information on Nation Books and The Nation Institute, please visit:

www.nationbooks.org
www.nationinstitute.org
www.facebook.com/nationbooks.ny
Twitter: @nationbooks